Also by Del Pe

Inner Powers To Maximize Your Performance
From Success To Fulfillment

HIDDEN DANGERS

of

MEDITATION

and

YOGA

HIDDEN DANGERS
of
MEDITATION
and
YOGA

How to Play with
*Your **Sacred Fires** Safely*

DEL PE

For general information on our other products and services, please contact our Sales Department within the United States at 1-800-352-6014, outside the United States at 1-936-273-9153, fax: 1-936-273-9230 or Website: www.mdpglobal.com.

Book design by Carolyn Wilder

First Edition Published: 2005

PRINTED IN THE UNITED STATES OF AMERICA

Library of Congress Control Number 2 0 0 5 9 2 4 2 6 0

ISBN 0-9717676-3-7

Disclaimer

This book presents the ideas, opinions, experiences and experiments of its author. This publication does not provide medical advice or diagnoses of health conditions. Readers, especially those with existing health conditions, should seek the advice of a medical professional and/or certified meditation or yoga instructor before engaging in any of the techniques or practices in this book.

The author and publisher are not liable for any loss, health effect or other consequence of using or indirectly applying any technique or practice in this book.

To all meditators and yogis of the world —
past, present and future

To founders of yoga and meditation systems,
their Guides and Lineages

To all yoga Masters and meditation instructors

To my family, students and co-workers

To my Teachers and Invisible Helpers — past and present

To the Absolute and Eternal Source of all experiences
in whom we live, breathe and have our being

Acknowledgements

It has long been one of my greatest aspirations to write a book that would allow me to share a big part of myself and my meditative life as a way to reach out to others and help them improve the quality of their own lives.

To say that this book is "by Del Pe" alone overstates the case. Without the spiritual training I received from my four early spiritual mentors, especially MCKS, this book would not be what it is today. Without books provided by Pranic Healing, the Theosophical Society, Lucis Trust, the Vivekananda Kendra Yoga Research Foundation and the Bihar School of Yoga, this book cannot stand on its own.

Thanks to the guidance of my Invisible Spiritual Mentors, who have empowered this book project and the mission to spread safe and effective meditations globally. I'd like to express deep appreciation to the many founders and lineages of the yogic traditions, whose ancient work continues to bear fruit in the enlightenment of humanity.

I am very fortunate to have a great dynamic team who worked tirelessly from the book's conception through to its production.

Special thanks to:

- Jenna Wayne, my editor and clairvoyant co-worker, for all her brilliant ideas and dedication to the book project

- Carolyn Wilder, my wife who designed the book's layout and cover, for her love and unfailing support for my spiritual mission
- Kain Sanderson, the model in the book's illustrative photos, for his selfless technical support
- Susan Powell, the copy editor, for her practical tips on the book's content
- Suzanne Jarvis and the ESOCEN and GLOCEN trainers and coach-healers for their unwavering commitment to spreading the science and art of meditation globally
- Joe Robbins for his photography

Thanks to my clients, who have given me and our international healing groups the opportunity to heal them, for sharing their stories of recovery from the hidden dangers of meditation.

In addition, I am grateful to my parents, children and family for their full support and belief in my mission.

I would like to thank many others whose names are not here, but who have given total support for the book's production.

And to those who study this book, thank you for being a part of humanity's growth towards the Light. It has been blissful writing this book, and I hope it has the same effect on those who will apply its teachings.

- Del Pe

Contents

TABLE OF DIAGRAMS AND ILLUSTRATIONS

Introduction

Today, more than ever, we have an overwhelming need for new tools like meditation to be able to live healthier, work smarter with less stress and be happier without artificial excitement through alcohol or recreational drugs. In my constant international travels and weekly spiritual mentoring, I have noticed tremendous demand for newer methods to understand and experience life's purpose – internally. Modern professionals are constantly seeking more robust strategies to grow faster and be ahead while maintaining balance, and the number of people, including youth, who are seeking practical ways to experience their spirituality outside their religion is growing exponentially. More and more people are turning to meditation as the answer to all this searching and aspiration.

But did you know that meditation and yoga have hidden dangers? Did you know that certain types are not safe for pregnant women and children? Were you aware that some forms can actually make ADD and ADHD worse? Did you know that some meditations and yogas can actually cause cancer and AIDS to spread faster? And did you ever hear that mixing different yogic techniques can produce unanticipated side effects that don't appear immediately?

This book shares insights and techniques resulting from the mastery I gained climbing to sacred spots in the Himalayas, studying and staying with a few advanced yogis and Sages in India, visiting many Saints and gurus in Nepal and the Himalayas and traveling all over India teaching meditation and the healing sciences. This has given me depth and exposure in these topics from their ancient roots, passed on through the many Indian yogic lineages and schools, which I appreciate deeply.

You won't find the unique wisdom offered here anywhere else because I had the good fortune to study and mentor with four enlightened Sages from Asia in my early years. All of my mentors' diverse backgrounds enabled me to create a synthesized approach to both the science and art of meditation, which is shared here. Most people are lucky to find just one Master mentor in a lifetime, so I am unusually blessed to have worked with four with varied training and mastery.

Two of my mentors from Southeast Asia are masters of healing, meditation and the spiritual sciences. Another is a master of Zen, mantric yoga and martial arts, and the fourth mentor is an enlightened yogi-guru in the highlands of the Himalayas. In fact, he is said to be an "immortal" who is more than 400 years old.

In my life's work so far, the indispensable training I received from my early spiritual mentor, MCKS, gave me some of the best preparation to write this book. I have also studied the books transcribed by Alice Bailey and the Theosophical Society. Finally, my current guidance from non-physical mentors is priceless.

This book also draws from my mastery of martial arts, especially the Japanese system, which provided the gifts of concentration, willpower and self-discipline — training that I include in the development of curricula for meditation students and clients. My early professional experience gave me the mind of an engineer and businessperson, which enabled me to convert the Eastern wisdom philosophies into day-to-day solutions and practical spiritual tools to solve life's modern problems. Thus, our meditations and strategies are intended for busy people, like most of you who will study this book.

Since meditation and yoga are gaining attention among parents, educators and students, I strongly recommend that parents and educators in particular read this book to study the side effects of meditation and yoga on children and to understand the appropriate ages for meditation and which types of meditation are safe for children.

One of the key points you will find here is that one meditation does not fit all people. Therefore, I have included an important chapter on how to choose the right meditation style and instructor for you.

This book is also useful for yoga and meditation instructors to teach both the science and art of meditation effectively. Since there are at least 12 types of meditation and 8 types of yoga, it is not easy for beginners to choose the right style and instructor for their needs and temperaments, thus instructors have a responsibility to guide their students properly based on a deeper modern understanding of meditation.

For advanced meditators and yoga teachers, this book provides ready-made, step-by-step solutions for the negative side effects of their spiritual practices, especially advanced esoteric meditations. These solutions can be grouped as a new form of yoga, the Yoga of Synthesis.

I had to write this book now more than ever before because many people are turning to meditation, yoga and the Eastern philosophies for self-improvement. Numerous private organizations and professional groups are considering these ancient teachings as immediate modern spiritual solutions to life's material problems. This increase in demand for meditation has triggered a new market niche, especially since the mainstream media is featuring meditation. For example, the January 20, 2003 edition of *Time* magazine was a special issue dedicated to how the mind can heal the body. The cover shows a woman in a yoga position. And the August 4, 2003 cover story of *Time* was dedicated to "The Science of Meditation" and included many supplementary articles on various meditation topics.

Many enterprising consultants and business coaches are taking advantage of this trend, grabbing new commercial opportunities by quickly learning some yoga, breathing and meditation techniques to teach executives and other clients. This is creating a problem, though: They are teaching without proper complete training.

Many overzealous people are authoring books on meditation as a cure for a variety of ailments, and several celebrities are commercializing meditation and yoga through their videos and CDs. These are all exciting developments, and we should be thankful for their good intentions, but people should share this knowledge with substantial understanding of the do's and the don'ts of meditation. Yoga and meditation instructors should be educated not only in meditation techniques but also in the potential side effects and precautionary measures. Meditators should understand what's going on internally whenever they use certain yogic *mantras* or prolonged breathing techniques. Without this knowledge, meditators are "playing with fire" and can eventually get burned.

But, by understanding the science and art of meditation and its unknown dangers, meditators can enjoy their practices more safely and effectively. By gaining insight into the different results and potential positive side effects of different meditations, and by understanding your existing strengths and weaknesses, you can wisely select meditations that will enhance your strengths and convert your weaknesses into virtues.

The teachings of this book are designed to benefit both beginner and advanced meditators. Some concepts and principles are not totally new since they are derived from the ancient wisdom of the Masters, but many techniques are re-engineered to be safe for modern-day practitioners while maintaining their original power. The meditations in this book are simplified integrations of yogic, esoteric, martial arts and healing science techniques that I have synthesized for people's material and spiritual needs by applying Eastern wisdom with Western practicality.

The principles and methods presented here are neither theoretical, speculative nor exhaustive. They are all harvested and distilled from more than two decades of study, experimentation, research, weekly practice, training of meditators and spiritual mentoring, which my teams and I have tested and proven with over 40,000 people, students and clients through my work in over 49 countries.

These meditations and weekly strategies when done regularly will help you live healthier, work smarter, be happier and grow faster and will accelerate of your inner development. My greatest wish is for you to benefit from the safe and effective meditations in this book to help you live your greatest life and achieve your life's purpose beyond your expectations.

Enjoy and be well.

- Del Pe

Part I:

MEDITATION IN MODERN LIFE:
Its Forms and Benefits

CHAPTER 1

Meditation:

Is It a Science or an Art?

You already have the hardware and software to be able to meditate! All you need to know is how to operate the hardware (your body) and upgrade the software (your consciousness) – and you will be on the path of meditation.

But is your meditation safe and effective? Are you going to use this meditation time in your already busy day wisely and with big benefits? Or if you are already a meditator, is your meditation meeting your expectations?

For any meditator to be safe and effective using meditation as a spiritual tool and practical strategy to live a successful, healthy life, meditation needs to be understood as a science and art, and the hidden dangers in its practices must be known.

The purpose of this book and its teachings is to educate about the hidden dangers and provide safe and proven meditation techniques designed for busy people like most of you to help you:

- ◆ Live healthier
- ◆ Work smarter
- ◆ Be happier
- ◆ Grow your personal and professional life faster

This may seem like a tall order to achieve, but it can be done faster than most people think with a systematic application of meditation as a way of life.

WHAT IS MEDITATION?

Most people have heard about meditation and many are studying and practicing it lately, but few practitioners actually understand it well. Knowing how to meditate is not good enough. You need to understand not only its external form and rituals, but also what's going on internally when you are meditating. You should know what meditations are safe and effective for you and your children according to their age group. You should have criteria to shop for the best meditation style or yoga instructor suited to your needs, temperament and health issues.

To help illuminate meditation in all its applications, this book defines it as a science and art and presents their many forms.

MEDITATION: *Different Meanings to Different People*

Meditation has different meanings to different people, depending on their level of exposure to it and their level of spiritual development. It can mean a method to relax and release daily stress through breathing techniques. In its spiritual context, it is usually interpreted as yoga or a tool for enlightenment. To many practitioners, it can mean a ritual of concentration and inner awareness leading to spiritual expansion of consciousness.

Zen meditators and Buddhist lamas use "mindfulness meditation" to focus on eating or working to fully enjoy the experience. Busy executives are great meditators in the modern world even though they may not be aware of it. Their form of meditation is one-pointed concentration employing the mind to design business plans and solutions for organizational problems.

Scientists also use a form of meditation through continuous mental focusing on their subject of research to unfold new discoveries.

Another general type of concretizing meditation occurs when people use their emotions, mental and spiritual faculties to focus their energy on the achievement of material and spiritual goals. The spiritual Masters consider this type of meditation important for their disciples, but traditionally, meditation has been limited to meaning sitting down in a lotus posture with closed eyes doing breathing techniques and *mantras*. This style is actually closer to the yogic method.

This book expands and modernizes the concept of meditation and presents meditation not only as a spiritual technique, but also as a pratical tool for material success and to enhance health and well-being.

MEDITATION AS A SCIENCE

Meditation becomes a scientific path and method when there is a clear understanding of its do's and don'ts. Meditation is made into a science when the procedures are designed with predetermined results and a complete understanding of the causes and effects.

Meditation as a science is like medicine: The contraindications of a protocol are known as well as the uses. Meditation is a spiritual science when its effects on the physical anatomy, emotions, mind and spiritual consciousness are studied properly with structured understanding.

Therefore, to achieve this level of scientific approach, we will include a more thorough study of both the visible physical and invisible spiritual anatomy behind the meditation science in Chapter 4.

8 FORMS OF THE SCIENCE OF MEDITATION

The eight forms of the science of meditation are:

- Abstraction meditation
- Concretizing meditation
- Meditation for understanding
- Healing meditations
- Inner powers meditations
- Esoteric meditation
- Meditation for the Masters
- Group and global meditation

Let's look at each form in further detail.

Abstraction Meditation

This is also called "meditation without seed thought" because the goal is to go beyond the mind. It is a systematic step-by-step process that allows the practitioner to expand their consciousness from grosser levels of experience to more subtle states of awareness. These procedures can bring a meditator from a normal state into an altered state, which may or may not include an out-of-body experience. This meditation can transform a very stressful, agitated person into a very calm state in a matter of 5 to 15 minutes of practice. Thus, it is very useful for busy people. This meditation normally includes:

- Sitting in a comfortable position
- Closing the eyes
- Special inner breathing techniques
- Sometimes chanting or sounding of *mantrams*
- Other techniques to heighten awareness

There are many variations of this meditation, but most of them lead to the same expected result – a more peaceful, expanded state of consciousness. This is a typical Raja yoga meditation.

Concretizing Meditation

This is also known as "meditation with seed thought" because the mind is continuously focusing on ideas, visuals or any chosen subject of meditation. This form of meditation is done with eyes open, but it can also be done with eyes closed initially when an idea is being penetrated for analysis. It does not require any special sitting posture. Most of its uses help focus the mind for decision-making and problem-solving, so it can be particularly effective for businesspeople and leaders. Its daily practical application for executives is to use the mind with one-pointed concentration to map options and solutions to business problems. Many thinkers, like engineers, can use this to transform ideas into:

- Concepts and principles
- Strategies
- Processes and systems
- Steps and protocols
- Product lines
- Services

This is how great ideas turn into technology or business. The powerful application of the mind leads us to our technological success today.

This same type of practical meditation is employed by social entrepreneurs to convert a philosophy into a vision, mission and plans that result in a nonprofit organization. This form of meditation is also recommended for mystical people who have already mastered devotional meditation so they can improve their ability to translate their good intentions into practical service to humanity and the world. After perceiving higher ideals through the abstraction meditation, the next step is concretizing meditation to put the ideals into intelligent action.

After "self-realization", one needs "self-actualization"
to complete the evolutionary process.

In another form, the concretizing meditation includes visualization meditation that concentrates on imagery, sacred geometries or other symbols to physicalize their magical powers.

Meditation for Understanding
This meditation can be used as a technique to become a philosopher without formal academic schooling or to cultivate wisdom in life. It is the opposite process of the concretizing meditation because it abstracts concrete events, situations or physical components of reality into a digested principle, philosophy or wisdom behind the physical circumstances.

Most people see life and happenings on the surface, but the experts of meditation for understanding are able to penetrate the underlying principle and wisdom in any event. The meditator can extract the causes behind the known effects.

Meditation can train you to be a true visionary thinker to predict incoming trends. By knowing the past and present trends and by understanding certain principles, you can draw conclusions through the Law of Cause and Effect.

Historians should master this type of meditation to develop the abstract power of the mind so they can understand the moral lessons behind history. Then they can illuminate humanity through new presentations of history books that highlight "karmic lessons" so the mistakes of the past are not repeated. The destructive lessons of war, for example, are lessons of history that have not been understood. Children and teenagers should also be taught this meditation to reduce the preventable seeds of failure in adult life.

Spiritual Masters are experts in this form of meditation. That's why they are called "the wise ones". Buddhism (*Mahayana*) teaches *Vipashyana*, the closest name for meditation for understanding. Vipashyana is the mental examination of the true nature of things that results in enlightened insight or illumination.

Healing Meditations

There are many varieties of this meditation used by different schools of healing. They include inner breathing techniques to release the energy of diseases, followed by visualization and concentration on different energy centers of the body to detoxify, revitalize and balance them. They also involve a systematic circulation of vitality and healing force into the different organs and auras of the human energy system. In the future, many people with ailments will use this form of meditation to recover their good health faster. Many meditations in Chapters 9, 10, 12, 19 and 21 will provide you with these techniques.

Inner Powers Meditations

These forms of meditation are designed for human faculty development. They help systematically develop your seven intelligences:

- Instinctive intelligence
- Emotional intelligence
- Concrete mental intelligence
- Abstract mental intelligence
- Psychic intelligence
- Spiritual intelligence
- Divine intelligence

These techniques not only stimulate the energy centers of the human energy system, which is your invisible spiritual anatomy, but also include certain exercises and practices that awaken your "inner fires" called the *kundalini* to permanently fertilize the new human faculties you gain through meditation. This systematic meditation will be incorporated into the new education system for our new generation to accelerate the learning process dramatically. The development of the seven intelligences will also be very helpful in shaping future leaders' advanced human faculties in the political, educational, business and scientific worlds.

Chapter 13 will provide some meditation methods to work smarter in any chosen career by applying some of these principles.

Esoteric Meditation

This form of meditation is also called "occult meditation" because it is the most advanced form and is not for the novice. Because this meditation generates so much energy, it is hidden from the public. It is usually taught by the spiritual teacher to the student through direct instruction accompanied by regular supervision and monitoring. These meditations are recommended only for students who are disciplined, prepared and mature enough to use the acquired inner powers for the good of humanity and world evolution. This group of advanced meditations is normally taught in different levels according to the spiritual development of the meditator.

Esoteric meditation applications include the use of the energy from meditation for spiritual blessings and esoteric service.

The results of these meditations include a high stimulation of the entire personality and the esoterically-known "kundalini fire", which is highly awakened with a pre-determined "spiritual burning process". Thus, the esoteric meditations are regarded as "playing with sacred fire".

Most gurus and spiritual teachers don't endorse these types of meditations unless there is direct supervision. Likewise, there is a need for the student to use the tremendous increase in energy for spiritual service.

This book includes some safer levels of esoteric meditation like those presented in Chapters 20 and 21, but advanced practices are only available with more direct training and monitoring.

Meditation for the Masters

This is a complete esoteric science and spiritual technology not only to awaken the power of the Soul, but also to awaken the Divine Powers of the Spirit. It is only applicable to beings who have reached above the Sainthood level, called the "Sages" or "Super-Sages". It is a path of meditation for Ultra-Human evolution towards human perfection. Meditation for the Masters is a higher version of the Esoteric Meditations. It is not allowed to be published in books for now.

Group and Global Meditation

A higher spiritual application of meditation is through group meditation, which can be used to support a global concern. When many people are focused simultaneously on an idea or good cause with one-pointed sustained attention, the power is magnified. This group ritual, either expressed as a group appeal to God or an invocation for a certain Divine quality like peace, is categorized as a group or global meditation.

The most common global meditations have been introduced through the United Nations, and the most popular spiritual group meditations are full moon monthly meditations. Group and global meditations are discussed in detail in Chapter 23.

MEDITATION AS AN ART

Meditations without structured procedures, or mystical meditations that do not use a systematic technique, belong to the art form of meditation. Even when mystics are young, they already have a natural way of meditating. This is commonly known as daydreaming. I call it out-of-body experience where their consciousness is projected somewhere else. Some of our mystical children today who are spacey in school are considered to have Attention Deficit Disorder (ADD). They can't concentrate and listen attentively because they are in an altered state — just like in meditation. They are not grounded to learn in the usual way.

Meditators who are more emotionally-sensitive and non-mental prefer the art of meditation because they can bypass the mind easily and are naturally in receptive awareness for spiritual impressions from their Souls called the intuition and psychic faculties.

4 FORMS OF MEDITATION AS AN ART

The four forms of meditation as an art are:

- Relaxation meditation
- Mindfulness meditation
- Devotional meditation
- Channeling and invocative meditation

Let's look at each form in further detail.

Relaxation Meditation

This is very useful for people who have a stressful and busy lifestyle. The problem for many in the process of learning how to meditate is how to sit and relax and stop mental chatter when at rest. People who are naturally good at quieting themselves like this technique. They go to a favorite relaxing spot at the end of the work day and gradually relax and let go of their usual daily concerns. They do this either lying down or in a relaxed sitting position listening to classical music or to the sound of a fountain. Stressed and busy people can achieve a similar effect in their office by taking a "mental vacation" away from work just by projecting their minds for five minutes to a beautiful place and enjoying the nice feelings. This type of relaxation meditation has no definite science to it. It's an art, and you can't force a person to relax without a good yogic technique. Most mental type people have to use other techniques because this way is not suitable for their temperament. But for mystical types of meditators, the relaxation type of meditation is very easy.

Mindfulness Meditation

Meditators who want to be aware and conscious about their daily activities, including eating, walking in nature and working, tend to enjoy their lives more than performance-oriented practitioners. This is because they are mindful of the meaning of their daily existence. Many Zen practitioners and Buddhist monks usually incorporate this method in their spiritual practices. They are the masters of mindfulness meditation. One of my earlier spiritual mentors, SHJ, is an expert at this meditation. His father was a Zen master in Korea. He also had two other Zen teachers until he mastered the mindfulness meditation and seven Oriental arts himself. Everything he does has meaning, and he is fully aware internally and externally. It is not easy to teach mindfulness to very busy mental types of personalities. Mindfulness meditation is easier for meditators who have natural sensitivity and inner awareness.

Devotional Meditation

This is sometimes called mystical meditation, the path of love and devotion or yoga of the heart within the practices of Bhakti yoga. This is the easiest form of meditation for people who are heart-centered and not mentally polarized. The meditator contemplates on the Divine qualities of their idols, either Saints, Sacred Deities, gurus or higher ideals. After constant meditation on their idols' spiritual qualities, including the Divine aspects of Godliness, they acquire those consciousnesses and qualities themselves. They follow the principle, "What you meditate on, you become". Most of our earlier Saints in history did not have to demonstrate creative mental intelligence to be considered holy. They were the devotional types who contemplated the love and compassion aspects of life and service until they were enveloped with that energy and became agents of service to help humanity. That's their process of illumination: to be absorbed into the ideals to which they surrender themselves.

Fanatical groups also use the same principle of one-pointed meditation. They focus on their ideals and contemplate the mission of their leaders – whether it is positive or negative. Then they can become fighters for their cause, including terrorism and wars. This devotional meditation is used by both evolutionary and involutionary forces.

Channeling and Invocative Meditation

People like mediums or psychics who are very spiritually or psychically receptive and sensitive are naturally apt to use this meditation. They use invocations or incantations as an initial tool to raise their vibrations to connect to invisible spiritual guides or an overshadowing being. They can go into a trance and automatically write, talk about and download information they don't know or have not learned.

In some cases, they don't have any clue who is giving them the data. This is where the danger lies. The overshadowing being can be from the negative side and can possess or obsess the medium or psychic permanently. Many books and dance rituals were channeled this way. This is not a safe meditation for people who are not supervised by an advanced spiritual teacher or for those without esoteric preparation.

THE SCIENCE AND ART OF MEDITATION *Compared*

Meditation can be practiced as a science or an art, or it can be an integration of both depending on your inner development and needs. There are so many new forms of meditation today, but they can all be categorized as the science or art of meditation, or a combination of the two. Their big differences are:

- The science of meditation takes a systematic approach with predetermined results. It is safer because it is well understood and guided by the known do's and don'ts.
- The art of meditation is more of an instinctive and intuitive way of practice and is suited to people who have inner sensitivity and more heart development, are less mental and tend to be mystical.

FORMS OF MEDITATION AS A SCIENCE

FORM OF MEDITATION	APPLICATIONS/DESCRIPTIONS
Abstraction Meditation or Meditation without Seed Thought	Typical meditation used in advanced yoga, employing postures, breathing techniques, *mantrams* and hand *mudras* or energy locking mechanisms for a more peaceful, expanded state of consciousness.
Concretizing Meditation or Meditation with Seed Thought	Methods using mental focus, visualization and concentration to transform ideas into physical events, projects or products. It is employed in decision-making, problem-solving and tactical planning. It applies and trains the concrete power of the mind.
Meditation for Understanding	Methods employed to abstract and understand lessons, wisdom, principles and philosophy underlying physical events, situations or components of truths. They cultivate the abstract power of the mind and invoke the wisdom of the Soul.
Healing Meditations	Many variations of techniques to heal the energy centers of the body and auras of the human energy system. They employ visualization, breathing techniques and mentally-guided circulation of healing energy.

Form of Meditation	Applications/Descriptions
Inner Powers Meditations	Meditation techniques that culture your inner powers and advanced human faculties, including the 7 levels of intelligence. They involve a thorough knowledge of the invisible energy anatomy and a complete understanding of the spiritual psychology controlling human consciousness. The meditation involves systematically activating the 12 major energy centers or chakras.
Esoteric Meditation or Occult Meditation	More advanced forms of meditation that are not for the public. They are recommended only for more disciplined and spiritually-mature students.
Meditation of the Masters	Very advanced meditations using spiritual technology only for Ultra-Human development above Sainthood level of consciousness.
Group and Global Meditations	Meditations by groups to focus attention and energy on supporting a global concern like peace.

FORMS OF MEDITATION AS AN ART

FORM OF MEDITATION	APPLICATIONS/DESCRIPTIONS
Relaxation Meditation	Typical method for most people without specific training and techniques to relax, rest and let go.
Mindfulness Meditation	Method to be consciously aware of events, activities and the mind to fully experience the meaning of daily existence.
Devotional Meditation or Mystical Meditation	Love- and devotionally-centered meditation towards an idol or ideal, be it a guru, Saint, Deity or Divine qualities.
Channeling and Invocation Meditation	Meditation employing mediumship and psychic faculties to receive and transmit unusual information. It can also include remote viewing.

There might be some rare ancient or modern forms of meditation that cannot be classified under any of these general categories, but for modern-life meditators, the forms above will suffice for our discussions and study.

The practical use of meditation can lead people from a normal, mundane life to a life of spiritual and material balance. In our modern era, we need meditation as a new tool to advance not only our concrete knowledge, but also wisdom; not only success, but also self-fulfillment.

The next step for meditators is to upgrade their mystical meditation and yogic practices into more practical uses. Those who are doing ordinary meditations will prepare themselves for more advanced training employing the power of Esoteric Meditations. Search and study with an open mind. As an old adage says,

"When the student is ready, the teacher appears."

CHAPTER 2

How Can Meditation Help You?

The benefits of meditation are enormous. These benefits depend on what type of meditation you are doing, how long you have been practicing it and whether you have a spiritual mentor or not. The most common reasons people meditate are for general relaxation and to improve their health. More advanced meditators generally benefit from mental and spiritual development through their meditations.

To improve and broaden the applications of meditation, we'll include material and spiritual uses of both the science and art of meditation. Most other books and teachings on meditation focus more on the yogic side and inner aspects. This book will present a comprehensive and synthesized study of meditation for our modern life. Most of the meditation techniques will be discussed in Chapters 7 through 21.

THE BENEFITS OF MEDITATION
Live Healthier and Enjoy a Sense of Total Well-Being

Meditation has many benefits. Let's focus on nine important ones:

- Release your stress and negativities
- Beat your fatigue and sleeplessness and get revitalized
- Anti-aging and rejuvenation
- Oxygenation of the blood
- Overall sense of well-being
- Happier and improved quality of life
- Work smarter and be more productive
- Train the power of your mind
- Accelerate your inner development

Let's explore each of these benefits:

RELEASE YOUR STRESS AND NEGATIVITIES
In the long run, stress can weaken your immune system and increase the risk of heart disease, hypertension and other life-threatening diseases. Burnout can also cause accelerated aging and decreased performance in both work and family life. Simple meditations like breathing techniques to release toxic vibrations and negative emotional and mental energies are the inexpensive way to deal with all of these preventable predicaments. After purging the different levels of discomfort, relaxation is easy and natural.

This breathing-out meditation technique is not only beneficial to release negative feelings and thoughts, it also helps calm the nerves. Through controlled breathing patterns and relaxation techniques, which will be discussed in Chapter 12, your body can bypass the "fight-or-flight" response to stress, which stimulates abnormal heart rate, high blood pressure and production of excessive cortisol and adrenaline. This stimulation hampers the work of the immune system's antibodies.

BEAT YOUR FATIGUE AND SLEEPLESSNESS AND GET REVITALIZED
In many cases, fatigue can be related to stress. It can also be related to sleeplessness or an inability to rest properly. A person who is very tired but stressed and worried can't sleep, even if they want to. Whatever the triggering cause of fatigue and sleeplessness, meditation can help quickly. Techniques to improve fatigue and sleeplessness are discussed in Chapter 18.

Meditation can help your physical body, vitality, emotions and mind release energy blockages, and it enables them to recover lost energy fast. Certain meditations with deep breathing can boost your vitality and increase your will-power rapidly. Other meditations activate specific energy centers of your body, which switch on certain powers that awaken your internal stamina and help stimulate hormones for facilitating a deep, restful sleep.

I teach these methods to combat flight fatigue and jetlag. As a frequent flyer who takes more than 90 flights a year, I designed this meditation technique for myself first because I needed to recover fast after getting off the plane.

ANTI-AGING AND REJUVENATION
One of the practical modern uses of meditation is to reverse the aging process and improve longevity. Advanced yogis use certain breathing methods to regenerate the allotment of internal energy we are given for a lifetime. This is a key to anti-aging and rejuvenation. If the "genetic allotment of vitality" or *chi*, gets depleted, people die earlier or grow old rapidly.

The physical body, including the skin, is controlled by energy centers called chakras in yoga. By activating, detoxifying and revitalizing the chakras through meditation, the whole body gets rejuventated and balanced.

OXYGENATION OF THE BLOOD
The rapid full breathing techniques in meditation allow better displacement of carbon dioxide in the lungs and blood by increasing the amount of oxygen. This increase of oxygen saturation in the

body enhances metabolic processes and purifies the body more effectively. The conversion of food nutrition into energy harnessed by the cells becomes highly efficient.

OVERALL SENSE OF WELL-BEING

There are secrets in yogic meditations that include certain controlled breathing patterns to balance the right and left nostril breaths. When these breathing sequences, including the alternate nostril breathing pattern, are done properly, there's an awakening of an internal energy that promotes an overall sense of well-being. This is discussed in detail in Chapter 12.

MEDITATION MAKES YOU HAPPIER AND IMPROVES QUALITY OF LIFE

The prerequisite for a happier life and better relationships
is to get rid of all negative emotional hang-ups and feelings
that prevent us from opening our hearts
to give love or receive affection from others.

Our personal lives can be affected by many bad memories, and the emotions are the most difficult battleground for most people. Meditation and breathing techniques are a fast way to release all negative emotional influences in our lives such as anger, hatred, frustrations, fear, worries, phobias, jealousy, envy, anxiety, guilt, resentments, grief, loneliness and all other types of emotional disturbances, whether these emotions are from current situations or the past.

A simple and quick meditation, presented in Chapter 19, helps people heal their past, transform their present and energize their future. This technique involves opening the heart, plus experiencing forgiveness and self-acceptance.

When we are happy,
we tend to attract happy people and positive events.
We magnetize the same qualities that we have inside.

Meditation Can Help You Work Smarter and Be More Productive

There are two main kinds of workers: Those who are hard-working and those who are hardly working. But even hard work is not enough. I know many people who work hard, but are not happy or successful.

Working smarter is the key. You don't have to struggle too hard to be successful or to achieve great things in life!

How can meditation help you work smarter? You can acquire better human faculties by unfolding five of the seven intelligences mentioned earlier that are used by highly-developed Masters:

- Instinctive intelligence
- Emotional intelligence
- Concrete mental intelligence
- Abstract mental intelligence
- Psychic intelligence
- Spiritual intelligence
- Divine intelligence

In normal education, we only partially develop one or two of these intelligences, but there is a series of meditations in this book that enables you to gradually awaken the special faculties of instinctive, emotional, concrete mental, abstract mental and psychic intelligences. By using these inner powers and multi-intelligences in your decision-making, problem-solving and career, you can definitely achieve more in less time with less effort and fewer resources. With these added extraordinary qualities, you can accomplish in a few years what most others can't achieve in a lifetime. Future education, scientific and business training will change dramatically when these meditation techniques are used for advanced aptitude and attitude development. The best leaders of leaders in the future will need to have at least five of these intelligences to stay on top.

MEDITATION CAN TRAIN THE POWER OF YOUR MIND
Since balanced development of the concrete and abstract mental intelligences is important to unlock the power of a penetrating mind that can also abstract wisdom from our experiences, this book offers two forms of meditation to train the mind: concretizing meditation and meditation for understanding. Mental type meditation can help you:

- Activate your mental power to be one-pointed and develop the attitude to finish what you start faster
- Develop mental stamina and will-power
- Awaken your philosophical mind to understand life's events and purpose and allow you to access the Soul's wisdom

The mental type of meditation can gradually develop your aptitudes so you can become a mental powerhouse and a super-thinker. Meditation can also offer you peace of mind daily. Meditation to empower your mind is discussed in Chapter 13.

MEDITATION CAN ACCELERATE YOUR INNER DEVELOPMENT
If you are looking for a new practical spirituality to develop yourself and grow your life faster, abstract meditation or esoteric meditations are the answer.

One of the main reasons Masters
introduced meditation to humanity is for inner development.

Most teachings on yoga or spirituality talk about expansion of consciousness, self-realization and bliss or being one with God as the main goal. I think this is important, but it is limited when it becomes a personal desire and a personal obsession without the practical service of meditational practice.

What's beyond enlightenment, bliss or self-realization? A new concept or requirement of service or greater usefulness.

Meditation is only a tool, self-realization is only a process
and self-actualization is the next step
to bring down that which is realized as a higher truth or idea.
This is converted into a service for a bigger need
and for a larger whole.
The Buddha, the Christ, Muhammad, Albert Einstein,
Mahatma Gandhi and all great Spirits have done it this way.

This sequence of evolutionary experience is in fact a continuous process of inner development that can be measured by the depth of external service. Advanced meditation can facilitate this evolutionary process and spiritual development.

Service is an expression of inner growth and development.
It is the muscle-building for virtues.
It is the barometer of inner development and spirituality.

I have to be very straightforward here to meditators because I have met many advanced meditators who stop their exoteric service and social usefulness after meditating for years. They become more reclusive and indifferent to others. They are more inward, but not as socially useful. This can be a danger brought by lopsided development.

We don't need to leave our homes and families to live a spiritual life like a renunciant or monk. In fact, the modern science and art of meditation calls on meditators to flower and serve where they are planted — in politics, education, business, the arts, science, law, medicine, religion and institutions in any career and social duty.

This book's teachings advocate a science of meditation that develops meditators with one foot in Heaven and one foot on Earth. When done properly, meditation will allow you to grow faster, both spiritually and materially. In Chapter 20, you will be given a meditation to experience your Soul and be spiritually aligned and balanced. For more spiritual, less materially grounded types of meditators, Chapter 21 will bring more material balance to your spirituality.

CHAPTER 3

Comparative Study of Meditation and Yoga

What's the difference between meditation and yoga? Generally speaking, meditation is a technique or series of techniques within a yoga system. Thus, yoga is a series of rituals and practices that include meditation as a step or steps.

But meditation can also stand on its own as a path and spiritual science without the practitioner doing all the other steps of yoga. In fact, in our busy modern era, meditation is easier to practice than a whole yoga system because of the time constraints in people's lives.

In the Himalayan Mountains where the yogis and lamas have a great deal of time without families and exoteric duties, it is easier to do yoga for many hours anytime they want to. A single mother of three children who works 10 hours a day has almost no energy or time to exercise and meditate, much less do hours of complete yoga practice.

In order to apply practical meditation for modern life, we need to understand meditation and yoga without interchanging their meaning, let's discuss the 8 types of yoga and evaluate where meditation plays its roles.

YOGA AND ITS 8 TYPES

Yoga is generally applied to many practices of spiritual training, meditation and asceticism, whether related to Hindu, Buddhist or other religious traditions, including Christianity. But it is originally derived from the Sanskrit term, "*yuj*", meaning "to bind or yoke together". In Hindu philosophy, it is understood as the sense of harnessing oneself to God or seeking union with God. Therefore, all major religions are classified as yogas, predominantly the yoga of devotion.

Yoga can also be further defined as:

- A system of achieving Divine perfection by the union of the personality with the Soul, then eventually with the Spirit
- A spiritual training to withdraw one's consciousness from external senses and worldly experience to the subtle realities of the higher spiritual world
- A ritualistic method to attain enlightenment by becoming one with the consciousness of the Soul and eventually of the Spirit through a series of purifications, special postures, breathing techniques and meditation

The eight types of yoga are:

- Hatha
- Raja
- Bhakti
- Karma
- Jnana
- Mantric
- Tantric *kundalini*
- Integrated Yoga of Synthesis

Let's examine the eight types in detail:

HATHA YOGA

This is the most popular yoga practiced in the West. Many people associate yoga with Hatha yoga. It is one of the oldest yoga systems, composed of flexibility exercises done with body postures (*asanas*) and lots of controlled breathing techniques called *pranayama*.

Hatha yoga also includes special energy locks called *bandhas* and hand seals called *mudras* in their practices to control the flow of energy called *prana*. We'll explain the different breathing methods and body, leg and hand positions in Chapter 10. More advanced and esoteric practitioners regard Hatha yoga as preparatory to higher meditation.

One of the purposes of Hatha yoga is to train the physical body and organs to integrate with the energy body called the "vitality aura", which is made up of different types of *prana* or life force. Another aspect of this yoga is to be able to circulate *prana* or internal vitality throughout the different energy centers, called the chakras, to revitalize them and the organs they control.

In our modern world, Tai Chi, chigong, martial arts and sports are substitutes for this training. They don't give the same quality result, but they are good enough in the absence of the original Hatha yoga methods. In fact, these more active forms are more attractive and dynamic to modern practitioners and youth.

RAJA YOGA

Raja yoga is one of the most complete yoga systems. It is popularly called the "Royal Yoga". Sometimes it is known as Astanga yoga, referred to as the eight steps from the *Yoga Sutras (Aphorisms) of Patanjali*, an ancient Indian Super-Yogi.

The following are the general steps of Raja yoga:

1. **BEHAVIORAL RESTRAINTS OR ABSTENTIONS** (*yama*):
   The don'ts of yogic life like:
   - Non-violence (*ahimsa*)
   - Non-falsehood (*satya*)
   - Non-stealing (*asteya*)

* Non-sensuality (*brahmancharya*)
* Non-acquisitiveness (*aparigraha*)

All of the above should be followed as a form of character-building at the level of thoughts, words and actions.

2. **SELF-OBSERVATION AND SELF-DISCIPLINE** (*niyama*):
   What one should do like:
   * Cleanliness and personal hygiene (*shancha*)
   * Contentment (*santosha*)
   * Austerity (*tapas*)
   * Self-study (*swadhyaya*)
   * Devotion to an ideal or submission to God
     (*ishwara pranidhana*)

   This practice is about virtue development.

3. **POSTURE** (*asana*): The Hatha and Raja yogi uses special leg positions and body postures to do meditation like:
   * Simple cross-legged posture (*sukhasana*) (page 130)
   * Egyptian posture or sitting in a chair with feet flat on the floor (page 130)
   * Adept posture (*siddhasana*): Advanced cross-legged posture with left heel at the perineum and right foot partially inserted between the thigh and the calf of the left leg (page 132)
   * Lotus posture (*padmasana*): The bottoms of both feet facing upward with the left and right legs crossing each other and the feet resting in the lap (page 131)

4. **CONTROL OF BREATH** (*pranayama*): There are so many types of breathing techniques used in yoga, but a few are the most significant. They are all geared towards regulating the breath to affect the stimulation of *prana* (internal vitality) and the other sources of energy like the *kundalini* or sacred fire and the Divine light or Soul electricity. There are two major breathing techniques:

- *Kapalbhati*: rapid nostril breathing, including alternating breath through the two nostrils, which cleans the upper energy centers and the head area
- *Bastrika*: rapid bellows breathing to clean the lower energy centers and internal organs

The science of breathing will be discussed thoroughly in Chapter 12.

5. **CONTROL OF THE SENSES** (*pratyahara*): Raja yoga uses the faculty of will to withdraw the consciousness from the five senses. It also utilizes the mind to withdraw or abstract the attention from the external to the internal. It is the last preparation before the meditation proper.

6. **CONCENTRATION** (*dharana*): This is a technique wherein the mind is focused and riveted on an idea or object of stimulation like an energy center or chakra. It is done by putting the mind's one-pointed attention on a selected subject or focal point like a part of the body or an external object.

7. **AWARENESS MEDITATION** (*dhayana*): This is a sustained passive awareness requiring gentle sensitivity to a certain idea, object or energy field. This step needs a letting-go attitude and non-focused receptivity. No will, force or tension is included in this process. It is overall diffused attentiveness leading to expansion of consciousness to a more refined state. This is a state beyond thinking. It is more of a sensing awareness.

8. **CONTEMPLATION OR TOTAL ABSORPTION** (*samadhi*): This is a high state of meditation wherein the object of meditation, the meditator and the process are absorbed or merged into oneness or non-duality. The observer and the observed merge and are absorbed in the process. This experience depends on the earlier meditation preparation, especially awareness meditation, the awakening of the meditator's *kundalini* and Soul development.

The total absorption in meditation, called *samadhi* in Sanskrit, also has layers of experience as follows:

- Emptiness (Zen's *shunyata* or the state of no-characteristic or meaning). It is related to the experience of nothingness.
- Freedom from attachment or state of Divine dispassion (Zen's *animitta*)
- Divine bliss or Divine alignment (*nirvana*)
- Union with the Absolute (*nirvikalpa*)
- *Samadhi* or Divine at-one-ment is the climax of Raja yoga and advanced meditation.

We have described Raja yoga deeply because it is one of the most complete systems, and it is the yoga style that clearly delineates the difference between yoga and meditation. Steps 1-5 (*yama, niyama*, postures, control of breath and control of senses) are all preparatory in nature, and steps 6-8 are the meditation portion called *sanyama* in Raja yoga.

BHAKTI YOGA
This is also known as yoga of devotion and the path of love. It is a path of intense reverence or veneration directed to a spiritual teacher, Saint, ideal or God. The persistent, continuous thinking, tuning in and connectedness of the devotee to the object of devotion facilitates the merging of consciousness of the devotee to the idol or ideal.

The esoteric principle,
"What you meditate on, you become", holds true.

Thus, the devotee's energy and consciousness get absorbed by the power and quality of the idol, be it an aspect of Divinity or a guru's aura.

In the general sense, Christianity, Buddhism, Islam, Judaism, Hinduism and other devotional religions can all be classified as bhakti yoga with devotion as their main path. But Bhakti yoga, one of the original Indian systems, can be sub-categorized as:

1. Devotional surrender to a guru (*guru-bhakti*)
2. Strict and total adherence to the teacher's instruction (*vaidhi-bhakti*)
3. Continuous unimpeded devotion to God (*raga-bhakti*)
4. Supreme love of God (para-bhakti)

Bhakti yoga is an easy path for loving and devotional types of meditators, especially mystics. Many people who support good ideals, like the betterment of humanity and environmental improvement, whether they are doing meditation or not, are on this path.

Laya yoga, another sub-class of *tantric* or *kundalini* yoga, can be categorized as Bhakti yoga. Laya yogis have highly intense meditations of continuous daily veneration and love towards a Divine aspect of God or their spiritual idol. In the process of being so energized with this connection, their *kundalini*, the sacred fire, is awakened, triggering high expansion of consciousness and enlightenment.

KARMA YOGA

This yoga aims to train practitioners to have skills in action for active service, especially through physical work. The Karma yogi achieves inner development and spiritual realization through life's labor and action while offering the results to a higher ideal or to the Divine Source of Life, be it the Soul or God. The fruits and rewards of the practitioner's intelligent hard work are dedicated to higher good and evolution. This is done with selflessness and without the negative influence of the ego.

The Karma yogi does not only pray or perform lip service. He or she acts upon higher ideals. Geoffrey Hodson, in his book, *The Yogic Ascent to Spiritual Heights*, offers a good example of Karma yoga:

A little girl's brother set a trap to catch birds.
She thought it wrong and cruel. She cried at first
and then her mother noticed she became happy again.
Mother asked, "Why?"
"I prayed for my brother to be a better boy."
"What else?", asked her mother.
"I prayed that the trap would not catch birds!"
"And what else?"
"Well, then I went out and kicked the trap
to pieces." [1]

In India, the practitioner starts performing Karma yoga in the ashram or the yoga center to serve selflessly, helping with the chores or administration or support of projects as a form of service meditation. Young Karma yogis also are asked to be good servers in their homes or communities.

In our modern cities, business executives, social workers, political leaders and public servants – whether they are in high or low positions – can be classified under Karma yoga if they work to uplift human or world evolution.

The only missing quality in many of these action-oriented workers is lack of awareness of and alignment to the fact that their results and rewards need to be transmuted with selflessness guided by the virtues of sacrifice and detachment. But as their hearts grow and their spiritual inspiration is harnessed, these "down to earth" servers will become the real Karma yogis of our modern times.

Karma yoga fulfills the Law of Cause and Effect – what you sow, you reap. If you serve, love and work for the upliftment of others, you receive the same qualities and favors, like a positive boomerang back to you as the server, with or without asking for it.

By continuous selflessness and conscious service, the practitioner develops the heart and also neutralizes many of the "karmic debts" that come along with each person. The result is that higher spiritual development is accelerated.

Karma yoga, when put into constant action, also rapidly develops:

- Will-power by working out difficulties in one's life and performing one's duty
- Mental creativity and power to materialize goals and projects
- Devotion and love for one's mission and work
- Group consciousness to work in teams
- Global consciousness to understand world affairs as part of one's responsibility and strategy (in international politics and business, for example)

As modern executives and career professionals work with their family group, career group and social and cultural affiliations, they are exposed to relationships, both good and bad, to realize their positive and negative qualities of behavior to be worked on. There is an interaction in these relationships through which a person can't escape self-auditing, realizing and rectifying the imperfections in their personalities and the environment.

Empathizing with the upheavals and vicarious suffering of others through relationships leads professionals to align their personalities and intentions to higher ideals and greater causes and eventually to refine their service with bigger global significance. Some executives or career professionals become philanthropists and even international legends through this process as a result of their selfless service and sacrificial attitude. Their work and service act as their meditation and spiritual path, but modern Karma yogis need to learn and practice meditation techniques to empower their next steps and expand their consciousness further.

JNANA YOGA

This yogic path seeks to develop the mind, both concrete and abstract, to gain knowledge and deepen understanding of life and its purpose, leading to enlightenment.

By constantly employing the mind to penetrate and reflect on causes and effects shaping one's condition, circumstances or life, the "microcosmic answers" or realizations mirror "macrocosmic truth" and principles, which brings illumination and expansion of consciousness.

Your mind can awaken fully by using it constantly and positively, guided by your Soul's wisdom, leading to higher degrees of enlightenment. Thus, the Jnana yogi becomes the real super-thinker with a higher vision implementing greater service for a greater whole.

Advanced Jnana yogis are the true visionaries because they can access the future goals of human development with their intuitive minds and also download blueprints and tactical plans with their brilliant concrete minds to manifest their global service.

In today's modern world, the Jnana yogis are represented by our scientists and technical inventors, who always surprise everyone with their new breakthroughs and discoveries. The pioneering technology we have today is all part of the physical materialization of Divine principles and laws discovered by the scientists, who put them into physical use to uplift human life.

Take the use of cell phones, radio, TV, the Internet and satellite systems: These are physical magic expressing the principle of Divine omnipresence. They are also products of humanity's level of omniscience. The harnessing of the power of the atom, expressed in nuclear power, is an expression of humanity's mental creativity to access Divine laws of omnipotence.

All of these super-technological advancements, and many more, are the output of modern Jnana yogis, the scientists, whether they know the term yoga or not. The added quality they need to bring them to the spiritual path of Jnana yoga is the selflessness of their actions, dedicating their work to the greater good in the service of world evolution.

The term self-realization has traditionally referred only to tapping into the Divine subtle meaning of existence, but the macrocosmic life of the Divine also includes the physical plane. Thus, there's a need to acknowledge the importance of the everyday world, improve it, respect it and enjoy living in it – even using the new technological inventions as part of the Divine Plan.

A Jnana yogi is a great example of a practitioner who has a degree of self-realization (of Divine Laws of Creation) and who has self-actualized these realizations.

The other aspect of Jnana yoga is the realization and actualization of advanced concepts, noble principles, masterpieces of art and philosophies of abstract thinkers. Their trained minds can penetrate the realm of the abstract world through deep reflection.

Jnana yoga is composed of two major meditations: the concretizing meditation and the meditation for understanding. These are very important tools for your modern life to be able to work smarter and grow your careers faster.

The work and path of the modern Karma yogi and Jnana yogi can be integrated to become one of the most powerful paths of our modern society. From their ranks will come the modern Saints and spiritual initiates who will be the crowning glory of the Occidental cultures.

The mystical saints were the cream of the crop from the masses produced by the East in a prior age through the practice of Bhakti or devotional yoga. Great yogis and Sages were the most evolved representatives of the Eastern cultures developed by advanced people in their eras. In this modern era, the scientists, politicians, businesspeople, professionals and world leaders practicing Karma and Jnana yoga – consciously or unconsciously – will represent the best of the best in humanity's evolution.

MANTRIC YOGA

This yogic system is an art and science in itself. It is a mantric science if the yogi or practitioner knows and understands the esoteric meaning and purpose of the recited *mantra* or chant, including the required technical breathing and intentions while using these sacred words.

Mantric yoga is considered an art if the Mantric yogi is using the mantra without technical knowledge or awareness of the do's and don'ts of its use. Most religions employ Mantric yoga as an art through their chanting of religious songs or recitation of religious prayers in their rituals. Christians use the Holy Rosary. Muslims use prayer time to recite the qualities and names of Allah, loudly and simultaneously. Buddhists and Hindus use *sutras*, and other religions have their own mantric ceremonies.

The foremost unifying sacred words used by religions are Amen (Christianity and Judaism), Amin (Islam) and Aum or Om (Buddhism and Hinduism). Religions are very similar in this respect. They all practice Mantric yoga. Mantric yogis from different religions also use tools like the 108 yogic *mala* beads and the Roman Catholics' rosary beads. The beads are used to focus the attention and to count repetitions of *mantras* properly.

Mantric yoga in general is a system of practice involving the chanting or repetitive recitation of mantras or sacred sounds. These *mantras* or sacred sounds were received by ancient Sages and spiritual teachers during their highest meditation states and consecrated through their constant use for yoga ceremonies or service.

These special collections of sounds and sacred words have been handed down from spiritual teachers to their disciples from generation to generation. *Mantras*, when recited or written properly, have many effects:

◆ They attract different types of energy and blessings from the lineage of the *mantra* to empower the practitioner.

- They automatically invoke the attention and blessings of angelic beings called *devas* in yoga that provide power and spiritual substance to the Mantric yogi or group of practitioners.
- The vibration of the recited *mantra* or chant alters and increases the vibration of the practitioner's aura and energy centers, including the energy of their brain, nervous system and other parts of the physical body. This effect elevates the consciousness of the practitioner and when directed to the chakras or energy centers, the *mantra* awakens the practitioner's latent powers.
- The continuous recitation of the *mantra* or singing of chants harmonizes the vibration of the vitality, emotional, mental and spiritual auras (see Figure 1 , page 50) and enhances the person's health and well-being. The different components of the human energy system will be discussed in Chapter 4.
- *Mantrams* and sacred sounds purify and revitalize the consciousness of practitioners, thereby preparing them for higher awakening of spiritual energy, including their inner sacred fire, the *kundalini* (see Figure 13, page 105), located at a point above the perineum. When awakened, this energy serves as a fertilizer for inner development.
- Special *mantras* can be used in meditations for blessing situations and healing of oneself, others or the environment.
- Foremost, the effect of *mantras* for meditation and yoga is expansion of consciousness when the practitioner is able to sustain awareness on the gap of silence between the *mantras*, especially Om or Aum. This is when illumination usually happens. The *mantra* serves only as a frequency elevator and focusing tool. The actual steps of this meditation are explained in Chapter 21.
- Spiritual Masters and teachers use special *mantras* to grant good wishes to their students, employing the power of spoken or written words. A special hand *mudra* or gesture can be used with this application. Special spiritual beings also use mantric science for the destruction of obsolete forms and things.

Mantric yoga can be associated with the practice called *japa* where the practitioner does *mantras* using four different mantric methods:

1. **AUDIBLE MANTRA** (*baikhari*): Vocalized audible recitation of a *mantra* to elevate the yogi's consciousness and render the mind and emotions calm and aligned. This prepares the practitioner to go to higher meditation.
2. **WHISPERING METHOD** (*upanshu*): Done by whispering the *mantra* so that only the yogi can hear it. *Upanshu* is done when the *mantra* is to be kept secret or is so powerful that it can adversely affect other listeners. The yogi can also choose to use this whispering method to conserve his or her voice if the duration of the mantric practice is long.
3. **MENTAL RECITATION** (*monasik*): Done for more inward meditation with more subtle effects. This silent recitation is better done after mastering the audible and whispering methods. You can also use this for healing and blessing purposes when you don't want to be too obvious in the process. In public, mental recitation of a *mantra* is encouraged rather than audible or whispering recitation.
4. **WRITTEN MANTRA** (*likhit*): Writing the *mantra* with deeper concentration and alignment is a powerful physicalizing technique. It has to be done with a good sense of inspiration and intention, preferably using blue, red or gold ink except for calligraphy *mantras*, which are done in pure black ink. It is not recommended to use the written *mantras* for most cases if you can use the other methods.

Mantric yoga is a very powerful method that is usually incorporated in most of the other yogic systems. This is one of my specializations, and I teach mantric yoga to many students.

TANTRIC *KUNDALINI* YOGA

In its general form, this yoga system deals with the awakening of the yogi's sacred fire called the *kundalini*, which is symbolized by the Indian feminine deity, Shakti. The caduceus in medicine is also a graphic symbol of this inner fire. In Indian philosophy, the Divine light, or the masculine aspect, is symbolized by Shiva.

The purpose of Tantric *kundalini* yoga is the deliberate stimulation and awakening of the two spiritual forces, Divine light and *kundalini* energy, to be alchemized properly and brought upward to the Soul via the upper chakras and middle energy meridian, the *sushumna*.

This alchemized energy serves as food for the Soul and Spirit to grow. This spiritual mixture of energy causes the expansion of consciousness and is the fertilizer for the higher experience of enlightenment. Without it, there is no true "continuum" (of inner development), which is the literal meaning of *tantra*.

To achieve this awakening of *kundalini*, there are many processes involved:

1. Kriya yoga: A sub-category of Tantric yoga involving physical, emotional, mental and spiritual purification through breathing techniques and other yogic rituals
2. Activation of the chakras or energy centers through special breathing methods and physical exercises
3. Awakening of the *kundalini* by:
   + Chanting method with breath control
   + Sexual methods with or without a partner called tantric sex
   + Physical exercises with breath control
   + Meditation techniques with circulation of internal energy
4. Higher abstraction meditation to withdraw from the personality consciousness to the spiritual realm resulting in self-realization or enlightenment

There are many Tantric schools. Some of them involve the traditional Tantric rites like the use of the five elements: wine, meat, fish, grain and sexual intercourse.

Another group of tantric practitioners bases their system and study on four themes:

1. The creation of the world
2. The world's destruction and dissolution
3. Worship of God through Shiva (masculine) and Shakti (feminine)
4. Meditation and various methods for attaining Divine union, including sexual alchemy

The ritualistic tantric forms using five elements or the study of the four themes are the religious and exoteric aspects of Tantric yoga.

Even though they don't call it Tantric yoga, many Chinese teachings on practical Taoism can also be classified under this *kundalini* yoga because they use breathing techniques and sexual alchemy in their system.

Sexual energy, when stimulated to a greater degree,
is the energetic medium by which the kundalini *energy*
can be circulated to the upper centers towards the Soul.
Thus, we can conclude that the sexual energy is a spiritual gasoline
for higher development. When it is suppressed,
true higher enlightenment is not possible.

Excessive release of sexual energy is counterproductive, and excessive awakening of the *kundalini* force is not safe either. In fact, this is one of the dangers in yoga and meditation that we will discuss in Chapter 22.

INTEGRATED YOGA AND YOGA OF SYNTHESIS

Now is the right time for the new generation, which is more advanced than their ancestors because their body, heart, mind and spirituality are more integrated, to use a faster path and more systematic approach to personal unfoldment.

The Yoga of Synthesis emphasizes self-realization followed by self-actualization. What I mean is that the search should not stop after enlightenment or self-realization.

The practitioner should stay in society
to manifest and physicalize the new realized ideas
or aspects of Divinity. This is the real complete yogic work:
redemption of matter and physical life,
bringing Heaven to Earth.

Based on my observation and evaluations of yogis and meditation practitioners, including books written about yoga, many people want to go inward and escape the physical plane. They want to withdraw from physical life and abandon the earth and society. Their major concern is the Spirit or "up there". That is why there is less respect or concern for the physical plane, including physical care and beautifying the physical body in traditional yoga. Ascetics typically have this tendency.

I'm sometimes surprised that people on the modern spiritual path want to go live in the Himalayan caves, as if that is the ultimate goal of yoga or meditation. If all the enlightened people leave the cities and the management and ownership of society to the unenlightened leaders and business groups, what would happen to humanity's and the Earth's evolution? It would become even worse than now.

There is an urgent need for an integrated yoga that can apply the best of the Eastern practices and philosophies but with Western practicality: a modern yogic science that develops the mind rapidly, heals and stabilizes the emotions, cultures the physical body and awakens the power of the Soul. This new path combines the best of all yogas but in moderation and with a more universal approach.

This new yoga has to include sports and martial arts as a yoga of the body and will-power culture, which can substitute for some of the workouts of Hatha yoga. It also has to include mastering and perfecting the physical forms of life. Many new advanced children will be ready for a more universal approach to yoga and meditation. An Indian spiritual leader, Shri Aurobindo (1872-1950), realized some of these possibilities through his Integral Yoga (Purna yoga). My early spiritual mentor, MCKS, developed Arhatic yoga, which is similar to Raja yoga and is one of the best yogic teachings in modern society.

Having taught thousands of meditators in many countries, including yogis in India, I have observed several important patterns in meditators, yogis and their groups:

- **DEVOTIONAL TYPES OF GROUPS AND TEACHERS** attract devotional students and mystical meditators. These groups have the biggest membership. They are on the path of Bhakti yoga and religion.
  Observations: Too much love and mystical experiences delay the development of the mind. These yogis can be passive in service and have less material and social influence.
- **ESOTERIC TYPES OF TEACHERS** attract more advanced esoteric students and powerful practitioners with more will-power. They have the fewest members and students, but these students are more advanced and powerful for greater esoteric service. These groups are the most disciplined and focused. They are on the paths of Raja yoga, Tantric *kundalini* yoga and some groups of secret spiritual societies. They normally have more powerful development and energy mastery.
  Observations: There is arrogance and too much exertion of will-power with elitism and an excessive secretive tendency in their practices. They need to maintain development of love and wisdom to complete their development.

- **MENTAL TYPES OF TEACHERS** attract creative and intelligent students and members. Their membership is growing fast, especially with the new incoming generation, which is more mental, technical and scientific. Many of them are involved in research and new scientific discoveries. They are on the paths of Jnana and Karma yoga and scientific movements. They are very disciplined and concrete. They also have the most money and resources.
- **Observations:** Too much mind with less heart. Sometimes they lack energy and will-power. Many have personal traps of excessive pride, stress and materialism.

KARMIC YOGIS AND MANTRIC YOGIS are usually distributed throughout all the groups and yogic schools. The more advanced teachers attract a mixture of different types of students.

There's a weakness that comes from only developing the qualities that are natural along your preferred path. In general, this is acceptable for normal levels of development, but as you evolve, you need to integrate the different yogas. Therefore, the next modern yogic path for more advanced practitioners will be designed with integrated development of the three qualities of God or Divine Perfection, namely:

- Will-power (omnipresence)
- Love (all-compassionate love and kindness)
- Creative Intelligence (omniscience)

Both Christianity and Hinduism teach the trinity of Divinity. Yogic traditions also have three major Deities or personifications of God: Shiva (God the Destroyer with Divine will-power), Vishnu (God the Preserver with love) and Brahma (God the Creator with creative intelligence).

The new Yoga of Synthesis must revolve and evolve around mastery of three Divine qualities through a modern systematic path:

- The science of will-power development

- The science and art of love development
- The science of advanced concrete and abstract mental development

It will climax as a new system integrating:

- The science and art of Soul unfoldment, including the sciences of awakening the sacred fires and the proper construction of the *antahkarana*, the Soul's cable of light
- The science and art of Divine Synthesis, including tiers of advanced Esoteric Meditation, bringing integration of the personality, Soul and Spirit

8 CORE VALUES OF THE MODERN YOGIC LIFESTYLE

Instead of the traditional do's and don'ts of yogic virtues (*yama* and *niyama*), practical modern virtues for character-building will be the subject of personality purification and mastery of life. They are:

1. **BENEVOLENCE:** The key to achieving happiness, contentment and right human relations. Benevolence is the key to accessing greater inner powers.
2. **ALTRUISM:** The key and power behind prosperity and sustained abundance
3. **DISCIPLINE AND CONSTANCY:** The key to attaining greatness and achieving big results
4. **OBJECTIVITY AND PRACTICALITY:** The power to discriminate to achieve balanced results – the antidote to fanaticism. This is a virtue for advanced mental development and is required for global exoteric service.
5. **WILL-POWER AND VITALITY:** The key to speed and continuity of long-lasting performance. This is also a highly required quality for bigger service and higher spiritual development.
6. **GROUP CONSCIOUSNESS:** The big key to sustaining power and achieving bigger goals in less time. It is also a requirement for global projects and service.

7. **GOOD HEALTH:** The key to attaining and enjoying lasting success, fulfillment and service. It is required for higher spiritual training.

8. **VIRTUE OF SACRIFICE:** The key to great achievements and powerful service and the power to become a legend. This virtue has been mastered by more advanced spiritual initiates.

These eight core virtues of the modern yogic lifestyle are very practical and suit both spiritual and material goals without being too religious or cultural like traditional character-building. Those currently experimenting with this new Yoga of Synthesis applying Eastern wisdom with Western practicality include executives in banks, technology experts, physicians, healers, psychologists, educators, parents and other professionals. The new strategies are working successfully helping them master their modern life in five key areas: Family/Home, Career/Work, Social Life and Environmental Contribution, Health and Recreation and Spiritual Life.

The main principle to be understood is:

"Flower and bear fruit where you are planted."

Then you will be a modern yogi, mastering both material and spiritual life with great service and contribution to the world.

Part II:

Understanding Your Energy Anatomy:

A Key to Safe and Effective Meditation

CHAPTER 4

The Invisible Spiritual Anatomy Every Meditator Should Know

This is a very important chapter in this book because by studying the topics here, you will understand the real science of meditation and yoga and the difference between awareness and consciousness.

Just as physicians are familiar with the internal organs, systems and physical anatomy of the body, a meditator should know the invisible energy anatomy of consciousness to become an advanced meditator. Yoga or meditation instructors and spiritual teachers must be able to understand what's going on internally with their students at the physical, energetic, emotional, mental and spiritual levels for every technique they teach, especially for advanced meditation. In this chapter, we'll mainly discuss:

1. The human energy system and the different layers of the auras
2. The anatomy of the personality, Soul and Spirit and the triplicity of a human being

COMPLETE HUMAN INNER ANATOMY

There are three major components of a human being, functioning as a triplicity, namely:

1. **THE PERSONALITY**, made up of the physical body, vitality, emotions and concrete mind
2. **THE SOUL**, composed of the abstract mind, love-wisdom (intuitional aspect or *buddhi* in Sanskrit) and Soul's will-power (*atma* in Sanskrit)
3. **THE SPIRIT**, the Divinity within every person that has the trinity of life: Divine Will, Divine Love and Divine Creative Intelligence. These aspects are the three Divine qualities in one God within, mirroring the God transcendent. This is the Christian mystery of the Trinity: three personifications in one God and the statement that we human beings are made in the likeness and image of the Creator.

Let's start studying that part in us called the personality, portrayed below.

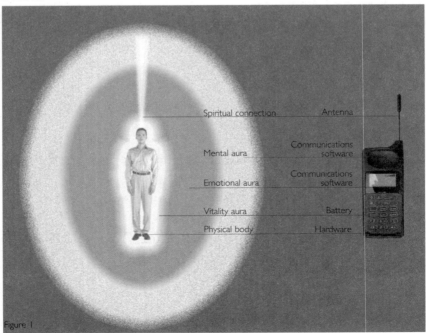

Figure 1

Your Physical Body is Your Hardware

The first part of your personality is what we see visibly as the physical body with its solid, liquid and gaseous construction. The physical body has been studied substantially by medical scientists and is recognized by almost everyone as their human self.

The physical part of ourselves is the grossest and lowest vibrational aspect of our bodies. When a person dies physically, the body gradually turns into physical earth substance. The emotional and mental energy bodies continue to exist for some time in their own planes.

Like a cellular phone, if the body gets physically sick, we bring it to the hardware specialists – physicians, massage therapists, chiropractors, osteopaths, herbologists and other healthcare practitioners.

Your Vitality Aura is Your Battery

The second component of your personality, the vitality body, is commonly called the "etheric body" in healing and yogic literature. It acts like our battery. This energy is the controlling factor of vitality and stamina. If we use vitality without replenishing it, we become depleted. When this vitality is constantly drained, which can be caused by stress, it accelerates the aging process, or a person can become ill.

As with different models, some people are born with long life and others are drained easily. This depends on their vitality and emotional, mental and spiritual development. The good news is that almost everyone can charge or increase their vitality through special methods like inner breathing, physical exercises, sleep, proper diet and meditation.

Visible solids vibrate at 360-750 trillion light vibrations per second. Gamma rays vibrate at approximately 3 billion billion light vibrations per second, and our vitality body vibrates even faster, making it invisible to the normal range of eyesight. The vitality body is invisible to the naked eye, but many children and psychics can see it using their inner sight. That is, they can perceive the vitality aura, even with eyes closed or by not looking directly at you. They can see a light around a person.

The etheric body has many layers of refinement. The densest part is seen as the exact shape of your body and extends beyond the body a few inches for most people. It is bigger in more advanced and powerful human beings. This denser part of the etheric body is sometimes called "the etheric double" because its shape follows the contour of the physical body.

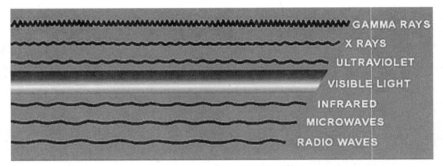

Electromagnetic spectrum: the full range of electromagnetic radiation from the longest to the shortest wavelengths and the lowest to the highest frequencies.

Figure 2   Source: Diane Boyack, 2000

The natural energy from the sun, air, ground and food, which are made up of *prana* or "bioplasmic life force", can charge the etheric body. The yogic tradition describes five types of *prana*, and we'll elaborate on this in Chapter 12.

When we do deep breathing, not only does the oxygen revitalize our blood and body, the *prana* from the air is also absorbed by the etheric aura, empowering the pranic or energy body. The physical body and its parts are controlled, purified and revitalized by the etheric body and its chakras and meridians (or pathways of *prana* and vitality). The health and power of the physical body depend primarily on the etheric body and its energy centers.

PIONEERING SCIENTISTS' WORK WITH ETHERIC OR PRANIC ENERGY

In 1929, a Russian electrician and scientist invented Kirlian photography with his wife, which can show light emanations, coronas and energetic sparks around objects photographed with the Kirlian apparatus. This is not exactly an aura, but an electrical pattern and reflection of one's auric pattern electrically and chemically appearing as a sensitive emulsion.

Many experiments using improved Kirlian photography show that frightened or anxious people have a differently colored auric pattern than calm people. Today, we have many improved Kirlian machines hooked up to computers. Dr. Hiroshi Motoyama, in his book, *Theories of the Chakras: Bridge to Higher Consciousness*, reported many interesting discoveries about the chakras, meridians and accupunture points, which readers may want to study.

For example, he invented the AMI apparatus for measuring the function of meridians and corresponding internal organs and discovered what advanced healers and clairvoyants already know – that there is such a thing as human energy.

At the Fourth International Conference on Psychotronic Research held in Sao Paolo, Brazil in 1979, Dr. Motoyama declared the results of his experiments[2]:

1. Psi-energy (etheric or pranic) is emitted through the healer's fingers and palms.
2. Psi-energy (pranic healing energy) is first converted into a form of physical energy which, in turn, generates changes in various physical variables.
3. A close relationship between *nadis*, meridians, *prana* and the sympathetic nervous system seems to exist.
4. Psi-energy and physical energy have mutual interactions through the intermediary of the chakras (invisible energy centers).

Another exciting scientific finding on the existence of the human energy system called the aura is reported in the book, *Psychic*

Discoveries Behind the Iron Curtain, by Sheila Ostrander and Lynn Schroeder. The book describes scientific investigations conducted in the former Soviet Union such as:

1. At Kirov State University in Alma-Ata, a group of biophysicists, biologists and biochemists concluded that the bioplasmic body (etheric aura) is not only some sort of plasma-like constellation of ionized, excited electrons, protons and possibly some other particles. It is also a whole unified organism in itself, which acts as a unit giving off its own electromagnetic fields.[3]
2. If a person loses a finger or an arm, he or she still retains the bioplasmic finger or arm so that sometimes it feels like the limb is still there.[4] This explains the phantom pain in amputees.

Thus, the vitality aura is closely interrelated with the physical body and is important to understand in terms of what is happening when you meditate.

YOUR EMOTIONAL BODY IS YOUR EMOTIONAL SOFTWARE

The esoteric literature calls the third component of your personality the "astral body" — an energy field made up of the substance of feelings. When we experience an emotion, we are utilizing the emotional substance in the emotional body. Love, happiness, peace, compassion, conscience, hatred, anger, fear, irritability, jealousy, aggressiveness, sentimentality and stress are all located in or connected with the emotional body and its energy centers. People express positive or negative emotional attitudes because their emotional body has various emotional substances. These have been inherited from ancient lives as well as through their parents during the process of insemination or during pregnancy. This phenomenon is illustrated by the fact that even babies and toddlers display varied emotional qualities at an early age.

You may have experienced effects on your emotional body without knowing how to explain it. For example, sometimes when someone is angry at you but hasn't communicated the negative feelings towards you verbally, you can feel it, especially in the stomach or solar plexus area. Likewise, when you enter a very stressed office, haven't you felt your stomach knot up or get nauseous? This happens because you are feeling the negative vibration through your emotional body, the energy body that receives and processes feelings, especially at the stomach or solar plexus area.

Another good example is mothers who are sensitive to the needs or problems of their children. Even at a distance, mothers can feel their children's issues or needs. Why? Because mothers can perceive feelings from their loved ones through their emotional bodies.

You can purify the negative feelings of your emotional body and recharge it with positive, pleasant emotions using special breathing and visualization techniques. As with the etheric body, the emotional body's densest vibration is shaped following the contour of the physical body, but extends beyond the outline of its etheric body counterpart. Since the emotional body is more refined than the etheric, its vibration interpenetrates it and is more expanded.

YOUR MENTAL BODY IS YOUR MENTAL SOFTWARE

The mind is not the brain.
The mind is the software and the brain is the hardware.

This fourth part of your human constitution is one of the most important because it differentiates your bodies of existence from the animal kingdom. To date, animals use only their physical and emotional instincts while humans use their minds.

The mental body is the energy field for creating, processing, receiving and projecting thoughts. When you are thinking, which is different from feeling, you are using the substance of the mental body. As with the emotional body, most people have already experienced some of the inner powers of the mental body. Have you ever thought about what prompts you to suddenly have a strong urge to call someone like a family member or friend? It turns out that you call the person who was thinking about you or sometimes you end up calling each other simultaneously. Have you experienced this? When someone is thinking about you – if you are sensitive and receptive at that time – you can receive the information they are thinking or at least know that the person is thinking about you and wants you to call him or her. What's happening is telepathic rapport.

The mental and emotional bodies serve as the software and energetic programs operating the entire personality, especially for normal everyday activities. For more advanced people, the Soul uses the software of the mind, emotions and vitality to empower the personality and daily life of the individual with more noble principles or advanced human faculties. Thus the difference between a Sage and a Saint, an intellectual and an average human being. The Sage is regulated and inspired by the Divine Spirit, whereas the Saint is regulated and empowered by the Soul. The intellectual person is regulated by their mental body and partially by their emotions. The average person is functioning and active at the level of the lower emotions and physical body and is engrossed with excessive physical appetites.

The mental body has many layers of frequencies. The densest can be seen psychically as the same shape as the physical body, but bigger and more expanded than its emotional and etheric counterparts. The mental body can be purified and recharged through many methods, including inner breathing techniques, affirmations and visualization. By using the faculties of the mind constantly, it is being exercised to develop mental powers and stamina.

When the mind is not used for a long period or stretched regularly with bigger ideas and new concepts, it starts to crystallize and atrophy. In a comatose person, the mind is disconnected from the brain. The mind – as distinct from the brain – will be a subject of massive new research and study in the coming generation.

The different auras and energy bodies are the sensors of meditation experience: When we speak of consciousness, it is a function of the auras and the human energy system. These many layers of frequencies serve as the perceivers and receptors of experience during meditations. The mind is used for concretizing and understanding type meditations, whereas the emotional body and vitality aura are naturally employed during awareness meditation.

More advanced meditations utilize all the auras and energy centers (chakras), including the Soul's influence. The consciousness of the meditator depends on what aura or energy body is being used or stimulated. The meditator can be aware of the energy bodies during meditation to facilitate greater expansion of consciousness.

YOUR SPIRITUAL ANTENNA OR CABLE OF LIGHT

The usefulness of a cell phone is affected by the antenna signal. It's the same for you. Even with a good mind, stable emotions and a strong physical body, there can be an absence of Soul inspiration, which is experienced as deep loneliness or apathy when your spiritual antenna is weak or has "bad reception". Your wisdom and intuition can be developed by improving your "spiritual antenna signal".

The ability to get out of body or expand our consciousness during meditation depends on the development of the spiritual cable of light. What we call intuition is the simultaneous accessing and downloading of the Soul's wisdom and advanced data via the spiritual cable to the mind. The bigger the size of this "cable of light", the more accessible the Soul's power and essence. The path of enlightenment is through this spiritual cable. It's as simple as that!

Your cable of light is a "Divine modem of consciousness" esoterically known as the *antahkarana* in Sanskrit. This cable of light serves as your modem to communicate with the Soul. It is a passageway of consciousness from the personality to the Soul (first part) and from the Soul to the Spirit (second part). These bridges of consciousness grow when we meditate, especially using advanced meditations.

Evolutionary progress and inner development are very fast after this connecting cable of light is constructed. Intuition, cosmic consciousness, wisdom, Divine oneness, advanced human faculties and advanced powers (called *siddhis* in yoga) are available after this stage.

HIGHER COMPONENTS OF THE HUMAN SPIRITUAL ANATOMY
The Soul

A human being is not a physical body with a Soul and a Spirit. It is indeed the other way around.

> *A human being is a Spirit using the Soul*
> *to incarnate through the personality*
> *to implement goals that allow the*
> *Spirit to become the master of life.*

YOU'VE GOT A DIVINE ELECTRICAL CORD

There is a Divine life and electricity supplied from the Spirit to the Soul and from the Soul to the incarnated personality. This supply of power and Divine life passes through a passage called the *sutratma* in Sanskrit.

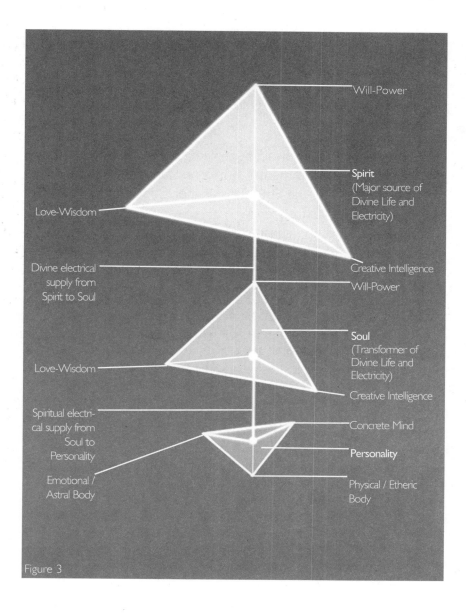

Figure 3

*How is the brain connected to the mind
and the mind to the Soul?
How does the personality connect to the Soul,
and the Soul to the Spirit,
and the Spirit to the Macrocosm we call God?*

These are common questions, even among advanced students. The incarnated person has three energy bodies that control the human energy system: the concrete mental, emotional and etheric or vitality. The Soul has different connections to all of these energy systems as follows:

+ The center of the head, approximately at the pineal gland, is the anchor of the mental light connecting the brain, the concrete mind and the Soul. This anchor is located at the higher levels of mental frequency.
+ The center of the chest along the body's central axis approximately at the heart area is the anchor of physical and etheric light connecting the etheric body with the Soul. This is located at the higher levels of etheric frequency.
+ The center at the solar plexus area below the sternum near the tip of the liver is the anchor of the emotional light connecting the emotional body with the Soul. This is located at the higher levels of the emotional frequency.

ANCHOR POINTS OF THE SOUL IN THE DIFFERENT BODIES

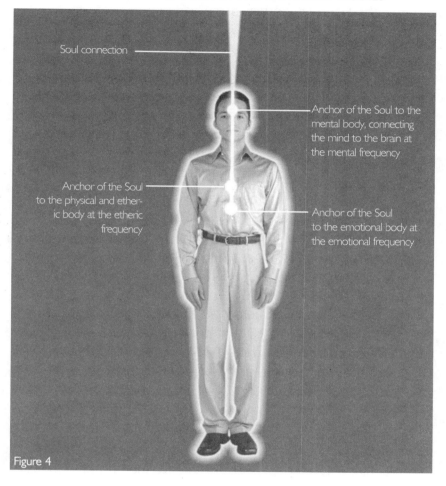

Soul connection

Anchor of the Soul to the mental body, connecting the mind to the brain at the mental frequency

Anchor of the Soul to the physical and etheric body at the etheric frequency

Anchor of the Soul to the emotional body at the emotional frequency

Figure 4

All of the different energy bodies have connections and correspondences at the Soul levels. The Soul as a being also has energy centers, which are qualified with spiritual will-power, love-wisdom and creative intelligence. The Soul also has equivalent connections to the Spirit or Divine Self. The Spirit is connected to the main power supply, which is the Planetary Divine Macrocosm, the Source of Divine Life and Light. In the English language, we call this source God.

This constitution explains the connecting points of a human being to the Planetary Source of life and power. Let's look at the human body like an electrical system to see how all of this works:

- The lighted electrical lamp is the personality
- The transformer station is the Soul
- The major power plant and source of Divine electricity is the Spirit

When the Soul wants to withdraw from the personality at physical death, it pulls its power supply from the physical and vitality bodies. Therefore, just like the electrical lamp, it's switched off. The ability to channel, absorb, assimilate and use the Divine Power, Love and Light is the real key to *samadhi*, enlightenment and true spiritual empowerment, leading to greater service and usefulness in life.

All the great achievements utilizing abstract and concrete intelligence and the ability to concretize great ideas, projects and plans are by-products of the stimulation and empowerment brought by the Soul or the Spirit to the incarnated person.

The expansion of consciousness in advanced meditators occurs at the Soul level. This experience of the expanded state is a quality of the Soul at its own level, which the personality experiences during *samadhi*. The advanced Masters experience this expansion of consciousness at the Spirit level.

THE SPIRIT
The Spirit is the Divine Self or the God within. It is the "I am that I am" within every person. It has three Divine qualities: will-power, love-wisdom and creative intelligence, which are mirrored from the Divine Macrocosm. The Spirit or Divine Self is the giver of life and light to the Soul.

The Spirit is a seed of Godliness in every human being, which is a fragment and aspect of the Divine Macrocosm. It is indeed an essence connected to and centered in the Supreme Divine Life on Earth. The Spirit serves as the basic seed or germ of divinity that sustains the will to live and evolve, containing the purpose of planetary life. In Sanskrit, it is called the *Monad*, the one God within with three divine qualities expressed in yoga as:

1. Shiva (God the Destroyer) qualified by Divine will-power
2. Vishnu (God the Preserver) qualified by Divine love and wisdom
3. Brahma (God the Creator) qualified by Divine creative intelligence

This highest center of Divine life where perfection happens in a person is latent and unmanifested until the Soul and incarnated personality have evolved to merit from and contribute to its functionality. In most people, the *Monad* or Spirit is asleep and in dormancy whereas the Soul is starting to vibrate and awaken in many people, especially in advanced meditators.

*The age of the Soul determines the level of
samadhi experience and expansion of
consciousness during meditation.*

OTHER ASPECTS OF THE SOUL THAT MEDITATORS NEED TO UNDERSTAND

1. The Soul is a being with consciousness that mirrors the qualities of will-power, love-wisdom and creative intelligence from the Divine Self or Spirit. The trinity of the Soul is reflected from the trinity of the Spirit.
2. For ordinary human level development to the Saint level, the Soul serves as the transformer and transmitter of Divine electricity, spiritual power and life from the Spirit to the incarnated personality. At the Sage level or higher, the incarnated

personality is already integrated with the Soul, and this new system is directly aligned to the Spirit or *Monad*.

3. The Soul is the transmitter of experience and lower presence from the incarnated personality to the Spirit. After a long series of lives as an incarnated human being, the accumulated substance and essence of experience are absorbed by the Higher Soul, which will eventually feed the development of the Divine Self or *Monad*.

ENLIGHTENMENT IS A SCIENCE

Expansion of consciousness, enlightenment and *samadhi* or higher yogic experience occur via the *antahkarana*. Ascension of consciousness is the elevation of awareness and a trip through this cable of light to the many levels of the Soul frequencies or the Divine levels of the Spirit as experienced by advanced Sages and yogis.

Once the science of Soul development, along with the science of the construction of the *antahkarana*, is known and practiced, enlightenment will become a science in the educational system. But this requires a lot of preparation and is very dangerous for the curious student without an advanced spiritual mentor.

One of the foremost requirements to progress to this advanced stage is very advanced service like esoteric work to use the excess energy you collect from meditation.

What we call expansion of consciousness, samadhi or Divine oneness with God has many levels and meanings.
Think of it as what floor of the tall building your elevator is on.
The Soul and the Spirit have many layers of consciousness within the Divine Macrocosm that even advanced yogis or Sages have yet to discover.

YOU HAVE A DEPOSITORY OF PERSONALITY EXPERIENCE IN THE SOUL

The Causal Body is a part of the Soul that accumulates the substance and essence of experience from a person's many lives. The by-product of each incarnation that brings additional consciousness and essence is deposited in the Causal Body. It is like a sac containing the substance of experience and is made up of varying colors and densities of light (see Figure 9, page 83).

When the Causal Body is substantially developed and filled up, there is an automatic brightening of the different bodies, especially the abstract mental body. A person's spiritual development is directly proportional to the amount and intensity of light and substance in the Causal Body. That is why there is a concrete description of advanced humans as old Souls and average human beings as young Souls. This refers to the level of development of the Soul as manifested in the Causal Body's emptiness or fullness of the energy substance of experience.

The purpose of the Divine Self investing its Divine life and electricity into the Soul and the incarnated personality is to gather experience and absorb it back as consciousness and substance of enriched life. It is like saying that the investor, the Divine Self, will gain its capital, plus interest or profits. The Divine Self, after the purpose is achieved, will also evolve and grow into a more mature being, which then becomes a brighter filament of light on the higher planes of Earth's existence. The physical, etheric, emotional and mental bodies are temporary sheaths and vehicles for the Soul to control the personality. These bodies change in each incarnation to suit the Soul's goals until the entire Soul's purpose is achieved. By that time, the Soul chooses to withdraw completely from the Earth's lower planes or comes back as another enlightened personality for planned Earth service.

Your knowledge and proper understanding of the human inner anatomy and a new spiritual psychology will provide you with wiser, deeper and safer ways to approach meditation, yoga and enlightenment. This is a must for advanced spiritual development, especially for those who will teach or are teaching meditation.

Now, our next step is to study and understand the complete chakra system in the following chapter.

CHAPTER 5

You've Got 12 Chakras, Not 7

The true essence of meditation, yoga and enlightenment can only be clearly understood and appreciated when the 12-chakra system is studied. Without this information, all yogas and meditations are just basic art or ordinary levels of practice.

Esoteric and advanced meditation requires a thorough comprehension of the three layers of the chakra system and their functions.

I believe that the great avatars like Lord Buddha and the Christ offered more advanced teachings during their physical incarnations aside from the philosophies taught by Buddhism and Christianity today. Their different religious scriptures serve as foundation doctrines in the spiritual path for their devotees, but Lord Buddha and the Christ must have trained their disciples with advanced techniques employing the chakras and *kundalini* awakening.

If you are planning to teach or master the path of yoga or meditation, I strongly recommend that you fully understand the human energy anatomy, the 12 chakras or energy centers, the *kundalini* and the new spiritual psychology of culturing the Soul.

If you are in charge of a big group, especially for esoteric meditation, it is a must for you to learn healing science — not just self-healing techniques — to be an energy healer with a complete understanding of the science of colored vibrations.

Most spiritual teachers and yoga gurus are not trained in healing technology by their lineage except for simple *pranayama* (breath method) or meditation strategies. If the meditator is "fried" and over-stimulated and the nerves are high-strung, the last thing a person needs is another meditation or breathing technique. The solution is not to add more stimulating energy, but to subtract and inhibit the chakras or release excess energies from the auras.

Mastering healing energy science is a must for spiritual leaders and teachers as an effective tool to help meditators with certain side effects, which will be discussed in detail in Chapter 22.

HUMAN ENERGY CENTERS OR CHAKRAS

There are many chakras or energy centers in your system connected by invisible meridians. These meridians, or *nadis* in Sanskrit, act as the "energy pipelines" to circulate *prana* or internal life force throughout the entire aura and organs.

In this current period, these human energy centers look like wheels or vortices of invisible light that form petal shapes of different colors. The roots of the chakras stem out from an axis of light passing through the center of the body. Most of the larger chakras extend horizontally to the front and back of the body; a few unfold upward and downward.

FUNCTIONS AND DESCRIPTIONS OF THE CHAKRAS

1. The chakras act as switches or keys to access inner faculties, spiritual powers and virtues like those we have discussed earlier: will-power, vitality, discipline and constancy, love, benevolence, altruism, creative intelligence, objectivity and practicality, group consciousness, sacrifice and good health.

2. Some energy centers are utilized by the Soul or spiritual consciousness to control certain physiological and psychological functions, including what we call good and bad situations in life like good luck or diseases.

3. These power centers regulate vitality, emotional attitudes and mental aptitudes. These faculties are tabulated on pages 84-86.

4. These invisible vortices of vibrations and forces serve as transmitters of energy and information within, into and out of the auras.

5. The energy centers act like energy software and subconscious programs for the proper functioning of the body's organs and systems, thus controlling health.

6. They serve as security gates for unwanted vibrations and negative forces, preventing these negativities from entering the energy bodies.

7. The chakras, especially the crown, when opened and activated, serve as special portals to uplift the consciousness to the Soul or Spirit.

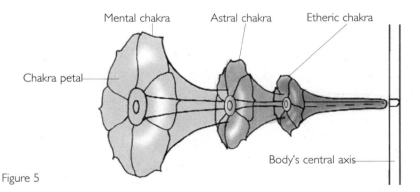

Mental chakra   Astral chakra   Etheric chakra

Chakra petal

Body's central axis

Figure 5

During meditation, you can energetically switch on many energy centers in your auras to stimulate your human faculties, aptitudes, attitudes and virtues gradually or rapidly.

When the chakras are more developed, trained clairvoyants or psychics see them as having brighter light, higher speed rotation and a bigger diameter.

EXAMPLE OF CHAKRA IN MOTION

Etheric Navel Chakra Advanced Human Being (8 Petals)
Colors: Mixture of red, yellow, orange and gold in advanced human beings

Figure 6

CURRENT FORMS AND FEATURES OF THE HUMAN CHAKRAS

The chakras have different stages of development according to a person's evolutionary level. As the person becomes a Saint or a Sage, a transfiguration of the total human energy system and the chakras occurs. Therefore, the shapes and features change. Chakras can be described as follows:

- They are formed by the aggregate crisscrossing of invisible forces and energy fields in the different energy bodies. In the current period of the Earth, humanity's chakras are circular and anchored in the central axis of the body like funnels or vortices of light. In more advanced human beings, their chakras modify into a multidimensional energy structure.

- The chakras move clockwise when admitting energy and counterclockwise when releasing energy, as seen from outside the body. The continuous rotation back and forth with all the interacting energies and forces creates spokes or petals, similar to a kaleidoscopic effect. The faster the rotation of the chakras, the bigger the vortex created, and this factor determines the chakra size and rate of vibration.

- The chakras have different colors, which are vibrations that stimulate certain physiological functions of the organs and also trigger the person's psychological behavior.

- There are three layers or tiers of chakras starting at the etheric frequency and continuing into the emotional and mental bodies.

- There are three sizes of chakras: the major, minor and mini-chakras. The major chakras are anchored along the body's central axis, extending to the front and back, with a few at the top and bottom. The organs have smaller-sized chakras, and some parts of the body like the fingers have mini-chakras.

- The higher the evolutionary development of the person, the bigger their chakras. The following is a list of approximate etheric chakral sizes according to level of human development:

SIZES OF CHAKRAS

Early humans	2 inches or less/5.08 cm
Average humans	3-4 inches/7.62-10.16 cm
Intelligentsia	5-8 inches/12.7-20.32 cm
Advanced humans	9-15 inches/22.86-38.1 cm
Saints	16-24 inches/40.64-60.96 cm
Sages	25 inches or more/63.5+ cm

In most cases, a person's chakras are not perfectly balanced or aligned (i.e., some of their chakras are bigger than others). Also, within the range of each of the above groupings, there are many sub-levels of development, thus the difficulty of approximating chakral size.

Let's discuss each power center briefly.

THE 12 ENERGY CENTERS AND THEIR GENERAL FUNCTIONS

TOP-OF-HEAD OR CROWN ENERGY CENTER

This center is located at the top of the head. When this chakra is highly stimulated or activated – especially regularly for many years – it harnesses the powers of intuition, unconditional love and wisdom, and it brings inspiration down from the Soul. It is one of the most important energy centers to activate and empower for advanced meditation, higher faculty development and to experience enlightment or expansion of consciousness.

For higher yogic meditation experience, including universal consciousness, the sacred fire or *kundalini* should be able to circulate to the crown center and even above it towards the Soul for higher illumination. The crown energy center stimulates the virtues of benevolence, altruism, sacrifice and group consciousness on a global scale. It is very developed in Sages, Saints and world servers.

The crown center controls and is in charge of central brain functions, including the pineal gland, which is like the CEO of the endocrine glands.

SYMBOLS OF THE TOP-OF-HEAD POWER CENTER

The cone shape on the head of the Buddha, which symbolizes full illumination and wisdom with a complete set of 1,000 all-seeing eyes equivalent to complete enlightenment. The Buddha is the embodiment of full wisdom and enlightenment.

The crown of Jesus the Christ with 12 stars and points. When seen with inner sight, this power center has 12 golden petal-like energies and, when fully developed, 12 opened petals like a crown or open lotus flower. The Catholic symbol of holiness and spiritual leadership is a miter worn on the head by the Pope and bishops. This crown symbol is also embodied in the three kings of Christianity who visited Jesus the Christ when he incarnated in Bethlehem.

The Shaman's many-feathered headdress, which symbolizes spiritual leadership as the tribal head.

The crown and halo of saints and Christian angels, which is the artist's portrayal of the crown center

Figure 7

FOREHEAD ENERGY CENTER

This power center is located at the forehead area and is responsible for the faculties of memory, intuitional insightfulness and greater awareness. It is a hidden energy center that most yogis, meditators, spiritual teachers and healers do not know about. Emotional excitement and the ability to sense pleasure, including orgasm, are also partially regulated by this power center, which controls the pleasure and pain center of the brain, the limbic system. Mystics and psychics have more active forehead power centers than scientists or concrete-minded people. This is why they can develop their psychic faculties more easily.

The forehead center regulates and controls the pineal gland, the nervous system, the limbic system and frontal brain functions.

MID-BROW OR *AJNA* ENERGY CENTER

This power center is between the eyebrows. It is symbolized externally in some cultures: for example, Indian women who wear a red dot between the eyebrows and the headdress of Egyptian pharaohs with cobra and vulture heads at the mid-brow area representing their more developed *ajna* power center and the third eye. Most yogis, healers and internal martial artists emphasize stimulating this point for mental will-power and abstract mental intelligence.

The *ajna* center is not the third eye, but is only one component of it. When practitioners do meditation for understanding, the *ajna* and the throat center (see below) are activated.

The *ajna* center controls and is in charge of the pituitary gland, the master gland of the endocrine system.

THROAT ENERGY CENTER

This center is located at the middle of the throat. It is closely associated with objectivity and practicality and is the center for the expression of the concrete mind. It is also related to concrete intelligence and discrimination. A well-developed throat power center is necessary to transform ideas into plans, organized activity and results. If this power center is over-developed without the heart, the person becomes over-critical and too meticulous.

Many scientists, accountants, lawyers and businesspeople have more developed throat chakras than mystics and loving type people. Jnana yogis have very developed throat and *ajna* chakras. The throat chakra controls and is in charge of the thyroid glands.

HEART ENERGY CENTER (Front and Back)

Bhakti yoga meditators' and yogis' heart, crown and forehead centers are the most active. The center of power probably most familiar to people is the heart, which is related to emotional intelligence, charisma and the love nature. The ability to love and be loved by people is one of the most powerful instruments to sustain leadership and influence. The faculties of love, compassion, altruism and benevolence utilize the heart center, especially guided by the unconditional love nature stimulated by the crown chakra. This is commonly depicted in portraits of religious Saints as the brightness and beam of golden light emanating from the center of their chest.

When we fall in love or do good things for others, we feel a pleasurable, warm sensation in our chest area. Likewise, when a person hurts others, the chest feels heavy, constricted and closed. This center of love expands or contracts depending on the activity and emotion projected or received by the individual. By activating this power center, you can feel love, peace and happiness, and the ability to forgive others becomes natural. Mystics and saintly people are naturally endowed with a big, active heart center, thus they are emotionally sensitive.

Many scientists, technically-minded people and business executives need to develop this center more so that their heart centers are as developed and active as their throat and *ajna* chakras. Businesspeople who are turning to philanthropic work are already opening their hearts. It is one of the keys to happiness and enjoying what you have in life.

The front heart center chakra controls and is in charge of the thymus gland, the immune system and the physical heart. The back heart chakra controls the lungs.

SOLAR PLEXUS ENERGY CENTER (Front and Back)
This energy center is located at the center of the abdominal area just below the sternum. This power center is the seat of passion, desire and lower emotions – both positive and negative. It is so important because it stimulates the energy for courage, commitment and determination, three qualities that very successful people have developed. It also usually accumulates stress, fear, anger, nervousness and guilty feelings. That is why people experience pressure

or a burning sensation in the solar plexus area when they are in a negative state.

When this center is over-stimulated, the person becomes unstable and emotionally reactive, sometimes leading to abrasiveness and stress. In most people, this power center should be regulated because its energy also exacerbates greed and self-centeredness, which work against the qualities needed to attain life's fulfillment. A well-developed, active heart can transform the negative impact of the solar plexus center.

This chakra controls the internal organs in the abdominal area, including the diaphragm and pancreas. It also serves as a clearinghouse for upper and lower energies.

NAVEL ENERGY CENTER
This power center is used most by the meditation masters, martial arts masters and advanced yogis in their inner practices and meditation. By breathing slowly and focusing on this power center, you can improve the following:

- Internal power for stamina and the body's rejuvenation
- Absorption, assimilation and circulation of internal vitality as a reserve of power
- Speed, instincts and agility in your physical reactions and movements
- Good gut instincts and timing in decision-making
- Sexual potency

This energy center is weak and underdeveloped in many people who are easily devitalized or sexually impotent, move slowly or have poor timing in decision-making.

The degree of navel chakra development separates the superathlete from the ordinary. If you look at the best golfers and basketball players clairvoyantly, they share one thing in common: Their navel chakras are more active and developed than in most players.

The faculties of the navel center apply in the business world as well. When a trained clairvoyant or good psychic examines the energy and auras of the best business decision-makers and great leaders, they can see that the navel power centers are bigger, brighter and more developed than their subordinates' or peers'.

Why then do these good decision-makers sometimes commit serious mistakes if they have good gut instincts? Because there are different degrees of penetrating truth, and the navel center instinct is just one of them. Sometimes higher mental discrimination is need-ed to override instinctive knowing. These higher faculties are devel-oped from the crown, forehead, mid-brow, throat and heart cen-ters.

Not only is the development of the navel power center impor-tant, so is the amount of energy stored in it. When the vitality of the navel chakra is low, instincts are off. Therefore, there is a need to constantly activate and energize the navel center.

I have experimented with activating and energizing the navel power center of athletes, and I have found that it definitely improves their performance immediately. In the future, internal energy employing the navel center will catch the attention of Olympic and professional athletes to break records easily in their chosen sports.

I also use navel center breathing techniques with our groups on Himalyan Mountain trips. As a result, they don't need to acclimate during mountain climbs because we boost internal strength and stamina through the breathing methods to improve mileage dra-matically, especially at high altitude.

I also teach these techniques to sexually impotent clients and after several weeks, their problems are solved. And imagine if this navel breathing were taught to astronauts who travel to outer space: I believe their health would improve and the negative side effects of long space trips such as muscular or skeletal deterioration could be minimized.

The navel chakra is an important center for advanced meditation, including storing of alchemized energy.

BACK-OF-NAVEL ENERGY CENTER

This center is located directly at the back exactly at the level of the navel. It controls the adrenal glands and kidneys. It is not usually mentioned in yogic texts in Indian philosophy, but the Chinese utilize it, especially in Oriental martial arts. It is also called the *meng mein*.

The function of this chakra is very important in the activation of internal energy. It helps circulate energy upward through the back along the back meridian. It serves as a pump of energy from the base-of-spine chakra (see below) upward to the other chakras. It is also directly related to the sex and spleen centers (see below).

If this center is over-activated, it can increase blood pressure. This is the danger of its use. But when an advanced meditator uses it to help circulate the alchemized *kundalini* energy upward, it is a very important chakra.

Most meditators and yogis should not attempt to energize this energy center unless they are experts in advanced healing science who know how to inhibit the back-of-navel chakra if it is over-awakened.

SPLEEN ENERGY CENTER

This center is a generator of vitality and helps the body purify toxins. It is a very important chakra for maintaining your good health. It is located below the floating rib cage to the left of the stomach area. When this chakra is weak, people tend to be depressed and their energy level is affected by poor weather conditions, especially when there is minimal exposure to the sun. The spleen center definitely has to be active, psychologically and spiritually, and healthy to sustain high output in life and great staying power.

This chakra is responsible for absorbing air *prana* or life force, digesting the *prana* into many colors and delivering the colors to the other chakras through the different meridians.

SEX ENERGY CENTER

This center is located in front of the pubic area and reproductive organs and is responsible for sexual vitality, procreativity and, indirectly, creativity. There is a direct relationship between sexual energy, creativity and success. Creative people are usually sexual in nature, and they tend to be smart, innovative and artistic. A well-developed sense of humor is also an expression of creativity and is connected to sexual energy.

Personal magnetism can be enhanced by the power of the sex center, along with the magnetic energy of the heart. This is normally called "sex appeal". In many instances, success and fulfillment are connected to personal charisma and a magnetic presence that enhance motivational leadership and the power of influence.

There is a technique to use the energy of the sex center to energize the brain and the mind to prevent senile decay that comes with age. Wouldn't it be nice to grow very old, still sexually appealing and mentally brilliant until our last breath?

The sex chakra is very important for awakening the kundalini fire.
A person's energy can be compared to a tree:
The sex energy is like the water to bring the minerals (kundalini) up
the trunk (center meridian) to make the flowers (chakras) blossom.

Tantric *kundalini* yoga employs sex energy through sexual activity called "Tantric sexual alchemy" to transmute the energy up to the higher energy centers to vivify them.

BASE-OF-SPINE ENERGY CENTER

The base-of-spine power center is located in the coccyx area at the base of the spine. It governs the basic will to survive and the ability to materialize goals. Wealthy and powerful people have well-developed and strong base-of-spine chakras. This power center is also associated with the strength and health of the hips, legs, knees, feet, muscles and bones. The base-of-spine center is necessary for a grounded, practical approach to life that balances spiritual fulfillment with material success.

Many yogic texts and books on healing confuse this chakra with either the perineum or sex centers. The inaccuracy of interpretation comes from studying a front view photo or drawing of the yogi. Therefore, they associate the base-of-spine center (*mooladhara* chakra) as the chakra in front of the sex region.

If these yoga schools and students count the chakras, the sex center is chakra number 1, which is erroneous. Any technique based on this error can be misleading. The root chakra (base-of-spine or *mooladhara* chakra) is located at the base of the spine with the vortex of whirling energy facing out from the back of the body. The base-of-spine center controls and regulates the repair and regeneration of body tissues, the muscular and skeletal systems and the spine. It is a very important chakra not only for physical health and instincts for material survival, but also for the awakening of the *kundalini* fire. It is also directly related to the sex, perineum, navel, back-of-navel and *ajna* chakras. Any weakness of the base-of-spine center affects these other centers.

EGOIC CENTER: *The Esoteric Chakra*
This chakra is not known by most yogic practitioners, meditators and many spiritual teachers. If it is known by some, it is generally not well understood or used in meditation. Yet this is one of the most important chakras in esoteric meditation for more advanced meditators.

Until the secret of the egoic center is discovered for meditation, most meditators are not doing advanced meditation yet.

In some yogic schools, instead of using the egoic center for meditation, the spiritual teacher utilizes the "light inside the head", approximately at the pineal area, which serves as a substitute for the meditator to be aware of the Soul light. They sometimes call this the "blue pearl meditation". This light inside the head that anchors the mind has a bluish color. It is as small as a pearl in more advanced meditators and very tiny in less developed people. This is a major component of the third eye or the advanced inner sight.

The egoic center, sometimes known as the chakra of the incarnated Soul or the Ego, serves as the major incarnation software for the total personality. It is not active in most people unless they start developing and utilizing the abstract or higher mind. It is located about 12 inches (30.5 centimeters) above the top of the head vibrating at the higher abstract mental frequency.

In Christianity, the story of the Pentecostal fire that descended upon the head of the apostles is a representation of the egoic center being awakened into a flame-like shape above the head of the spiritual aspirant. In this case, the apostles of Jesus experienced a group initiation that awakened not only their egoic centers during their group meditation (the Bible calls it prayer), but also their *kundalini* fire. After this event, they were more illumined to teach the doctrine of Jesus. The flame-like tongue of fire depicted in this event is the egoic center activated by the "descent of the Holy Spirit" or the Soul electricity.

Christian teachings claim that Master Jesus came to perform baptism with fire whereas John the Baptist performed baptism by water. The 'Pentecostal fire and awakening of the apostles' *kundalini* fire is indeed a spiritual baptism (group initiation) as far as I understand it. In more advanced spiritual aspirants like the apostles, the egoic center is the size and shape of a flame that continues to grow bigger until it is like a blossoming lotus flower in Saints and junior spiritual initiates. Therefore, if you see the Buddha or an enlightened Sage sitting atop a big lotus flower, these Beings are highly enlightened and have total control over the incarnated personality or Ego. Their consciousness is permanently above the egoic center, either at the Soul or Spirit levels.

The following illustrations are schematic cross-sectional drawings of the egoic centers for different levels of human development. Figure 9 on the following page shows the placement of the egoic center in the spiritual anatomy of a human being. The egoic center is the twelfth chakra for our present study. The Soul has three more energy centers higher than the egoic center.

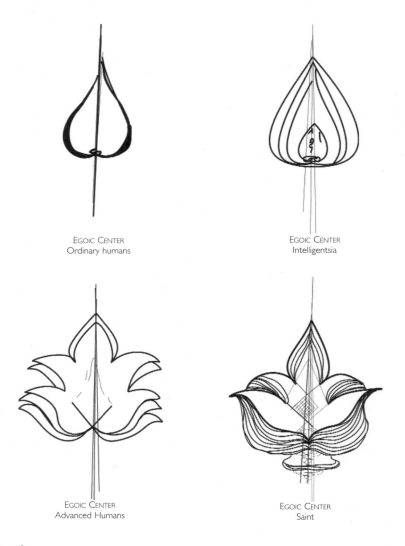

EGOIC CENTER
Ordinary humans

EGOIC CENTER
Intelligentsia

EGOIC CENTER
Advanced Humans

EGOIC CENTER
Saint

Figure 8

SCHEMATIC DIAGRAM: SPIRIT, SOUL AND INCARNATED PERSONALITY

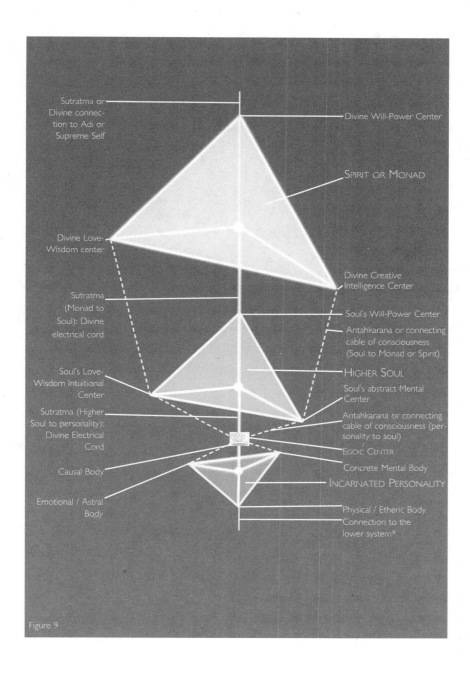

Figure 9

ENERGY CENTERS AND CHAKRAS

Keys to Awaken Your Advanced Human Faculties and the Secret Portals to Access Your Soul Power

POWER CENTERS	LOCATION	FUNCTIONS, APTITUDES, ATTITUDES AND VIRTUES ACTIVATED
Egoic Center	12 inches (30.5 centimeters) above head (abstract mental frequency)	• Soul's software to incarnate in the personality • Serves as the transmitter of Divine power, love and light • Mediating chakra between the Soul and personality
Crown	Top of head (center)	• Unconditional love, inclusiveness, benevolence, altruism, virtue of sacrifice and detachment • Global consciousness • Intuition, spiritual vision, wisdom, serenity, bliss and inspiration
Forehead	Center of forehead	• Insightfulness, spiritual vision, awareness, higher clairvoyance • Emotional sensitivity to pleasure and pain • Memory and imaginativeness

POWER CENTERS	LOCATION	FUNCTIONS, APTITUDES, ATTITUDES AND VIRTUES ACTIVATED
Mid-Brow or *Ajna*	Between eyebrows	• Abstract and principle-based thinking and philosophical mental aptitudes • Capacity to mentally understand and creativity through higher ideas • Mental stamina and will-power, ability to focus and be one-pointed • Virtue of discipline and constancy
Throat	Middle of throat	• Concrete and critical thinking, capacity for details • Communication skills and accurate mental perception • Virtue of objectivity and practicality
Heart	Mid-chest	• Personal love nature, compassion, emotional intelligence, joy and inner peace • Virtues of benevolence, altruism, sacrifice and group consciousness • Emotional magnetism and power to inspire • Ability to attract successful relationships
Solar Plexus	Center of abdomen below sternum	• Courage, emotional commitment and determination • Passion and desire (both positive and negative) • Happiness
Spleen	Left side of abdomen below the floating rib cage	• Vitality and good health • Purification of toxins

POWER CENTERS	LOCATION	FUNCTIONS, APTITUDES, ATTITUDES AND VIRTUES ACTIVATED
Navel	Navel or belly button	• Instincts, agility, timing and guts in decision-making • Vitality and internal energy/stamina • Rejuvenation
Back Navel	Directly at the back of the navel	• Serves as an energy pump at the back meridian helping bring the lower energies upward • Helps boost internal energy for the lower centers and the whole body • Energizes and awakens the sex energy center
Sex	In front of pubic area and repro-ductive organs	• Sexual appeal and personal magnetism • Energy fuel for creativity, artistic ability, sense of humor and spiritual growth • Happiness through fulfilling sexual relationship
Base-of-Spine	Base of spine at the coccyx	• Practical instincts, especially for financial and material results • Physical health and stamina • Ability to materialize goals

Ordinary human beings' chakras currently have whirling vortex or flower-like designs, but as we go into a higher level of development (like the enlightened beings), there will be modification into more diamond or geometrical shapes.

The chakras also have different colors depending on the tier or layer of the chakra: etheric/pranic level, emotional, mental or higher levels. We will include only the etheric level chakra features in this book.

Chakra	Number of Petals	Etheric/ Predominant Color
Egoic Center	12 (3 systems)	Varies according to predominant Soul and personality type/temperament. Generally golden with pinkish-reddish-blue core in current humanity. Colors and quality are different in advanced people with newer designs and more esoteric training.
Crown	960 outer 12 inner	Rainbow colors, predominantly violetish with mostly golden core
Forehead	144	Predominantly purplish, bluish, red, orange, green, a little yellow
Ajna	96	Yellow and violet, sometimes green and violet
Throat	16	Green, blue
Front Heart	12	Pinkish-golden-yellow, a little red
Back Heart	12	Yellow, red, orange, gold
Solar Plexus (Front/Back)	10	Green, blue, red, yellow, violet, orange
Navel	8	Red, green, yellow, blue, violet
Back-of-Navel	8	Orange, red, yellow, a little blue
Spleen	6	Green, yellow, red, violet, white
Sex	6	Red, orange, yellow
Base-of-Spine	4	Red, orange, yellow

Further reading on the nature of the chakras and auras is available in:

1. *The Chakras* by C.W. Leadbeater (Adyar Madras, India: The Theosophical Publishing House, 1927)
2. *The Etheric Double* by A.E. Powell (Wheaton, Illinois, USA: The Theosophical Publishing House/Quest Books, 1969)
3. *Miracles Through Pranic Healing* by Master Choa Kok Sui (Makati, Philippines: Institute for Inner Studies, 1997)
4. *Esoteric Healing* by Alice A. Bailey (New York, New York, USA: Lucis Publishing Company, 1953)

My book, *Inner Powers to Maximize Your Performance*, is a complete guide for readers who want to study the deeper functions of the chakras for physical, emotional, mental, psychic and spiritual development with more than 100 techniques and strategies.

My upcoming book, *Spiritual Technology for Advanced Inner Development*, will also be a complete reference even for advanced meditators. It is not only a treatise on the human energy system, but also on the "spiritual technology" behind the three tiers of chakras (etheric, emotional, mental), esoteric tool development and advanced Soul science.

OTHER ASPECTS OF THE AURAS AND CHAKRAS MEDITATORS NEED TO KNOW

MERIDIANS

These are energy channels, called *nadis* in yoga, that act as conduits of vitality or *prana* throughout the entire aura. These meridians act as irrigating pipelines and circulation pathways of life force. They are not only in the etheric body, but also in the emotional and mental energy bodies. They connect the different chakras.

There are three major meridians and thousands of micro-meridians. The three major ones are:

1. **FRONT MAJOR MERIDIAN**, which runs in the front area from the crown down to the perineum
2. **BACK MAJOR MERIDIAN**, which runs from the perineum up to the crown at the back
3. **CENTER OR MIDDLE MERIDIAN**. This is like a central axis of light, called the *sushumna* in yoga, running inside the center of the body from the perineum up to the crown. In more advanced people, this extends beyond these points in both directions. There are two circulating energy streams that affect the center meridian: The *ida* or feminine force and the *pingala* or masculine force. When these two flowing forces are balanced, the center meridian is induced to flow upward smoothly, accompanying the awakening of the sacred fire (*kundalini*) at its main seat somewhere above the perineum. We'll discuss this further in the chapter on *kundalini*.

The Taoist version of Tantric *kundalini* yoga named the complete loop of the front and back major meridian the "microcosmic orbit". Tantric yoga includes sexual alchemy techniques using this complete meridian loop to circulate internal energy and *prana* around all the chakras and organs to revitalize the human body and the aura.

CHAKRAL AND AURIC ENERGY FILTERS

We have studied and identified the different energy bodies and their chakras, which are made up of varying intelligences, intensities of light, frequencies and consciousness. And we have pointed out that the chakras are portals of different levels of consciousness in our whole being.

The chakras and energy bodies with their auras have separate functions and connect to different energy frequency stations or Earth dimensions and energy fields as follows:

1. The human vitality or etheric body is interpenetrated by the Earth's etheric aura and functions within this substance and vibration.

2. The human emotional body is enclosed by the Earth's emotional field and aura and functions within this emotional world.
3. The human mental body is interpenetrated by the Earth's mental energy field and aura and functions within this mental world.

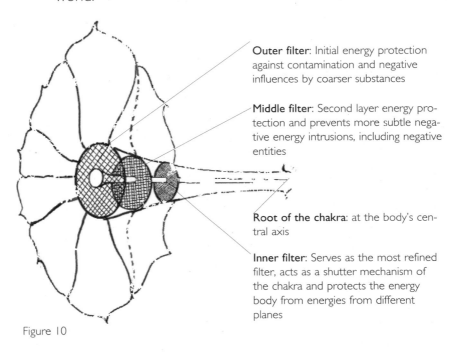

Outer filter: Initial energy protection against contamination and negative influences by coarser substances

Middle filter: Second layer energy protection and prevents more subtle negative energy intrusions, including negative entities

Root of the chakra: at the body's central axis

Inner filter: Serves as the most refined filter, acts as a shutter mechanism of the chakra and protects the energy body from energies from different planes

Figure 10

FUNCTIONS OF THE ENERGY FILTERS

The energy filters, acting like thresholds that separate the different bodies and chakras, have several additional functions:

- They are intelligent energy filters that screen incoming energies, allow harmonizing vibrations and reject unwholesome energies or negative entities and forces.
- They also act as separating veils preventing one's psychic faculties from always seeing the other side of the veil – meaning they are like shutters on a camera or video recorder. They function like a curtain to protect the person's consciousness and development from what they are not prepared to see.

Why is understanding the energy filters important for yoga and meditation?

The so-called expansion of consciousness
and the ability to integrate emotional, mental
and spiritual consciousness depends on the intra-communication
among the different auras and energy bodies.

When a person is ready after much purifying of the auras and chakras, the *kundalini* fire is aroused and circulated in the three major meridians, causing not only a revitalization but also a "burning of the filters" process.

When this burning of the filters and veils is done properly, the Soul's energy field and consciousness are "penetrated" or accessed during deep meditation. This allows the normal consciousness to expand to the realm of the Soul. The meditator can plug into the higher consciousness of the "inner world". This experience is labeled by some as Divine oneness or omnipresence or everything-ness (similar meaning to emptiness or "suchness"). This is one of the missing pieces in most teaching tools in most yogic schools.

The puncturing or transcending of these different veils
of consciousness between energy bodies,
especially between the Soul and the personality,
is the key for advanced esoteric meditation.

This advanced but risky strategy results in a deliberate ascension of awareness into the higher spiritual realm. This technique is used at will by the masters of esoteric meditation. The dangers in using this technique are great for the uninitiated and the curious.

People who use hallucinogenic substances also destroy these protective filters between their physical, etheric, emotional and mental bodies. Since many of them are not energetically purified and spiritually ready, instead of expansion towards the higher refined world, their bodies are contaminated and sometimes negatively influenced by negative entities in the lower etheric, emotional and mental worlds.

Due to the tearing of the veils or the energy filters in their auras and chakras, these people have "psychic experiences" expressed as either paranoia or hallucinations. They are just accessing the inner world without shutting their doors and walls to other consciousness. When the energy filters are damaged with holes, one can hear and see the inner world without understanding it. The worst case is the person who gets possessed by negative forces due to the damaged energy filters.

CHAKRA'S ENERGY PROTECTIVE FILTERS AND THEIR CONDITIONS

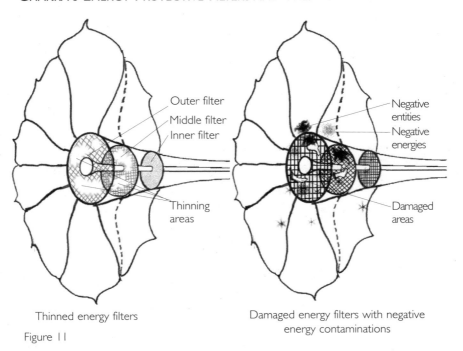

Outer filter
Middle filter
Inner filter

Thinning areas

Negative entities
Negative energies

Damaged areas

Thinned energy filters

Damaged energy filters with negative energy contaminations

Figure 11

To illustrate functions, aptitudes, attitudes and virtues activated by the power centers, let's look at the comparative case study below of world leaders and executives. Trained clairvoyants have determined the activity level of the power centers of these leaders and executives.

LEADERS OR EXECUTIVES	POWER CENTERS THAT ARE VERY ACTIVE AND MORE DEVELOPED
Mother Teresa (before she died)	Top-of-head, forehead, heart, solar plexus
Mahatma Gandhi (before he died)	Top-of-head, forehead, mid-brow, heart, solar plexus, spleen, navel
Martin Luther King, Jr. (before he died)	Top-of-head, throat, heart, solar plexus, sex
Winston Churchill (before he died)	Mid-brow, throat, solar plexus, navel
Bill Gates (Microsoft CEO) (On December 15, 2003)	Top-of-head, mid-brow, throat, heart, solar plexus, spleen, navel, sex, base-of-spine
Jack Welch (Former CEO, GE) (On December 15, 2003)	Mid-brow, throat, solar plexus, navel, sex, base-of-spine
Steve Jobs (CEO, Apple) (On December 15, 2003)	Top-of-head, forehead, mid-brow, throat, heart, solar plexus, spleen, sex, base-of-spine
Bill Clinton (Former US President) (On December 15, 2003)	Throat, heart, solar plexus, navel, sex
George W. Bush, Jr. (US President) (On December 15, 2003)	Mid-brow, throat, heart, solar plexus, base-of-spine
Mikhail Gorbachev (Former President of The Soviet Union) (On December 15, 2003)	Mid-brow, throat, heart, solar plexus

Note: The tabulation of leaders and executives does not reflect the development of the above leaders and executives compared to each other, but rather demonstrates the comparison of the different power centers within the person's own development, triggering balance or imbalance. The more power centers that are active, the more balanced the individual, especially when both upper and lower centers are active. The spiritual power center, the top-of-head, should match the size of the base-of-spine material power center for a balanced material and spiritual life.

The centers that stimulate material existence, objectivity, inner experience and spirituality are as follows:

MATERIAL AND CAREER SUCCESS:	Mid-brow, throat, solar plexus, navel, sex and base-of-spine centers
INNER FULFILLMENT:	Top-of-head, forehead, heart, navel, sex and base-of-spine centers

The future approach and new psychology for material life,
spiritual fulfillment and inner growth will inevitably
employ the new science of the chakras and meditation.
The matrix and actualization of this new paradigm will be
sculpted and shaped by the application of Eastern wisdom
methods of yoga and meditation applied with Western practicality.

Advanced human faculty development through meditation with the deeper understanding of the chakras, the human energy system and Soul science will bring a new revolution in learning and holistic education for the new generation. I envision that all these super-learning sciences will be part of the new education curriculum for the new millennium. They will be taught in high school up to the post-graduate level as a cornerstone of the education process. The science of the Soul will be a major subject, including the science of the chakras and meditation.

CHAPTER 6

Where Do Your Soul and Spirit Reside

Where do we go when we get out of body during meditation or when we die physically? When we say that our consciousness expanded during meditation, where and to what level of the Soul have we reached in that expansion? What is the difference between experiencing the Soul versus the Spirit? Where do our Soul and Spirit reside? Do these greater aspects of our personality belong somewhere?

Most of these questions can be answered by understanding the inner world, where our Soul and Spirit dwell. The Soul and Spirit are anchored in different frequencies, with the Spirit existing at higher planes than the Soul. The Soul and Spirit are beings with energy centers, and they are vibrating at different levels.

OLD SOULS VERSUS YOUNG SOULS

The single most important indicator of an older Soul is the activity and sizes of the energy centers, not only in the three layers of the personality but also at the Soul levels. The bigger and brighter the energy centers, especially the egoic center, the more advanced the person.

Another significant indicator of,the development of an old Soul is the degree of awakening of the *kundalini* fire. If this sacred fire has been substantially activated and brought upward to the Soul via the middle meridian (*sushumna*) and cable of consciousness (*antahkarana*), the Soul is starting to be fertilized to evolve faster. Therefore, during advanced meditation, the level of experience and the real expansion of consciousness occurs at the level reached by the alchemized *kundalini* via the *antahkarana*, the cable of light.

For example, if the *kundalini* energy has reached the abstract mind center, then the person has expanded to that higher level where the higher mind dwells. If the meditator has successfully brought the *kundalini* up to the Soul's love-wisdom chakra or *buddhic* center, the consciousness has expanded to that same level, which will give the meditator an experience of the Soul's love and intuitional nature. The meditator interprets this experience as one-ness with the love of God, which he or she calls bliss.

When the advanced meditator has brought the alchemized *kundalini* energy up to the Soul's will center called the *atmic* chakra, then the highly developed initiate or Master has experienced the will of the Soul or the "will-of-the-God-within", which is interpreted as the serene characteristic of the consciousness and Divine Oneness.

Zen meditators call this Soul's state "emptiness" or "suchness" or "nothingness" – not because there is nothing up at that level of consciousness, but because the brain and mind cannot process and interpret these levels and so the experiences are rendered "meaningless" to the personality.

Advanced Sages who have the equipment to reach and interpret the higher consciousness of the Spirit call it "I am that I am".

It's not easy to explain or label things at these levels without esoteric training and reference to a mentor who has been there.

Some esoteric literature about the different experiences of yogis describes these spiritual states with the different aspects of God as:

- ◆ Becoming one with the mind of God: expansion at the abstract mental level
- ◆ Becoming one with God's love: experiencing the Soul's *buddhic* or love-wisdom plane

◆ Being one with the will of God: experiencing the Soul's will or *atma* during meditation

YOUNG SOULS DON'T HAVE SPIRITUAL CABLE MODEMS YET!

Young Souls, even those who practice advanced meditation, can hardly experience higher expansions of consciousness because their "spiritual cable modem" is not yet connected — meaning their *antahkarana* or cable of consciousness is still not constructed. Therefore, there's not much experience during the meditation.

There is a big danger if young Souls are awakened too fast. It's like overwatering a small young plant. Instead of growing, it dies or gets stunted.

WHERE THE SOUL AND SPIRIT RESIDE

When meditators get out of body during meditation, their energy bodies — either the emotional or mental or both — are projected to the inner world, or their consciousness might be elevated to the Soul level. This is called the abstraction of consciousness in meditation or yoga. So what is called *samadhi* in Sanskrit or the "contemplation" experience of *nirvana* are progressive experiences of the meditator in the realms of the Soul or Spirit. But where do they reside? Somewhere within the 49 subplanes or dimensions of the Earth.

EARTH AS A MACROCOSM

The Earth is a living being, just like you and me. It has an invisible energy anatomy with energy centers, auras, a Soul and a Spirit, just like a human being. There are different levels of consciousness within the Earth energy system that we can experience during meditation.

The Earth, serving as the Macrocosm of higher spiritual beings, human beings and all kingdoms of nature, provides varying levels of consciousness, spiritual energies and substances that empower every being — visible or invisible, higher or lower — residing within it. Even the Super-Beings, Super-Sages, Sages and Saints are still inside

the planetary Earth consciousness. They reside at the range of frequencies within the Earth planes where their energy bodies are
located and vibrating. The Spirits and Souls of human beings are also
accommodated in different levels of the Earth planes or dimensions.
The Earth's population and different occupants of the Earth as a
macrocosm reside in the following planes of existence:

- Supreme Earth plane or *Adi*
- *Monadic* or Divine Spirit Earth plane
- *Atmic* Earth plane
- *Buddhic* Earth plane
- Abstract mental and concrete Earth planes
  - Abstract mental Earth plane
  - Concrete mental Earth plane
- Emotional Earth plane
- Physical and etheric Earth plane

All these planes or dimensions of the Earth are like energy
worlds within themselves, thus the more refined levels interpenetrate the other less refined dimensions. The Spirit resides in the
Monadic plane and the Soul from the *Atmic* to the abstract mental
plane.

SUPREME EARTH PLANE OR *ADI*

This is called the *Adi* in Sanskrit or highest Divine plane composed
of seven layers of frequencies. The Super-Beings, like the Buddha or
Christ with consciousness functioning at the *Adi* energy center,
wield the power of this plane, already employing a perfect quality as
far as the Earth evolutionary level is concerned. This is loosely called
"the seventh heaven".

MONADIC OR DIVINE SPIRIT EARTH PLANE

This plane is where the *Monad* or the Spirit of human beings is
housed. It is called "the sixth heaven". It is made up of seven layers
of frequencies. Those whose *Monadic* energy centers are active and
functional get their energy and power from this plane.

ATMIC EARTH PLANE

The *Atmic* plane has seven layers of frequencies and is considered the "fifth heaven". It houses the *Atmic* or spiritual will-power centers of human Souls. This plane stimulates will-power, fearlessness, detachment and spiritual centeredness. In advanced Sages, this plane is the source of all of the abovementioned powers and qualities.

BUDDHIC EARTH PLANE

This plane also has seven layers of frequency and is called "the fourth heaven". The energy quality at this Earth plane includes universal love, wisdom and intuition. The Soul's *Buddhic* or love-wisdom center is housed in this dimension.

Abstract Mental and Concrete Mental Earth Planes
ABSTRACT MENTAL EARTH PLANE

This plane is called "the third heaven" and is composed of three layers or frequencies of abstract mental substance. It is the start of the spiritual plane of the Earth, housing the abstract mental energy centers of human Souls. The powers available in this plane are the abstract ideas and seeds of creative concepts with universal applications. This is where philosophers and abstract thinkers get their new information and advanced principles.

CONCRETE MENTAL EARTH PLANE

This is considered "the second heaven". This plane has four layers of frequencies of concrete mental substance. The higher fourth level of frequency serves as a transition to the abstract mental plane. The powers available in this plane are logical and sequential thinking and the power of reason. Many aggregate and accumulated thoughts of humanity are deposited in the concrete mental plane of the Earth: positive, negative, true and illusionary. This is the big issue for this plane because of the contamination of lower vibrations of thoughts from all kinds of sources, including the thoughts of past civilizations, present humanity and polluting negative programs from anti-evolutionary forces. Therefore, the power tapped from this level deals with both good and bad sources and qualities.

EMOTIONAL EARTH PLANE

This is also called the astral plane with a total of seven layers of consciousness: the three highest layers of frequency are considered "the first heaven", the lower frequencies at about the fourth and fifth layers form the state of purgatory and the lowest frequency houses the state of hell.

PHYSICAL AND ETHERIC EARTH BODIES

These are the densest planes of the Earth. The etheric part of the Earth has four layers of frequencies: first etheric, second etheric, third etheric and fourth etheric. The physical aspects of the Earth are the gases, liquids and solids.

EARTH BEING AS A MACROCOSM

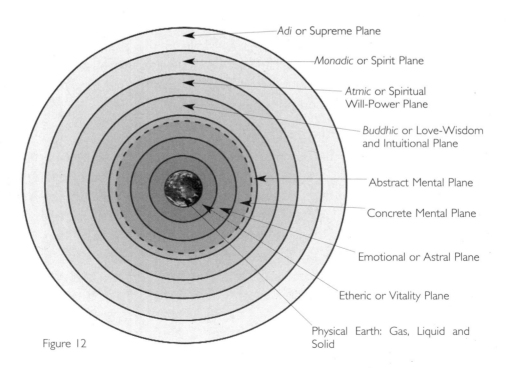

Adi or Supreme Plane

Monadic or Spirit Plane

Atmic or Spiritual Will-Power Plane

Buddhic or Love-Wisdom and Intuitional Plane

Abstract Mental Plane

Concrete Mental Plane

Emotional or Astral Plane

Etheric or Vitality Plane

Physical Earth: Gas, Liquid and Solid

Figure 12

The more subtle and refined the frequency or consciousness tapped from the Soul and the Earth planes, the greater the expansion of consciousness and Divine oneness. Thus, the science of advanced meditation requires a better understanding of the following:

- The science of constructing the *antahkarana* (cable of consciousness)
- The science of awakening the Soul
- The science of activating and culturing the chakras
- The science of awakening the *kundalini*

This chapter has given you an overview of where the personality, Soul and Spirit are housed inside the Earth. By understanding the different Earth dimensions, which can be penetrated through meditation, then true esoteric knowledge and expansion of consciousness during advanced meditation are meaningful.

In order to learn and grow through more advanced meditation, we need to study the anatomy and use of the *kundalini* in the next chapter.

CHAPTER 7

Kundalini:

How to Play with Your Sacred Fires Safely

The *kundalini* fire and its awakening are some of the most sought-after topics in yoga and meditation, but the *kundalini* is also one of the most misunderstood of all topics. Why? Because the *kundalini* or sacred fire is one of the major fuels to awaken the latent powers of the personality, Soul and Spirit.

Kundalini is a Sanskrit term that literally means snake, referring to the serpent-shaped flowing form of the *kundalini*. This creative force is anchored in people at the junction of the perineum, sex and base-of-spine centers.

In the present human design, its shape is like coily springing flames. That is why it is called the serpent fire. But as a person advances, the shape of the *kundalini* seat changes into more sharp geometric designs.

THE *KUNDALINI* OR SACRED FIRE

A tree needs minerals and water to stay alive, grow and bear fruit. Super-Beings, Sages and human beings also need spiritual minerals or spiritual food and spiritual water to grow and bear the fruit of enlightenment. The sexual energy is like the water that brings up the *kundalini* as the fertilizing mineral to all the energy centers and bodies.

In ancient times, the *kundalini* was symbolized as the dragon spitting fire and the snake coiling up around a staff or cane. In India, some statues of advanced yogis show cobras at the back of their heads. The number of snakes signifies how advanced the yogi or how many *kundalini* channels are opened. The wisdom of ancient medicine was symbolized by the caduceus — two snakes coiling around and ascending a staff with two wings and a rounded top.

As there are seven Earth planes with seven frequencies each, totaling 49 frequencies, the Super-Beings at the highest level of human development have to reach a total of 49 degrees of *kundalini* awakening.

Every human being has a certain level of *kundalini* development. It is a matter of the degree of opening of the sheaths covering the *kundalini* path. The opening of the *kundalini* sheaths is analogous to the peeling of the layers of an onion, but from the inside. The more sheaths removed through the inner fire burning process, the greater the volume of *kundalini* flow.

The real source of stimulation of consciousness at all levels is determined by how many of the *kundalini* layers are opened. It also depends on the level of energy centers and energy bodies of the incarnated person, Soul or *Monad* the *kundalini* has reached. The greater the opening, the higher the development of the meditator and the more advanced the experience and expansion of consciousness.

Schematic Illustration of the *Kundalini* (current model)

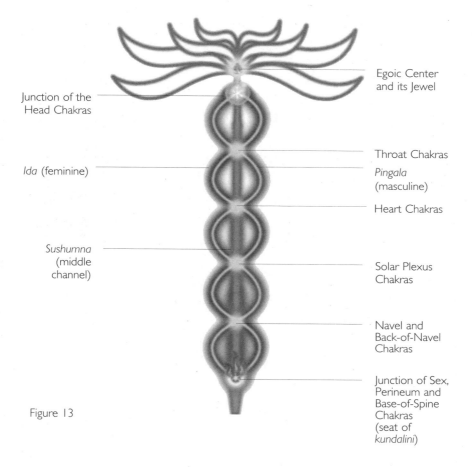

Egoic Center
and its Jewel

Junction of the
Head Chakras

Throat Chakras

Ida (feminine)

Pingala
(masculine)

Heart Chakras

Sushumna
(middle
channel)

Solar Plexus
Chakras

Navel and
Back-of-Navel
Chakras

Figure 13

Junction of Sex,
Perineum and
Base-of-Spine
Chakras
(seat of
kundalini)

Cobras as a Symbol of the *Kundalini*

Super-Being Level with 49
layers of *kundalini* awakening symbolized by 7 cobras
at the back of the head

Figure 14

The faculties, inner powers, energy levels, sizes of the chakras, development of the energy bodies and the degree of world influence of any person or being are directly proportional to their *kundalini* awakening. Here are some of the major functions of the *kundalini*:

1. Catalyst and fertilizer to stimulate and activate the growth of the chakras and energy bodies
2. Serves to vivify the latent qualities and functions of the psychic and psychological powers, both positive and negative
3. Burns the protective webs or energy filters separating the different bodies from physical up to the *Monadic* and *Adi* for the human being to be perfected
4. By the alchemy of the *kundalini* mixed with different energies and forces from the energy bodies and chakras, the resulting substance is brought to the egoic center at first, then to the Soul's higher chakras in order to accelerate the Soul development. At a high stage of development like the Super-Sage and Super-Beings, the alchemized *kundalini* has to be brought to the *Monadic* level.

   This alchemized *kundalini* substance serves as a catalyst and fertilizer for the Soul to grow and for the different levels of the Soul's and Spirit's development to manifest. This last stage of development applies to Saints, Sages and Higher Beings.
5. The *kundalini,* resulting in the awakened development of the meditator, serves as a substance to fill up the *antahkarana* or spiritual cable connector. The fertilizing action of the *kundalini* mixed with other energies fills up the substance of the *antahkarana*. Thus, there is no true construction of this cable of consciousness without the alchemized *kundalini* energy. Enlightenment and higher evolution are not possible without advanced *kundalini* development.
6. The *kundalini* path, when developed, acts as a rod or electrical conductor, optical passageway and transmitter of vast amounts of information and data when perceived as spiritual

technology equipment. The *kundalini* pathway also serves as a power supply. It is a super communication and electrical equipment when highly developed and activated.

7. The substance of the *kundalini* is the power that materializes thoughts, intentions and goals at a faster speed and with greater potency.

ENERGY FORM AND MYTH OF THE *KUNDALINI*

If you study the medical caduceus symbol deeply, you can see that it represents the inner path of the sacred fires latent in every human being. The central line is equivalent to the middle energy meridian passing through the central axis of the body. The intersecting snakes in the caduceus represent the masculine (*pingala*) and feminine (*ida*) equivalent forces and the meridians traversing through the different roots of the chakras going upwards to the crown center. The wings on top of the caduceus are the equivalent symbol of the faculty of intuition and higher expansion when the *kundalini* is able to reach to the egoic center or higher. The rounded top of the caduceus is equivalent to the mental seed of consciousness seated at the pineal gland area inside the head. Once meditators understand this universal symbol, the spiritual practitioner or yogi can achieve greater heights of experience and inner powers development. Ancient Sages and Enlightened Beings have used this knowledge to develop techniques to harness the sacred fires and develop the inner powers in all the energy bodies and centers.

The story of Prince Charming kissing and waking up Sleeping Beauty is a great fairy tale that hides the inner meaning of how to awaken your *kundalini,* sometimes called the sleeping serpent or dragon. Prince Charming is the Divine Light from the Soul, and Sleeping Beauty is the dormant energy (in most people at their current level of development) at an area slightly above the perineum. This energy moves upward with a spiral action in humanity as of this period. There are three major ascending paths of the *kundalini* fire or substance in the energy bodies:

1. The middle path or axis called the *sushumna* in yoga
2. Active force or the masculine aspect expressed as *pingala*. This is the path of the sacred fire that is affected by right-nostril breathing.
3. Passive force or the feminine force expressed as *ida*. This is the path that is affected by left-nostril breathing.

The advanced yogis and Sages have found that by balancing these two flowing forces or meridians (*ida* and *pingala*) through the balancing of the breaths through the nostrils, the *kundalini* naturally flows outward.

The current configuration of the *kundalini* and its path are still valid as of this time. But it has been observed that features and patterns of flow are being altered, especially in more advanced humans.

Once the sacred fire of the *kundalini* circulates outward, it vivifies and fertilizes all the centers and their psychological as well as spiritual powers. This is what advanced meditators and yogis are technically doing to achieve great inner powers and advanced faculties. Even without formal schooling, their faculties of wisdom and higher qualities get developed.

WHAT CAUSES THE AWAKENING OF THIS SACRED FIRE?

When you inhale fully and hold your breath for a few seconds, the Divine light descends through the crown chakra and floods the bodies. When you exhale fully and hold for a few seconds, the *kundalini* is stimulated and increases its activity. By doing this alternately for 3-5 minutes for each nostril, there is already a substantial awakening of this sacred fire. The outcome is increased internal energy in your bodies. This creative fire also vivifies and fortifies the chakras and bodies that it reaches.

Of all the topics that engross esoteric schools and advanced schools of yoga, the *kundalini* has been a source of fascination and also a source of menace and fright to those who are ignorant about it. The true esoteric scientists, divine alchemists and white magicians are masters of the *kundalini* science. This power is the secret behind extraordinary faculties in some yogis and spiritual teachers.

The right dose and quality of the *kundalini* awakening depend on one's level of spiritual development. It is very dangerous to awaken the *kundalini* power without proper guidelines and guidance from a knowledgeable teacher. Working with the *kundalini* requires the same type of strictness needed in handling the power of a nuclear bomb compared to handling a gun. The greater the force and power, the greater the safety measures and knowledge required for their care and use.

The technical requirements of awakening the powers of the *kundalini* are:

1. Knowledge of the *kundalini*, its nature, function and mechanisms, including the do's and don'ts of handling it
2. Purification of the energy bodies and energy centers and removal of energy obstacles along the front, back and middle meridians of the bodies
3. Character-building to eradicate negative attitudes and behaviors, which get amplified by the awakening of the *kundalini*. The *kundalini* is like a fertilizer facilitating both the personal "weeds" and "flowers" to grow fast.
4. Preparation of the physical and energy bodies by proper diet and culturing them with special exercises and breathing techniques. People with vices like smoking, alcoholism and drug abuse cannot practice the awakening of the *kundalini* safely.
5. Outlets for the excess additional powers and energy as a result of the *kundalini* awakening for greater service and a bigger purpose in life. When the *kundalini* gets activated, tremendous power is added to the meditator's normal energy level. If this is not utilized for a good cause, it can result in congestion or over-stimulation affecting one's health. Also, additional energy and power are supposed to be sought for greater service or nobler applications, not just to feed a hunger for power. Good intention is important right from the start.

Greater service guarantees that if a meditator's negative karma is accelerated as part of spiritual development and inner purification, the good karma generated from service can neutralize difficult situations.

6. Activation and alignment of the chakras, especially certain important parings and triangulations. This involves the three energy bodies.

7. Proper meditation and breathing techniques: The practices of many exoteric schools of yoga, internal martial arts and spirituality still need to be organized and esoterically integrated to warrant a gradual and safe awakening of the *kundalini*. In most systems, many steps and ingredients are missing. Either the teachings are too slow or cautious or techniques are done improperly and sometimes blindly. Also, too much advanced meditation without service and external applications makes people mystical and too centered on inner practices rather than focusing on their externalized usefulness for social or world development.

8 Guidance from a spiritual mentor who understands the *kundalini* technically and scientifically is the foremost requirement. If people need fitness coaches for very simple tangible activities like body-building, how much more important is it to have a guide for culturing invisible energy, which is very abstract? The spiritual teachers have already walked this path; therefore, they are the best guides.

There are a few modern esoteric schools that are really safe and scientific in their approach to dealing with more advanced awakening of the *kundalini*. Spiritual teachers and yoga masters must be able to do esoteric healing to manage or prevent the negative side effects of meditation or yoga. But it's surprising that many of them are not equipped with these healing tools. For this reason, I felt the need to help spiritual teachers, yoga masters and practitioners by establishing a school, ESOCEN, to teach advanced healing systems.

This book includes several safe and simplified methods of gradually awakening your *kundalini,* including yogic breathing, exercises, *mantrams* and the use of your Soul light, in upcoming chapters.

The *Kundalini* Has Colors and Density

The more advanced a person, the more intense the *kundalini* colors and the higher the density. The *kundalini* color ranges from reddish-yellow-orange to a more intense golden-red-orange in more advanced practitioners.

In very advanced yogis and meditators, their *kundalini* substance is highly compact with more intense colors and metallic hues. In super-advanced Sages or spiritual initiates, this sacred fire becomes a crystalline or diamond rod of power that acts like electrical, electronic and conductive equipment connecting the personality, the Soul and the Spirit. It is not just the spiritual fuel line at this point, but rather the "path" of Divinity itself.

Let's summarize the *kundalini* experience and awakening by level of human development:

LEVEL OF HUMAN DEVELOPMENT	KUNDALINI EXPERIENCE AND AWAKENING
Early or primitive people	*Kundalini* seat just formed and dormant
Average people or masses	*Kundalini* seat starting to vibrate slightly, almost awake
Intelligentsia	*Kundalini* starting to awaken with more vibratory movement. *Kundalini* substance, as it arises upward through the spine, is sensed by the meditator as a bubbling thin, airy-like flow.
Advanced people	Watery to milky density feeling flowing up the spine
Saints	*Kundalini* flow feels like condensed milk, thick syrup or a liquid-cheese density
Sages	Thick, fiery, lava-like or molten metal flow
Super-Sages	Energetically, the *kundalini* looks like hardened mercury or platinum, but with different texture configurations like diamond structure depending on whether the Super-Sage is of the old or new system.

KUNDALINI CHANGES AS YOUR LEVEL OF DEVELOPMENT EVOLVES

Source of The Kundalini Fire
The Earth as a being is the source of the power and energy in every person's *kundalini* seat. The Earth has seven layers of *kundalini* and seven sub-layers, and a person's *kundalini* seat is housed within the Earth's *kundalini* system.

The upward flow of this primordial force depends on the speed, size and available energy at the sex, base-of-spine, perineum and navel chakras. The higher their speed and integration, the higher the flow.

HOW TO PLAY WITH KUNDALINI FIRE WITHOUT GETTING BURNED

The safest methods to awaken the *kundalini* without many side effects are:

1. A lifetime of character-building and purification of negative habits, lifestyle and spiritual toxins
2. Making your body, vitality, emotions and mind more resilient through exercises, breathing techniques, meditation and energy healing
3. Awakening the upper energy centers through certain techniques to regulate the lower animal nature of the lower chakras. The higher principle of life should control or transform the lower principles.
4. Stimulating and employing the Soul's Divine light to awaken the *kundalini* by bringing it down to the *kundalini* seat. Then the alchemized mixture should be circulated or transmuted upward through the upper centers and released to the Soul. This is the right way. Most practitioners and yogis, including some Taoist practitioners, almost always awaken the *kundalini* by forcing it to push upwards. Some Tibetan lamas even force it by repeatedly dropping themselves and bumping their buttocks onto the ground or floor to jolt the *kundalini* seat. This is unsafe and physically tiring with lesser results.

There is a common symbol in Indian philosophy representing enlightenment achieved by bringing alchemized *kundalini* energy to the crown center. This is Ganesh, an enlightened deity with an elephant head. Why this symbol? Because in yogic mythology, the base-of-spine chakra is represented by an elephant due to its physical power. Most yogis believe that the *kundalini* seat is at the base-of-spine or *mooladhara* (sometimes spelled *muladhara*) chakra. This is not totally accurate because, as we mentioned earlier, the *kundalini* seat is in the junction of the perineum, sex and base-of-spine at the center axis.

When this *kundalini* rises to the top of the head at the crown center, the yogi gets enlightened (to a certain degree). Thus, the elephant-head Ganesh symbolizes the risen *kundalini* at his crown.

The idea that bringing the *kundalini* to the mid-brow or *ajna* chakra will develop enlightment or construct the third eye is another partially incorrect idea. The third eye is constructed by the integration and fusion of all the chakras in the head, not just the *ajna,* plus the vivification of the alchemized *kundalini* energy. The action of the Soul light is much needed to complete the technique of third eye development.

As a rule of thumb, the Soul's Divine light should awaken and regulate the *kundalini* force. Then it is safe. That is why the fairy tale of Prince Charming and Sleeping Beauty is correct. The original storytellers who created this tale knew the secret of this spiritual alchemy. After Prince Charming and Sleeping Beauty are married (mixed and alchemized Divine light and *kundalini* energy), they lived happily ever after (the mixed energy rises towards the Soul and becomes part of the Soul's quality of immortality).

Chapter 22 offers more instruction on the dangers of *kundalini* awakening and solutions to these dangers.

The first part of this book has served to inform and educate novice and advanced meditators about the simple to advanced concepts of meditation and yoga, including their types. We also studied the spiritual anatomy and the nature of the *kundalini.* We now have enough tools and data for the complete practice of safe and effective meditations.

Part III:

STEPS FOR SAFE AND EFFECTIVE MEDITATION

CHAPTER 8

How to Meditate Safely:

5 Steps for Safe and Effective Meditation

W e have covered the most important concepts and different types of meditations, including the spiritual anatomy. Now we can learn how to meditate safely. Since there are many types of meditation, we need to select and discuss in depth a general procedure for the typical meditation that most meditators will use, the abstraction meditation, which is similar to most yogic practices. This book is presenting the science of meditation, therefore we need to apply specific protocols. The five steps below offer a modern system for abstraction meditation.

Other types of meditations that are targeted to other purposes like for self-healing, concretizing, understanding and daily applicable models will be discussed separately in later chapters.

5 Steps of Meditation Every Meditator Should Know

Let's summarize the steps before discussing them in detail.

Step 1.
Prepare Yourself and Your Space for Your Best Meditation Experience

   a. Purify and organize your meditation space.
   b. Isolate yourself from disturbances like cell phones and noise.
   c. Condition and purify your physical body and auras:
     - Shower, bath or yogic cleansing rituals
     - Physical exercises to condition and unblock the body
     - Breathing techniques to purify and condition the auras and chakras
   d. Invocation for Divine protection, guidance and empowerment
   e. Proper body postures and meditation *mudras*
   f. Proper breathing techniques

Step 2.
Concentration Techniques

   a. Activate the energy centers with different methods.
   b. Awaken the Divine light, *kundalini* energy and pranas
   c. Alchemize the awakened energies and circulate them.

Step 3.
Awareness Meditation and Wisdom Development

   a. Transform concentration into awareness.
   b. Let go of the mind, withdraw from external senses and abstract to the Soul or higher world consciousness.

Step 4.
Higher Inner Experience Through Contemplation or *Samadhi*

a. Total letting go and allowing expansion of consciousness
b. Total receptivity to the Soul or Spirit or higher Divine Being's stimulation
c. Abstracting the meditator's consciousness to his/her highest point based on the Soul's and *antahkarana*'s development
d. Merging with a higher source of inspiration and empowerment

Step 5.
Post-Meditation Techniques Even Many Yogis Don't Know

a. Absorption, assimilation and storing of alchemized energies
b. Releasing energy and blessing different subjects or specific events as spiritual service
c. Thanksgiving to Divine Beings or your lineage and mentors
d. Physical exercises to ground back and physically circulate your energy
e. Go back to your daily life revitalized and balanced, and use your increasing power, love and light for greater exoteric service.
f. Self-mastery: Continue culturing your character through the eight core virtues.

Let's elaborate each of the five steps.

Step 1 Preparation
How to Prepare Yourself and Your Space for Your Best Meditation Experience

a. You're safer and more effective in your meditation if your body, vitality, emotions and mind are energetically clean and if your environment is physically clean and well-organized with higher vibrations. If you are a yogi, you can also employ yogic tools like the neti pot for cleaning nasal passages. A salt water bath is recommended before meditation when you are very stressed.

b. You are better off if you are not thinking of answering your phone during your meditation. Don't allow other people, animals, noise or any disturbances distract you. Quality meditation depends on quality time and environment. If you happen to get distracted, just focus back and continue the meditation without getting irritated. Just form a strong mental intention to isolate yourself temporarily.

c. If you are meditating outside, protect yourself from insect bites and other external disturbances. Make sure it is a safe environment.

d. Do not over-expose yourself to the sun, especially around noon and into the early afternoon. When you are meditating, you tend to absorb tremendous amounts of solar and air *prana*. Noontime and early afternoon sun will over-stimulate your system.

How to Purify and Clean Your Meditation Space

1. Burn incense and let the scent circulate through the space. Sandalwood and palo santo are great types of incense for energetically and psychically clearing up the negative vibrations of your immediate environment.

    The method of using scent is not only for aromatherapy, but the fire elementals from the incense attract purifying invisible elementals and beings to the space.

2. Special *mantrams* chanted or recited inside your space like Om Shanti Shanti Hum (invocation for peace) or Om (recited as Ooooooomm) or Amen (recited as Aaaaaaamenn) are also good to use.

3. Sunlight and ventilation with fresh air are natural ways to purify your meditation space.

How to Organize Your Meditation Space

Most yogis in India and many lamas don't care about the immediate physical environment. Many of them with whom I meditated can sit on the dirty wet ground and meditate.

I had a rough experience as part of my Himalayan training when one of my earlier mentors, SHJ, had me meditate very close to a cremation ground where they were burning the bodies of dead people. You could smell the burned flesh with the smoke traveling downwind where we were sitting. This was a test at a higher level of practice of withdrawing from the environment to develop detachment and will-power. But I don't recommend this to beginners!

Your Meditation Space Should Be Well-Organized

For most meditators, I would recommend:

1. A neat, simple and organized environment or meditation room that has been consecrated by your regular meditation.
2. The physical space should not be cluttered or disorganized with many items that are associated with unimportant superstitious rituals or obsolete symbols compared to your level of development. Just be simple and orderly as much as possible.
3. Avoid sharp objects pointed towards you because they tend to hurt your aura energetically.
4. Face East when you meditate. North is a second option. West is not preferable, and South is not recommended at all because it diminishes the upper centers and tends to reduce your energy. If you have a photo of your spiritual teacher, then face towards it. If you see old churches built by the Masons, the worshippers face East for maximum spiritual stimulation.

Additional Preparation Protocols for Advanced Meditation

To condition and purify yourself to be ready when you do more powerful and advanced meditation, you need to follow certain preparatory protocols:

1. **Take a bath with the salt water mixture**. Preferably finish with cold water to flush out negative congestion. It is more effective to use cold water than hot water. Mix 1 cup of salt

per 2 gallons (7.56 liters) of water. Put 10 drops of lavender or tea tree oil in the water if you have it. Soak yourself for 10-15 minutes before you rinse. It is not recommended to swim or bathe for three hours after meditation because of energy contraindications, which will be discussed in Chapter 22.

2. *Physical exercises are a must for advanced meditation.* One way of purifying your auras, unblocking your chakras and meridians and revitalizing your whole body is special types of exercises that incorporate full breathing synchronized with the physical movement. The integration of the breath is the key not only for more oxygen in the blood, but also for injecting more *prana* and vitality into the body.

When people meditate and are toxic and congested, they will not have a good experience. This is one of the dangers — lack of exercises to prepare the body to receive higher doses of Divine light and *kundalini* energy. Regular exercises with the breathing techniques also train the chakras to be more resilient to adapt to increased stimulation. Chapter 11 will give you detailed illustrations of the required exercises to do before your meditation. Physical exercises are preferably done outdoors or in areas with good ventilation.

3. *Breathing techniques to maximize your meditation experience.* Your breathing techniques should be understood and calibrated by the right ratio. There are so many breathing techniques like *pranayama* in yoga. If you study the science of breathing, you will be amazed by how breath control influences many aspects of your physical, vitality, emotional, mental and spiritual functions and consciousness. There are also different roles of breath from your right and left nostrils and a breathing variation when you breathe through alternate nostrils. Through the science of the breath, you can expand your awareness and heal yourself. These breathing techniques will be taught in Chapter 12 and applied in some of the upcoming chapters.

INVOCATION FOR DIVINE PROTECTION, GUIDANCE AND EMPOWERMENT

As people get older, there are three things that can happen:

1. Intensification of your affirmation and confirmation that your evolution is not an accident, that you are not traveling alone and that you belong to a lineage or a bigger Divine Source
2. Lack of interest in deeper philosophy or a connection to a greater whole or Divine Source because you're fed up with religion or you did not have much connecting experience with a spiritual lineage or Divine inspiration
3. In between intensification and lack of interest and still confused or wondering what's going on

My recommendation to people I mentor is for them to invoke before they meditate to be more spiritually connected to a Higher Divine Source with more empowerment of the inner experience. Although some meditators may be using a meditation technique from a book or DVD, if there is not much spiritual energy or blessing from a lineage or teacher, the meditation experience is not the same. Techniques alone without power are like machines without electricity or gas. You can use your own religious prayers or simply have the intention of invoking for Divine blessings, protection and guidance. Here's a sample invocation:

"I invoke for Divine Protection, Guidance and Empowerment for a successful meditation."

BODY POSTURES AND *MUDRAS*

The body has to be upright and in a position that is comfortable long enough to finish your meditation. It also has to be a posture where you won't fall if you are out of body or in an altered state of consciousness. Another significance of proper posture and hand *mudras* or gestures is the added science of using legs, hands and fingers to switch on certain inner powers and processes to empower the meditation. The body positions and postures will be discussed in the next chapter, and the hand, finger, eye and tongue *mudras* or gestures will be discussed in Chapter 10.

Step 2: Concentration Techniques
LEARNING TO CONCENTRATE IS EASY

We will learn many techniques of concentration in another chapter (page 13). Almost all of the practical techniques in the meditations in this book will include concentration integrated into the techniques.

Concentration is a mental technique to focus or rivet one's intention and attention to a specific topic, subject or target. It is done with a slight exertion of the will for the meditator to sustain one-pointed focus. That's why people with no will-power tend to disperse, because of lack of sustained attention.

There are also many other reasons why people can't focus. One of them is that the emotional and mental auras of the person are plagued with negative energies, chaotic vibrations and sometimes negative entities. Special healing techniques or breathing methods can be used to release these energetic disturbances.

Many of these strategies will be revealed later. There's no substitute for practice and more practice to master the techniques. Therefore, we've allocated a later chapter to train you further on this technique of concentration.

Step 3: Awareness Meditation and Wisdom Development
LEARN TO LET GO AND SUSTAIN INNER ATTENTIVENESS

This is easy for people with more love and devotion and those with a more passive nature. Whereas concentration utilizes will and focus, awareness meditation uses a gentle surrendering nature and more of a diffused sense of feeling. This can start through feelings and inner sensitivity without negative reactions. This is where the problem lies because when people are emotionally sensitive but full of painful feelings, they tend to react and feel worse after meditation.

Thus, even if it's easier for sensitive people to go for awareness meditation, they need to first flush out all disturbing feelings and negative thoughts before the meditation. The more aware you are, the more you can perceive and read your issues in life. Thus, the will also needs to be developed in order for "soft people" to be able to let go and go forward and enjoy an expansion of consciousness that leads to bliss.

There are many methods to practice awareness meditation. Especially for very objective and mental practitioners, it is not easy to let go of that "will-to-control" part of your nature. We've dedicated a whole chapter to this training on awareness and sensitivity.

Step 4: Higher Inner Experience Through Contemplation or Samadhi

Even though meditation and bliss are not the only goals for meditators, it is indeed a great idea to experience such a high state of awareness called *nirvana* or Divine oneness.

This inner experience depends on many factors, but here are a few important ones:

1. Spiritual development or age of the Soul
2. Preparation and entitlement to the high experience. People who have good karma and do spiritual service are usually more entitled than those who just think they deserve high experience without doing spiritual service.
3. Connection to a lineage or spiritual mentor or teacher
4. The safety and effectiveness of the techniques used
5. Whether the meditator is trained or not

This highest stage of meditation, *samadhi*, is the culmination of awareness meditation. After sustaining the "awareness" without effort in a high state of expansion, the consciousness of the meditator merges with the Soul light, which is already in a state of expansion at its own level.

The *samadhi* can be intensified if the yogi or meditator has a lineage or spiritual teacher because the Soul of the meditator is also connected to that greater being. Thus, the meditator can even merge with the light of the teacher or lineage. I'll explain this further in Chapter 15. There are a few methods to attain this, but it is in doing that you'll understand. There's no amount of discussion that can substitute for actual experience.

Step 5: Post-Meditation Rituals Even Many Yogis Don't Know
A MUST FOR SAFE AND EFFECTIVE MEDITATION

You need to absorb, assimilate and store the energy that comes through your meditation for improving your health, for intensifying your power and for spiritual blessings and service.

There are techniques to do this built into all the meditations that will be given to you in this book. After much energy is generated during the meditation, there's a need to share and bless this energy out to others and special events to heal and transform them. Thanksgiving or extending gratitude to your Soul or lineage and teachers is also important at the end.

To ground yourself back so you are not spacey, especially if you have to drive or go back to work, you need to do physical exercises, especially squats. This also helps you absorb and physicalize the generated energy faster and release any excess that you don't need. We'll discuss this post-meditation procedure further in Chapter 16. The techniques will all be easy, safe and effective.

POST-MEDITATION PROCEDURE VARIATIONS

In most types of yogic or abstraction meditation, all five steps we've discussed are highly recommended, but if you are currently doing basic or less intense meditation practices, you can modify the five steps as follows:

1. You can bypass Step 1 (preparation) in meditations that are not classified as esoteric or abstract meditation. You can also

abstain from physical exercises and breathing techniques if you just do a simple meditation or concentration method without awakening the *kundalini* fire.

2. If you are doing relaxation or mindfulness meditation, you can just do Step 5 (awareness) and bypass all the other steps.

3. Concretizing meditation or meditation for understanding can be done without doing any of the other steps. These two mental meditations can also be done without being in a meditation room, for instance in your office or anywhere you need to solve a problem.

This chapter has introduced you to the five important steps for safe and effective meditation. Chapters 9-16 will help you apply the key components of each of these steps with detailed procedures. Chapters 9-12 cover the four important preparations and elements in Step 1 of the 5-step process for safe and effective meditation, including:

* Body postures, or *asanas*, in Chapter 9
* Power switches for meditation, or *mudras*, in Chapter 10
* Exercises for safe and effective meditation in Chapter 11
* Breath, the heart of meditation, in Chapter 12.

Chapter 13 gives Step 2 of the 5-step process, meditation techniques to master concentration. Chapter 14 provides Step 3 of the 5-step process, awareness meditation to learn wisdom and life's lessons. Chapter 15 reveals how just about any meditator can achieve *samadhi* in step 4 of the 5-step process. And Chapter 16 completes the 5-step system with six critical post-meditation techniques you should apply to avoid "being burned" by meditation and yoga.

After learning the five key steps for safe and effective meditation (Preparation, Concentration, Awareness, *Samadhi* and Post-Meditation Techniques), Part IV of the book is dedicated to applying safe and effective techniques in various practical meditations, including weekly, monthly and yearly meditation schedules. And Part V will help you choose the right meditation or yoga instructor for you with valuable guidelines and a directory of safe and effective meditation and yoga instructors, centers and schools.

CHAPTER 9

Your Body Postures Matter

How you sit – whether your body tends to be upright, stooped or inclined at an angle – matters. In yogic traditions, body postures called *asanas* are the first training of yoga practitioners, especially in Hatha yoga. This chapter addresses the *asanas*, the first part of preparation for safe and effective meditation (Step 1 in the 5-step process that we discussed in Chapter 8).

There are so many variations of the different meditation postures, but for the purpose of this book, a few important, useful postures will be illustrated. Some of the postures are designed with energy locks or seals to control or regulate the flow of internal energy and *prana* using methods like chin-in throat lock, squeezing the perineum muscles or abdominal squeezing lock. These are called *bandhas*, and they'll be discussed in the following chapter.

COMMONLY-USED ASANAS OR MEDITATION POSTURES

The main purpose of meditation postures is to be able to sit and practice meditation properly for an extended time without being uncomfortable or falling when you get out of body. The *asanas* or postures also keep the spinal column upright and vertical while energies circulate throughout the whole system. At a certain point of altered consciousness, the body has to be maintained in the same position without conscious effort or attention. The following are recommended:

WESTERN POSTURE OR SITTING IN A CHAIR POSTURE

This is sometimes called the Egyptian posture or *maitrayasana*. It is suited for the cultures that are not trained to sit on the floor and are less supple. Westerners sit in chairs almost all day, everyday whereas Indians and Arabs can sit naturally and comfortably on the floor and in a cross-legged position. Therefore, this Egyptian posture is well-suited to Western meditators whose legs are not as flexible to do more complicated postures.

When using this posture, make sure your feet are flat on the floor with no tension in your legs, back and hips. It is important to not lean on the back of the chair. Rather, sit with your back aligned and vertical. Make sure that the chair allows your thighs to be relaxed and horizontal to the floor. I recommend this position for spacey types of meditators so that you stay grounded during the whole meditation. This Egyptian pose is also helpful if the meditator has sciatica or other leg problems and can't do the lotus position.

THE CROSS-LEGGED POSITION (*SUKHASANA* IN YOGA)

People with knee or leg problems can do the cross-legged posture instead of the more difficult lotus posture. This position can still lock the body in the same position even when you get out of body. The left foot should be under the right thigh with the right leg crossing under the left leg.

LOTUS POSTURE (*PADMASANA IN YOGA*)

This is the classic meditation position. It is one of the most popular poses, resembling the Buddha's meditation posture. Both feet are placed facing upward, one foot on top of the opposite thigh with the heels touching the pelvic bones. The connection of the soles of the feet is withdrawn from the Earth, thus the meditator is abstracted in a way from the more physical pull by Earth ground energy. This is very good for materialistic people to abstract their consciousness towards the spiritual. But for spacey people, this will make them even more spaced-out and lightheaded. This is one of the dangers of prolonged meditation using this position. The meditator tends to become impractical and less objective and instinctive.

ADEPT'S POSTURE (*SIDDHASANA* IN YOGA)

This is the advanced master's posture to lock the position of the meditator tighter. The sole of the left foot should touch the inside of the right thigh. Insert the right toes and foot tightly into the crevice between the thigh of the left leg and the left calf. The hands can be on the lap, or you can perform a closed hand *mudra* position at the navel level. A female form of this posture is called *siddha yoni asana* wherein the left heel is inside the labia majora of the vagina as a leg lock to redirect sexual energy upward. But *siddhasana* can be used for both men and women meditators. A simple variation of the *siddhasana* is the *swastikasana*. The difference is the left heel doesn't press the perineum so it allows energy flow not only upward but also downward.

SITTING ON HEELS POSTURE (*VAJRASANA* IN YOGA)

Sit on the inside of your heels while your knees are together. Your heels are at the sides of your hips. Your hands should be on top of your lap or knees, usually facing palms down. This is the prayer pose of Muslims and Japanese Buddhists and is even used in some martial arts meditations. This posture is said to alter the flow of nervous signals and blood in the pelvic and visceral regions of the body. This is good for meditators with sexual issues and sciatica. Another version of this is called the *bhadrasana*, which is the same as *vajrasana* except that the knees are separated widely.

STANDING POSITIONS

Most yogic books do not indicate the standing *asanas* as an option for meditation, especially in the Indian yogic system. But during the period in Indian history just before the Buddha's enlightenment, another spiritual leader propagated yoga and meditation in a standing position. He was Mahavira, the founder of Jainism. He proved that the standing posture can be used for enlightenment. In India, Jains meditate for days in a continuous standing posture with amazing stillness and composure. The Chinese system of martial arts normally uses the standing or walking style. That's why you seldom see sculptures of Chinese masters in a lotus position or sitting in a locked position. The Oriental ways of flowing movement like Tai Chi, chigong and martial arts focus on dynamic awareness concentration meditation as can be seen in the use of moving forms or *katas* in martial arts.

Let's look at a few stationary standing *asanas*.

STANDING POSTURE

The first standing position is straight legs with both hands on the side. This is the basic standing meditation to be aware of the continuity of Heaven (Divine light) and Earth (*prana* and *kundalini*). The eyes can be closed with consciousness withdrawn inward, or half closed and gazing at a selected spot in front of you for concentration. The concentration will turn into awareness until "oneness" happens to the standing meditator. This standing *asana* can be done with the awareness of the continuity of the inner core light of the body and Soul. This is a more advanced version and is not safe for beginners.

STANDING MEDITATION WITH NAVEL MUDRA

The meditator stands straight but with both hands held together pointing downward at the navel level. This is very important to ground you back after a high meditation and also to increase the flow of Divine light down into the auras and chakras. This should not be done for extended periods of time (10 minutes maximum) because it over-awakens the *kundalini*, especially if it is accompanied by deep breathing techniques. I recommend 5 minutes average. Finish with another 5 minutes of standing meditation with the *anjali mudra* with both palms joined together in the heart area, pointing upward.

STANDING MEDITATION WITH HEART AND NAVEL MUDRA

I designed this meditation technique with the following purpose:

- ◆ To activate the heart and navel centers for emotional and instinctive intelligence
- ◆ To help align the body and its energies
- ◆ To simultaneously circulate more refined energy downward to transform the lower chakras and energy of the lower chakras upward to feed the upper body and chakras. It is an alchemizing technique and should not be done for more that 5 minutes by beginners.

This meditation is done in a standing position with the left hand placed at the heart level against the chest pointing upward and the right hand placed at the navel pointing downward. Both palms should be lined up in a straight line in front of your body. Your concentration should be focused on your heart and navel chakras while breathing slowly. After 1 to 5 minutes, reverse the positions of your left and right hands. This is the second step to complete the technique. There is a different effect of the left and the right in the energy bodies, which will be discussed in Chapter 12. The complete technique for standing meditation will be discussed in Chapter 11.

STANDING MEDITATION IN A HORSE STANCE

This technique is done for 3-10 minutes as follows:

1. Do this stance by standing as though you were riding a horse with your knees bent and your feet shoulder width apart. More advanced meditators should bend their knees more for a deeper stance.
2. Perform a meditation *mudra* with both hands anchored at your navel (*dhayani mudra*) with the left hand on top of the right.
3. Focus on your navel center and breathe slowly and deeply.
4. You may close your eyes if you want to be inward. If you are a spacey person, half close your eyes so you stay grounded.

STAYING GROUNDED

It's not good to have "two feet in Heaven" while we are physically incarnated. This can result in lopsided development. One foot (the spiritual foot) in Heaven and the other foot (Earth root) on the material plane is better and more balanced. The horse stance technique achieves this balance and prevents another danger of meditation and yoga — a spacey, mystical and impractical life with financial challenges — by being rooted physically.

There's a certain pattern that you can observe from many of the yoga postures called *asanas*. The soles of the feet are facing upward. This has something to do with the withdrawal of the material Earth connection and roots through the soles of the feet, which are the connectors of ground *prana* for the body.

Most of the yogic postures facilitate deliberate abstraction of consciousness from gross to subtle towards the Soul consciousness — all upward. But if they are done by meditators who are physically and materially depleted or energetically dirty in the lower chakras, then they are not safe or healthy. This is a danger even many spiritual teachers don't recognize.

During meditation, these *asanas* should not be used because they bring dirty sexual congestion upward. Also, the ground in many cities is not physically and energetically clean. Sitting on the ground contaminates you and your *kundalini* seat. Therefore, sitting on a chair or doing the standing postures is safer, especially in energetically dirty places.

LYING POSTURE (*SHAVASANA* IN YOGA)

This is done by lying flat on your back with arms beside your body. Your feet should be slightly apart. This posture is used for relaxation and to sleep.

LYING ON THE SIDE POSTURE

This position is used to balance the flow of energy when one nostril is blocked. The key to a more powerful, aligned meditation and safer awakening of the *kundalini* is determined by whether the nostril breaths are balanced or not.

This is how to balance nostril breathing or open a closed nostril:

1. ### LYING ON THE LEFT SIDE TECHNIQUE

   This opens the right nostril if done for a few minutes. It is a good sleeping position for people who want to enhance more *yang* or active energy, including those who are depressed.

2. ### LYING ON THE RIGHT SIDE TECHNIQUE

   This technique opens the left nostril and promotes the more *yin* or passive nature. It is excellent for people with ADHD. I've used this technique with people who are more aggressive, and it calms them down if they sleep lying on the right side.

To open the blocked left nostril, do this technique for at least 3-5 minutes.

KNEELING POSTURE

In Christianity and other religions, the kneeling posture is common and used in many prayer rituals. Catholic worshippers use this *asana* a lot. The knee is the contact point with the ground or floor. This position symbolizes penance accompanied with reverence for the Saints or God. Kneeling is a demonstration of humility. It is also a gesture of putting oneself at a lower level to request mercy or the awarding of blessings. The more advanced kneeling position is with the heart or *anjali mudra* (see page 149) and the feet facing upward to disconnect the Earth energy root from the soles of the feet, thus facilitating upward flow of consciousness.

OTHER ASANAS

There are many more postures, but the above *asanas* are sufficient for beginner to advanced meditators. Augmentation with hand *mudras* (hand and finger positions) and body locks (*bandhas*) modifies the energy flow and higher power of the *asanas*. Several *asanas* like *nada anusandhana asana* (sitting posture over a rolled blanket or smooth log) is another useful position to be able to insert the fingers into the ears for Nada yoga (practice of tuning in to inner sounds). Another is the head stand to bring circulation of energy and oxygen to the head area and allow the flow of certain *prana* to the upper chakras. This is not safe for many people, especially for pregnant women and those with heart disease, hypertension or thyroid problems.

Your Tools for More Energy Power:
BODY LOCKS AND SEALS

Body and energy locks and seals (*bandhas*) are power tools and strategies. These special positionings of parts of the body like the throat, perineum and abdominal muscles are important for more intense breathing techniques with longer breath retention. They also facilitate the flow of *prana* and/or *kundalini* energy to certain predetermined areas or directions.

Here are some useful *bandhas* or locks:

I. THROAT LOCK (*JALANDHARA BANDHA* IN YOGA)

This lock restrains and compresses the pranic flow upward while holding the breath. This is also a safety lock not to over-strain the organs and tissues in the neck, especially the epiglottis (the flap of skin that hangs down in the back of the mouth). The throat lock is released by straightening the head to a vertical position from the chin-in position. This sudden upward flow of compressed energy brings expansion of consciousness and more velocity to the upward energy circulation.

2. ABDOMINAL COMPRESSION LOCK (*UDDIYANA BANDHA*)

This is a more intense locking of energy. After deep exhalation followed by long breath retention and the throat lock, the abdominal muscles are contracted upward and inward as far as possible and held in this locked position. Then the throat lock is released with the unlocking of the *uddiyana* (abdominal compression) to inhale. This activates the upward flow of *prana* and *kundalini* energy.

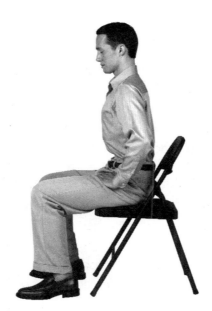

3. ROOT OR PERINEUM LOCK (*MOOLA BANDHA*)

This is done by inhaling deeply, retaining your breath longer and then exerting muscular contraction and compression of the perineum and anus muscles. Afterwards, the compressed energy is released as part of the throat lock technique procedure, which is described in detail in Point 4 below.

This is a very useful technique to activate the seat of the *kundalini* and pump it upward to alchemize and transmute it. It is also utilized to compress the pranic energy and *kundalini* not to go downward during the compression period. This causes the energy to move upward with greater force and intensity.

This lock is also useful to transmute sexual energy upward. This is particularly helpful for those who have pre-ejaculation problems: Simply squeeze and compress the perineum muscles in sets of 20-30 repeated 3-4 times. This can be done before sexual intercourse to prolong sexual performance. The perineum lock can also be done after exhalation, especially with the other two locks above. Women should not use this locking technique when they are menstruating. The root lock is also not recommended for anyone with sexually-transmitted diseases or women with tumors or cysts, especially in the form of cancer of the reproductive system.

4. **GREAT LOCK (*MAHA BANDHA*)**
This is a combination of throat lock, abdominal compressing lock and root lock. The sequence is as follows:
- Exhale all your air.
- Do the throat lock by exhaling your air while bringing your chin down towards your chest.
- Do the abdominal compression lock by compressing and holding your abdominal muscles.
- Do the root lock by contracting and holding your perineum and anus muscles.
- Hold your breath for a few seconds.
- Release the root lock.
- Release the abdominal compression lock.
- Release the throat lock by straightening your head upright.
- Inhale fully to the maximum. Then:
- Do the throat lock.
- Do the abdominal compression lock.
- Do the root lock.
- Hold your breath for a few seconds.
- Release your throat lock.

- Release your abdominal compression lock.
- Release your root lock.
- Exhale all your air slowly.
- Do a maximum of 7 sets.

This lock should not be done by pregnant women or people with heart ailments, hypertension, cancer, tumors, AIDS, digestive disorders, bleeding problems or glaucoma. Consult a certified safe and effective meditation or yoga instructor before participating in this type of breathing practice. This technique is dangerous for starting meditators without an expert's supervision.

The body postures, along with the body locks and breathing techniques, are all accessories to a successful meditation or yoga practice. They were instituted by the enlightened Masters and advanced yogis to facilitate practitioners' development.

Many initial introductions of yoga to the West have not been totally based on the exact meaning of yoga because many meditation and yoga instructors are just going for the commercial value, selling meditation and yoga for weight loss, anti-aging and fad market enticement without the spiritual philosophy. Of course, a few good teachers are very sincere in their mission.

Hatha yoga is what most Westerners know as "the yoga", and yoga studios most commonly teach and practice the *asanas* or body postures. The *asanas* are a very important component of meditation practice, so I encourage people to do them. I also encourage meditators already practicing them to apply higher meditation methods that go beyond the physical and health benefits. Your body posture and *asanas* matter for safe and effective meditations.

CHAPTER 10

Power Switches for Meditation:

Magical Secrets Revealed

T he magical hand tools called *mudras* are used by many religions for prayer and ceremonies. This chapter discusses the *mudras* used in meditation, the second part of preparation for safe and effective meditation (Step 1 in the 5-step process that we discussed in Chapter 8).

The special hand gestures or hand sealing techniques involving the fingers and hands are very important in meditation and yoga. Their functions are numerous, but in general they are external hand-finger switches of energy circulation in chakras and meridians within the human energy system. The fingers can also be used in different positions to direct energy or force within or outside the body.

The fingers are pathways and extensions of different energy meridians that pass through the auras and chakras. Different fingers activate different aspects of the energy field. In acupuncture, there are terminal points of meridians at the fingertips as follows:

- ◆ Finger-thumb for the lung meridian connections
- ◆ Index finger for the large intestines
- ◆ Middle finger for the heart constrictor vessel
- ◆ Ring finger for the triple heater meridian
- ◆ Little finger for the small intestines and heart[5]

According to the Bihar School of Yoga in Munger, India, the fingers also have a relationship with the five natural elements (*pancha bhutas* in yoga terms) and stimulate these aspects in the personality and higher correspondences in the consciousness:

- Thumb: fire
- Index finger: air
- Middle finger: ether
- Ring finger: earth/ground
- Little finger: water

According to my experiments that confirmed what my early mentor, MCKS, told me, the left and right hands have different variables in the hand *mudras*. The left hand triggers more of the subjective internal energy with effects coming from the Divine light. The right hand stimulates the energies and chakras from the lower sources and *kundalini*.

Therefore, the placement of the hands and fingers is very important to know. It also helps to understand at least to a certain degree what's going on internally when you are following certain yogic or meditation practices.

Many people self-practice without a mentor by haphazardly applying a technique from a video or book. Be careful applying breathing techniques plus hand *mudras*; their combination can cause a cumulative over-stimulation without immediately evident side effects, which can be dangerous in the long run.

INDEX FINGER-THUMB MUDRAS

The index finger when connected to the thumb stimulates the upper chakras more than the lower centers. This combination also activates the flow of Divine light more than the *kundalini*. When done along with the lotus meditation posture, *padmasana*, or any leg position with the feet facing upward, the withdrawing of lower body energy and consciousness is maximized. If this is overdone with certain breathing methods involving holding of the breath after exhalation accompanied by root, abdominal compression and throat locks, the "vacuuming upward effect" is amplified.

This is dangerous if the practitioner is already imbalanced (e.g., if the upper chakras are significantly bigger and more developed than the lower centers). Spaciness, lack of objectivity and practicality and financial starvation are probable consequences due to the combination of powerful leg, hand and finger *mudras* with breathing techniques.

There are five variations of the index finger-thumb *mudra*:

GYANA MUDRA

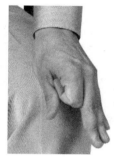

Index-thumb connection with palms facing downward on top of the knees or lap during meditation. The index finger touches the base of the thumb and the three other fingers are stretched outward. This is called *ehlohaynu* in the Kabbalah tradition. It is a more grounded index-thumb *mudra*. Sometimes it is used to hold the nostrils in the nostril-controlled alternate breathing method.

CHIN MUDRA

Index-thumb connection with palms facing upwards on top of the knees or lap during meditation either with *gyana* style or with the tips of the fingers connecting. This is a faster method to abstract from your senses to a higher level.

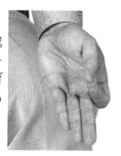

INDEX-THUMB MUDRA WITH THE FINGERTIPS CONNECTING

This is a variation of the two *mudras* above with the thumb touching the side of the index finger. This is a gentler way if you get tense with the other two *mudras* above. The effect is almost the same.

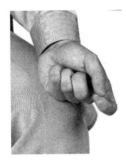

CHINMAYA MUDRA

This is the same index-thumb *mudra* except the other fingers are folded in touching the palm. The effect of the meditation is more grounded and stimulates the energy connected to respiratory functions more. The *mudra* is placed on top of the knees or lap during breathing techniques or meditation.

VITARKA MUDRA

The index finger and thumb are connected at the tip while the other fingers are relaxed and slightly stretched. The right hand faces front pointing upward at shoulder level, and the left hand faces front pointing downward at hip level. This is a mudra for spiritual blessing with both material and spiritual energy used by more advanced teachers or initiates for a larger number of subjects or bigger targets.

MIDDLE FINGER-THUMB MUDRA

The middle finger when connected with the thumb stimulates the lower chakras more than the upper chakras and also awakens the lower sources of *prana* and *kundalini* more compared to the Divine light. It can be used to offset the side effects of the index finger-thumb *mudra*, especially for people with extremely mystical, impractical and spacey attitudes in life. Meditators who are too materialistic and objective and can't leave their body during meditation, should minimize using this *mudra*. Use the index and thumb *mudra* above instead.

Some paintings depict the Chinese Avatar of Compassion, Quan Yin, with this hand *mudra*, symbolizing materializing good wishes for those who request them. This middle finger-thumb *mudra* can be used alternately with the index finger-thumb *mudra* for meditation.

The other combinations of the thumb with the other fingers will not be discussed here because they are not always used for meditation purposes.

TRIPLE FINGER *MUDRA*

In this mudra, the tips of the thumb, index and middle finger are joined, and the ring finger and little finger are folded in, touching the palm. This balances the upper and lower chakras with a more grounding effect. This mudra was introduced to me by my early spiritual mentor, MMCN.

ANJALI *MUDRA*: HEART MEDITATION GESTURE

This *mudra* is used either for deep prayer or for meditation. The palms and fingers are connected and held together at the center of the chest at heart level. This activates the heart center, uplifts the consciousness and connects the personality to the subject of respect or veneration. It is an attitude of yogis, *lamas* and some Asian cultures to use the *anjali mudra* as a gesture of inner salutation to the divinity of every person they meet. It is usually used to greet others, especially teachers, expressed as *namaste* (Indian style) or *namashkar* (Nepalese style). The respect-loaded words *namaste* and *namashkar* are uttered as the head is bowed slightly with the *anjali* hand gesture at the chest. This *mudra* can be used by people who are too mental to develop the heart center during meditation and to balance their mental nature with the loving nature expressed in Bhakti yoga. A variation is using only one hand in the *anjali*, especially the right hand.

There are other variations to this heart *mudra* like the ones used

in the deep prayers of mystics. Instead of fingers pointing upwards, the fingers are clasped together and folded with the tips at the knuckle area. This is an approach with a more grounded effect while still maintaining a deep sense of spiritual connection to the idol or subject of veneration. It does not fully circulate all the lower energy upward.

The *anjali mudra* also has several higher forms as follows:

AT THE FOREHEAD LEVEL

In this version, the palms are held together at the level of the forehead, approximately at the third eye slightly above the *ajna* center. This is a more advanced form of the *anjali mudra*, connecting the head centers, including the third eye if it is already constructed in the meditator, to the subject of respect or veneration. It can also awaken the power of the meditator's mind, through mental salutation to the spiritual lineage or enlightened teachers.

AT THE CROWN CENTER

In this version, the palms are held together pointing upward on top of the head. This is an even higher *namaste* or *namashkar* technique for two purposes:

- as a salutation of the total personality to a higher Divine Source
- as an activation and opening of the crown chakra, allowing transmutation of the personality power, including the *kundalini* energy upward to the *antahkarana* and the Soul

AT THE EGOIC CENTER OR HIGHER

In this version, the *anjali mudra* is stretched above the crown chakra at the egoic center (12 inches/30.5 centimeters) or higher (full arm stretch). This can be utilized to salute very high Divine Sources of inspiration, including Divine affinities to a "realized Divine Macrocosm" beyond the planetary scheme. This technique also develops the higher part of the *antahkarana*, but it is not safe for those who are not advanced esoteric practitioners. If you observe the yogic salutation to the Deity of the Sun (*surya namashkar*), this hand gesture is partially used, but is not "esoterically tuned-in" in most practitioners. The internal understanding and realization should accompany the external use of the *mudra*.

There are more varieties and upgraded versions of these *mudras* with new finger arrangements, but the ones included above are the safest to use for now.

DHAYANI MUDRA OR MEDITATION GESTURE

This is one of the most commonly used *mudras* for meditation, yet it is one of the most confusing in terms of application. There are many variations to this *mudra* for energy circulation while meditating.

Left Hand on Top of the Right Hand with the Tips of the Thumbs Touching

This hand *mudra* forms a circle whose center is in front of the navel. There are many purposes of this *mudra*, but the important ones are:

* It acts like a switch to circulate energy through the front and back meridians and in the different energy chakras while meditating. You'll avoid energy congestion in different chakras while meditating.
* This *mudra* allows you to accumulate and assimilate internal energy in the navel area for it to be alchemized and absorbed by the navel chakra and depository meridians in that area.
* You can apply this *mudra* to direct energy upward or downward by using the thumbs to point in an upward or downward direction. This is useful for

transmuting *kundalini* or sexual energy or bringing more Divine light downward to the lower centers.

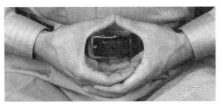

Right Hand on Top of the Left Hand

This is usually what you see in sculptures of the Buddha in the *padmasana* meditation posture.

Buddhist meditators regard this as a symbol of enlightenment with the right hand (state of enlightenment, *nirvana*) over the left hand (world of appearance or material world). But energetically, it is the reverse of the left over right *dhayani mudra* above. The right hand on top of the left hand *mudra* is not energizing but reversing the flow, thus releasing the pranic energies instead of accumulating. This *mudra* is useful if you want to decongest your stress energy or if you have too much energy that needs to be released as in the case of ADHD (Attention·Deficit and Hyperactivity Disorder).

This mudra will reduce your energy, so if you are already depleted, it is not good for you. This is one of the dangers unknown to practitioners when they follow the depictions of the Buddha using this hand posture. What's good for a very advanced yogi or meditator is not always good for beginners or depleted meditators.

MODIFICATIONS OF THE *DHAYANI* MEDITATION HAND *MUDRA*
Dhayani mudra *with the two index fingers held together with the thumbs*
This special modification serves two purposes:

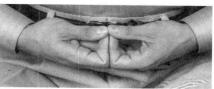

- To activate the upper chakras and Divine light more than the lower centers and *kundalini* fire
- To continue an ongoing circulation in the front and back meridians with a build-up of energy qualified with more Divine light

Dhayani mudra *with the two middle fingers held together with the thumbs*
This modification offers the same benefits of ongoing automatic cir-

culation of the front and back meridians except that the lower chakras are more activated than the higher centers, plus there's more stimulating power from the *kundalini* than the Divine light. This is good for practitioners who have over-developed upper chakras relative to the lower chakras. It is also beneficial to people with lower *kundalini* awakening to increase the power.

Dhayani mudra with the index finger, middle finger and thumb held together

This is a more balanced activation of upper and lower centers with

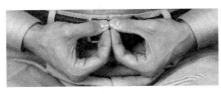

a boost of *kundalini* and Divine light while maintaining automatic circulation. It balances the energies of power, love and light in your system. It is recommended for meditators who have more capacity to generate and sustain more energy, but it is too jarring for beginners. It is like putting a spiritual turbo engine into normal meditators.

BHAIRAVA AND BHAIRAVI MUDRAS (RELAXING MEDITATION MUDRAS)

These two are done automatically by yogis or meditators while

relaxing or just letting go. They do not employ the thumbs connecting at the finger points; rather, the thumbs are resting with the other fingers. The hands are on top of the lap when one wants to maintain a meditative posture without the purpose of awakening the forces of the auras. This is a classic hand position. In the *bhairava mudra*, the right hand is on top of the left. In the *bhaivari mudra*, the left hand is on top of the right.

BRAHMA MUDRA (ALL FINGERS LOCKED MUDRA)

This is a very powerful *mudra* usually accompanying the combination breathing or maximum breath technique (abdominal, chest and 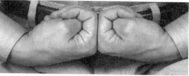 shoulder breathing combined). (See Chapter 12, page 210) The thumbs are inserted all the way into a fist with all the other fingers over the thumbs. Then both hands are pressed together with the knuckles touching and the hands placed in the lap. This is another power booster with a pranic turbo effect. It is not recommended for beginners.

There's a slight variation to this *mudra* called the *aadi mudra*, which is observed by practitioners to enhance respiration. The difference is that the thumb is not fully extended across the palm, but just the index finger is grabbing the thumb.

NASAGRA MUDRA (NOSE MUDRA)

This is commonly used by yogis who practice *pranayama* breath control. It is often used with the alternate nostril breathing with breath retention, which will be discussed in Chapter 12.

The nose *mudra* is done as follows:

- ◆ The index and middle fingers anchor on the point between the eyebrows. This also activates the *ajna* or mid-brow chakra as the breathing is done.
- ◆ The thumb controls the right nostril.
- ◆ The ring and little fingers regulate the left nostril.

There's a variation to the nose *mudra*, which is called *nasikaa mudra*. The right index and middle fingers are folded with their tips at the base of the thumbs. The thumb controls the right nostril, and the ring and little fingers regulate the left nostril. This is easier for beginners, and stimulation is not limited to the *ajna* or mid-brow chakra.

EYE MUDRAS

Just as the hands and fingers are switches of force and energy meridians, the eyes can also be used as triggering mechanisms of energy and consciousness.

There are four forms of the eye *mudra* for meditations.

MID-BROW GAZING MUDRA

Yogis call this *shambhavi mudra*. This is done by gazing or riveting your eyes towards the mid-brow spot and looking upwards as high 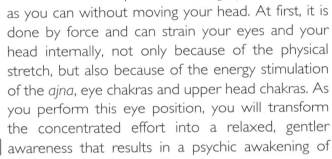 as you can without moving your head. At first, it is done by force and can strain your eyes and your head internally, not only because of the physical stretch, but also because of the energy stimulation of the *ajna*, eye chakras and upper head chakras. As you perform this eye position, you will transform the concentrated effort into a relaxed, gentler awareness that results in a psychic awakening of your upper centers, resulting in faculties like being able to see energy or the auric colors.

Aside from activating the ajna and upper centers, this *mudra* awakens your mental will-power while stimulating the construction of the third eye. It also helps transmute the lower body *pranas* into the higher chakras, especially the head centers.

This should be done with the proper sitting postures, hand *mudras* and breathing techniques. If you typically can't focus during meditation, this is a good practice to bring back your concentration.

This method crosses your eyes and represents the spiritual saying, "If thine eyes are as one, you can witness God" or experience higher Divine light through the faculty of the third eye. There's a science to the development of the third eye employing a combination of the above techniques.

NOSE TIP GAZING *MUDRA*

Yogis call this *agochari mudra*. This is the opposite of the mid-brow gazing. The tip of the nose is the target of eye gazing accompanied by the proper awareness, breathing, postures and hand *mudras*. This downward look utilizes the eyes as a switch to first concentrate on one point, the nose. Then the Divine light is induced to descend through the crown and down the chakras to awaken the *kundalini*.

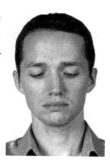

When done with awareness, this brings revitalization and healing with a grounded state. The Zen practitioners use the nose tip gazing *mudra* while doing breathing and awareness at the navel. It helps even beginners rivet their focus on three things: the tip of the nose, the navel center and the breath.

This technique allows practitioners to be absorbed into one-pointed awareness. The mind can't jump from one thought to another, and even noises can't disturb the meditator when this technique is used. Mindfulness or awareness attitudes can grow with the open eye nose tip gazing *mudra*.

MINDLESSNESS OR *UNMANI MUDRA*

This is a technique to help the meditator focus away from disturbances, especially the attitude of mental chattering typical of beginners. Zen and martial arts meditators usually do this *mudra* as follows:

1. Start with your eyes totally open.
2. Pick a small point of attention directly in front of you like a spot or a small physical object to center your gaze.
3. Continue focusing on the selected spot with slow, gentle breathing. If your mind wanders, return your attention to the spot you chose in front of you.
4. As you continue, slowly and gradually reduce the gap between your eyelids until they are more than half-closed. Maintain this position.

5. Continue the gentler, slower breathing, and transform the concentration into a gazing look until you are mindless and just aware.

6. At some point, you sense that you are "lost" and just aware of the spot, and eventually you merge with it. This is the purpose, to become one beyond the mind state of consciousness.

Note: This can be done for 5-10 minutes. There is an advanced version of this technique, but the basic mindlessness *mudra* is applied this way.

HIGHER CONSCIOUSNESS OR *AKASHI* MUDRA

This is a combination of the mid-brow gazing *mudra* and deep, slow breathing plus tilting your head backward until the mid-brow area is aligned with the neck on a vertical axis. The tongue *mudra* (tongue touching the palate) is also used to switch on the middle meridian of the body. The effect of doing this as a 10-15 minute meditation is a tremendous transmutation upward to higher consciousness of your normal physical senses. If you observe some meditators who are highly withdrawn from their physical body during meditation, they tend to lift their heads backwards, especially people whose third eye is being awakened. This is also useful for people who are unable to leave their body or are "consciousness-heavy" meditators who can't "spiritually ascend" easily.

TONGUE MUDRA

Yogis call this *khechari mudra*. This technique is very important and fundamental in yoga and meditation because of its three main purposes:

1. The tongue serves as a switch to connect the middle, front and back meridians to promote more circulation of *prana* and alchemized energy in the human energy system. This will result in more powerful meditation and awakening of the internal forces for inner powers development. There are many energy pressure points and glands that are massaged, triggered and switched on at the back cavity of the palate.

2. Meditators who use continuous and long breathing techniques have fluid secretions in the mouth, which they consider an elixir or "meditator's nectar" for rejuvenation. The tongue stimulates the creation of these secretions.

3. The tongue also acts as a conduit to supply saliva to the throat while rapid breathing techniques are being done. Extended rapid nostril breathing can dry out the nose and throat.

The tongue *mudra* is done by curling your tongue as far back as possible to the roof of your mouth, the palate. This tongue position is maintained during meditation and in most breathing techniques.

There are many variations of the tongue *mudra* like those used in Hatha yoga schools. Their version is more intense because they intentionally cut the tendon beneath the tongue to be able to curl it further back in the upper cavity of the mouth to close the air passage for certain rituals of breath control. For your practice, using the meditation techniques and *mudras* as discussed here is safer and more effective.

Your hands, fingers, eyes and tongue are physical organs, but with the science of *mudras*, they act as physical switches for power, energy and consciousness. It's amazing how a small part of the body can be used to access more Divine electricity from the Soul or more energy from your *kundalini*.

The science of *mudras* was revealed to ancient yogis and teachers of the ancient wisdom. They have been utilized not just for meditation practices, but also for healing, blessing and magical purposes. *Mudras* that are commonly applicable in weekly meditation have been included here. There are a number of *mudras* not used yet by the traditional yogic system, which are more suitable for the new human designs of consciousness, but they are not included in this book.

These secrets of the yogis and meditation masters revealed here are now yours to develop your power, love and light safely because you have deeper understanding about their functions.

CHAPTER 11

Exercises for
Safe Meditations

This chapter focuses on the third necessary preparation for safe and effective meditation: important exercises with breathing techniques that are required before you do advanced meditations. I can't over-emphasize the need to loosen up your body and unblock your energy system to have a safe and effective meditation. Even a few hours of meditation are rendered useless if the energy pipelines and pumps are clogged. The "water of life" – the *prana* – and spiritual fires do not flow properly. If your system is blocked and you force more energy to circulate, there's danger. It's like putting more water and pressure through a pipe after the valves and pipelines are closed.

Also, even after your system is unblocked, if energy debris is floating in your aura, it contaminates other parts of your energy bodies. Exercises synchronized with breathing techniques can help solve this problem.

There are two exercise programs designed to bring your meditation to a heightened experience:

1. **BODY THERAPY EXERCISE AND INNER POWERS MEDITATION** (20 minutes)

    This is a special 13-step strategy to release blockages in all your auras and chakras followed by a standing meditation utilizing hand *mudras* and inner breathing. This is a complete meditation in itself.

2. **8-STEP INTERNAL STAMINA EXERCISE** (5 minutes)
This is a shorter version of Body Therapy that can be done in 5 minutes or less. This is suitable for busier people who only have a few minutes to exercise. You can also pair this exercise with the Inner Powers Meditation below. If they are combined, it takes only about 15 minutes.

SPECIAL EXERCISES AND BREATHING TECHNIQUES TO BOOST VITALITY POWER

Inner Powers Exercise

The Inner Powers Exercise develops inner powers and internal energy through the use of exercises synchronized with breathing techniques and hand *mudras* to circulate vitality power (shown in , page 185).

I used to exercise two hours a day to stay fit for competition during my martial arts days. I employed physical training power more than internal power. But as I learned the secrets of internal energy through my healing mastery, I combined both of these methods to design a quick and effective way of purifying, revitalizing and balancing the human energy system. Twenty to 30 minutes of this method give more internal energy and balance than hours of my normal athletic and martial arts training.

The program was designed with these expected benefits:

◆ Rejuvenate the body and release stress and physical tension
◆ More oxygen in the blood and the body to enhance metabolism, accelerate weight loss and purify and detoxify the whole body
◆ Improve physical strength and stamina
◆ Increase vitality and improve its proper circulation throughout the entire body

- Release toxins and stress from all the internal organs and the energy body
- Activate and align the power centers of the body
- Special overall alignment of the body, emotions, mind and spiritual powers

Physical exercises, muscle-building and body movement alone are not sufficient to develop internal powers. The muscles can be toned and strong but lack inner stamina and internal energy. Certain additional exercises and physical biomechanical movements are necessary to release blocked stale energy and stress in the meridians and muscles. In culturing the body for advanced meditation, it is important not only to increase the energy level, but it is also essential to circulate oxygenated blood and energy throughout the whole body and human energy system for fast rejuvenation and to sustain internal stamina. You don't have to over-exert your body to accumulate energy faster and build stamina.

This Inner Powers Exercise was designed as a method integrating my mastery of martial arts, healing and spiritual sciences, bearing in mind that most people only have 15-30 minutes to exercise daily. This method does not require special equipment or accessories and can be done almost anywhere, anytime. You can do the exercises and breathing techniques in a business suit in your office, at a conference or during work breaks. This program is available on DVD so you can apply it easily, but let's discuss the details here.

Part 1 of the program offers simple physical exercises synchronized with full breathing. The exercises rejuvenate and detoxify all parts of the body from head to toe without making you tired. The exercises also oxygenate the blood and cells and enhance metabolic processes.

Part 2 provides advanced yet simple inner breathing techniques to activate and balance the body's energy centers and different auras. People who have been practicing the Inner Powers Exercise report not only experiencing internal power development but also better relationships and more creativity.

Part 1: Inner Powers Exercise
EXERCISES WITH SYNCHRONIZED BREATHING TECHNIQUES
(see Figure 17, pages 202-204)

PREPARATION
1. You may follow the DVD guiding this program.
2. You can achieve best results in a well-ventilated exercise space with plenty of clean, fresh air. Once you have familiarized yourself with the sequence, do it outdoors if possible.

PROCEDURE
1. **BODY SHAKE** (2 sets): to loosen up your entire body
   - Place your feet at shoulder width.
   - Shake your whole body to loosen up. Build up the rhythm.
   - After 1 minute of shaking, slow down until you stop.
   - Bend your knees slightly.
   - Concentrate on the top of your head and soles of your feet simultaneously and breathe slowly. This is to allow the circulation of energy in your whole body (30 seconds).
   - Repeat the whole Body Shake procedure one more time.

2. **EYE THERAPY** (10 times each direction): to enhance eyesight
   - Move your eyes up and down.
   - Move your eyes from side to side.
   - Move your eyes diagonally from the upper right to the lower left.
   - Move your eyes diagonally from the upper left to the lower right.
   - Rotate your eyes counterclockwise.
   - Reverse the rotation.
   - Rub your eyes and face gently for a few seconds.

3. **NECK THERAPY** (10 times each step, except neck rotations): to release tension in your throat and neck and revitalize your brain. People with neck injuries should not do this step.

- Tilt your head slowly from side to side.
- Turn your head from right to left.
- Inhale rapidly through your nose as you move your head up and exhale through your mouth vigorously as you bend your head down.
- Rotate your head slowly in each direction 3 times.

4. Shoulder and Spine Stress Release

(10 times): to release tension in your upper body and spine

- Place your hands together in front of your navel.
- Inhale rapidly as you pull your bent arms towards the back with your head tilted backwards and your back arched.
- Exhale rapidly as you curl yourself forward, chin in, and bring your hands back to the front.

5. Arms and Hands T-Exercise

(10 times): to empower your shoulders, arms, hands and fingers

- Extend your arms together in front of your chest.
- Inhale fully as you move your arms out to the side in a T-position.
- Hold your breath and rapidly close and open your hands 3 times.
- Rotate your hands around your wrists 3 times.
- Exhale fully as you return your arms to the front position.

6. Arm Swing

(10 times each step): to oxygenate your lungs and blood and empower your upper torso

- Extend your arms together in front of your chest.
- Inhale fully as you swing your arms around your shoulders by circling them up backwards.
- Exhale fully as you bring them back down to the front.

7. BUTTERFLY STROKE

(10 times each step): to further revitalize your lungs and blood and empower your upper body
* Extend your arms together in front of your chest.
* Inhale fully as you bring your arms down to the back and circle them around your shoulders.
* Exhale fully as you bring your arms back down to the front.

8. UPPER BODY TURNS

(10 times in each direction): to release tension in your upper torso and spine
* Place your feet at shoulder width.
* Join your knuckles in front of your chest.
* Inhale fully as you twist your arms and upper body to the far right and exhale as you swing back to the left 10 times, then reverse direction.

9. HIP ROLLS

(10 times in each direction): to loosen up your hips and flow vitality throughout your body
* Put your hands on your hips.
* Rotate your hips to the right in a circular motion 10 times.
* Then reverse direction and rotate 10 times.

10. INTERNAL ORGANS EXERCISE

(10 times): to detoxify, revitalize and exercise your internal organs (not recommended for pregnant women and people with internal organ problems)
* Place your feet at shoulder width and bend your knees slightly.
* Inhale rapidly while expanding your abdomen.
* Exhale rapidly while compressing your abdomen.
* Continue rapid and full inhalations and exhalations.

11. EXPANDING SQUATS

(20-30 times): for anti-aging, increased will-power and to enhance blood and vitality circulation throughout your body (not recommended for people with knee problems)

- Place your feet at shoulder width.
- Put your palms together at the center of your chest with fingers pointing upwards.
- Inhale fully.
- Exhale fully as you squat down, bending your knees and expanding your arms fully stretched to the side.
- Inhale fully as you come up, bringing your palms back to the center position.
- After completing the squats, stand steadily while simultaneously concentrating on the top of your head and soles of your feet.
- Breathe slowly and relax for 30 seconds.
- This technique facilitates the flow of vitality and power in your entire body.

12. WHOLE BODY STRETCH

(10 times): to align your entire body, release pressure on your spine and strengthen your lower legs and feet

- Place your feet together.
- Put your palms together at the center of your chest with your fingers pointing upwards.
- Inhale fully as you pull your hands as high as you can over the top of your head, stretching your whole body on tip-toe.
- Exhale fully as you return to the starting position with your hands back at chest level.

13. SIDE-TO-SIDE BODY STRETCH

(10 times): to loosen up the sides of your body and further oxygenate your lungs and blood

- Place your feet at shoulder width.
- Put your palms together at the center of your chest with your fingers pointing upwards.
- Inhale as you pull your hands over your head as high as you can.
- While holding your breath, bend your upper body to the right, then to the left and back to the center starting position.
- Exhale as you bring your hands down to the original position at chest level.

Inner Powers Exercise
BODY SHAKE   (2 SETS: 2 MINUTES)

Starting position

Shake your whole body
to loosen up and build
rhythm.

Shake to the right

Shake to the left

EYE THERAPY

Starting position   Move your eyes up and down (10 times)

Side to side (10 times)   Diagonally upper right, lower left (10 times)

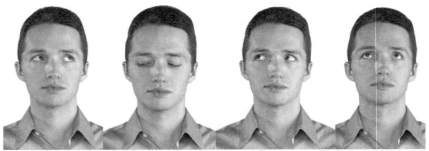

Diagonally upper left, lower right   Rotate eyes clockwise and
(10 times)   counterclockwise (10 times)

NECK THERAPY

Starting position

Tilt your head from side to side (10 times)

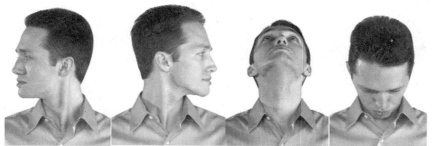

Face to the right, then to the left (10 times)   Move your head up and down with full
breathing (10 times)

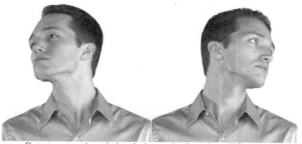

Rotate your head slowly in each direction (10 times)

SHOULDER AND SPINE STRESS RELEASE   (10 TIMES)

Starting position

Inhale rapidly as you pull your arms towards the back with your head tilted backwards and your back arched.

Exhale rapidly as you curl yourself foward, chin in and bring your hands to the front.

Ending position

ARMS AND HANDS T-EXERCISE   (10 TIMES)

Starting position

Inhale fully as you move your arms out to the side, hold your breath and close-open your hands 3 times.

Rotate your hands around your wrists 3 times, then exhale fully as you return your arms to the front position.

ARM SWING   (10 TIMES)

Inhale fully as you swing your arms around your shoulders by circling them up backwards.

Exhale fully as you bring them back to the front.

Starting position

Ending position

BUTTERFLY STROKE   (10 TIMES)

Starting position

Inhale fully as you bring your arms to the back and circle them around your shoulders.

Exhale fully as you bring your arms back to the front.

Ending position

UPPER BODY TURNS　(10 TIMES IN EACH DIRECTION)

Repeat in the opposite direction for another 10 sets.

Exhale fully as you swing to the left. Do this 10 times.

Inhale fully as you twist to the right.

Starting position

Hip Rolls   (10 Times in each direction)

Starting position

Rotate your hips to the right
in a circular motion 10 times.

Then to the left 10 times

INTERNAL ORGANS EXERCISE   (10 TIMES)

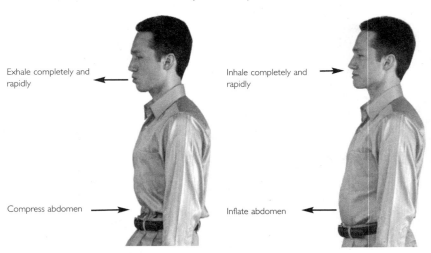

Exhale completely and rapidly

Inhale completely and rapidly

Compress abdomen

Inflate abdomen

EXPANDING SQUATS   (20-30 TIMES)

Inhale fully in the starting position.

Then exhale completely as you squat down.

Inhale fully as you return to the starting position.

Starting position

Squatting position

Keep back straight

WHOLE BODY STRETCH   (10 TIMES)

Starting position

Inhale fully as you stretch your whole body with your hands up as high as you can, on tip-toe.

Exhale completely as you return to the starting position.

SIDE-TO-SIDE BODY STRETCH   (10 TIMES)

Inhale fully as you stretch your hands over your head.

Hold your breath and stretch from side to side.

Starting position

Exhale completely as you return to the starting position.

Part 2: Inner Powers Meditation
INNER POWERS DEVELOPMENT TECHNIQUE
(see page 185)

This inner breathing technique has a great overall impact on the development of inner powers and internal energy. Certain faculties are particularly enhanced using specific *mudras* or hand positions from internal martial arts and advanced yoga practices. These steps were designed to activate and revitalize important energy centers of the body safely:

- Navel energy center for internal energy, stamina, good instincts and sexual vitality
- Heart energy center for love, compassion, happiness, inner peace and emotional intelligence
- Paired heart and navel center for integrated emotional and instinctive intelligence
- *Ajna* or mid-brow center for mental stamina and will, improved concentration and abstract mental intelligence
- Crown energy center for intuition, Divine inspiration, wisdom and universal consciousness

Developing and refining these qualities through the activation of the energy centers improves personal success and inner growth. Regular practice gives more vitality and stimulates the gradual development of inner faculties, which will improve the ability to perform a safer and more effective meditation.

INNER POWERS MEDITATION PROCEDURE
After completing the Inner Powers Exercise, proceed as follows (see page 185):

1. **HEART MUDRA** (*Anjali mudra*)
   Start by closing your eyes and join your palms together at the center of your chest, with your fingers pointing upward.
2. **NAVEL BREATHING** (1 minute)
   Swing your hands down to the navel with your fingers pointing downward. The sides of your palms should be touching

your navel area. This technique causes higher energies to descend to the lower parts of your body and auras. The energy flows wherever your hands are directed. Concentrate on your navel center while breathing slowly and deeply for 1 minute. This will activate and energize the navel energy center and your lower system.

3. **HEART BREATHING** (1 minute)
Swing your hands back from the navel to your heart energy center at mid-chest. Concentrate on your heart energy center at the mid-chest area while breathing slowly for 1 minute. This will activate the heart center, transmute your lower energies and energize your upper system.

4. **HEART-NAVEL BREATHING** (1 minute)
Maintain your left hand at the heart and swing your right hand down to the navel. Breathe slowly and deeply for 1 minute while concentrating simultaneously on your heart and navel centers. This technique will enhance and align your emotional and instinctive intelligence, which are good for decision-making faculties.

5. **NAVEL-HEART BREATHING** (1 minute)
Switch your hand positions so that the left hand swings down to the navel and the right hand swings up to the heart. Breathe slowly and deeply for 1 minute while concentrating simultaneously on your heart and navel centers. This will activate, energize and balance your heart and navel centers and circulate upper and lower energies.

6. **ENERGY FLOW** (18 times)
Swing your left hand back to your heart center, joining it with the right hand, fingers pointing upward in the *anjali mudra*. Swing your joined hands down to your navel and back up to your heart repeatedly 18 times. End at your heart center. This technique facilitates the flow of energy down to the lower energy centers and then upward until the lower and higher energy centers are balanced. This technique is very important to circulate and balance your human energy system.

7. **CROWN-HEART BREATHING** (1 minute)

Raise your left hand up to the top of the head at your crown center with your fingers pointing upward. Your right hand maintains its position at the center of your chest with fingers pointing upward. Breathe slowly and deeply for 1 minute while concentrating simultaneously on your crown and heart centers. This will activate, energize and align your crown and heart centers. This technique also stimulates and integrates the faculties of love, wisdom, intuition and universal consciousness and also improves the connection of your personality to your Soul.

8. **INNER SALUTATION TO LOVED ONES AND OTHERS** (4 minutes)

Bring your left hand down to your heart center. Join both hands together in the *anjali mudra*. Bow your head slightly. Feel love, gratitude and respect in your heart. Silently express these qualities to your loved ones, family members and those who have helped your life (1 minute). Express yourself as if this were your last opportunity to do so. Then express good feelings and wishes to your friends, co-workers and associates for 1 minute. Silently express an apology to people who have been hurt by you, and also silently forgive those who have hurt you in the past or are still hurting you. Mentally express your point of view without judgment. This technique and process will build a positive program for better relationships and to release pent-up emotions. Do this process of forgiveness for at least 2 minutes.

9. **INNER SALUTATION TO THE SOURCE OF LIFE** (2 minutes)

Keeping your hands in the *anjali mudra*, bring both hands up to your forehead area. The sides of your palms should be touching your forehead. For 2 minutes, silently express your love, respect and gratitude to the Source of Life as if this were your last opportunity to do so. If you have an affinity with spiritual teachers, Saints or Sages, you may include them in your inner salutation. Enjoy the positive effects of this technique.

10 . CLOSING

Gently bring your hands down to your heart center, palms together, fingers pointing upward. Open your eyes and smile. Enjoy the pleasant feeling, well-being and balance of aligning yourself.

SCHEDULE

The Inner Powers Exercise is recommended at least 3 times a week. You can do it after your morning shower before you go to work for lasting energy throughout the whole day. It is also helpful after a stressful day to revitalize yourself before spending time with your family. Experiment with the program for one week to observe how you feel compared to days you don't do it. This exercise will prepare you for your next level of meditation.

Inner Powers Development Technique

Inner breathing with hand *mudras* to activate and align the energy centers
(1 minute each position)

Starting position
Anjali Mudra

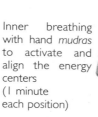

Navel breathing

Heart breathing

Heart-Navel breathing

Navel-Heart breathing

ENERGY FLOW

Return to the *Anjali Mudra* and swing your hands down to your navel and back to your heart repeatedly 18 times.

CROWN-HEART BREATHING

Start from the *Anjali Mudra*. Raise your left hand to the top of your head. Concentrate on your heart and crown centers while breathing slowly for 1 minute.

INNER SALUTATION TO LOVED ONES AND OTHERS

INNER SALUTATION TO THE SOURCE OF LIFE

| Return to *Anjali Mudra* | Bow your head slightly and silently express love, gratitude and respect to your loved ones, family and others for 4 minutes. | Bring both hands up to the forehead area, silently expressing your love, gratitude and respect to the Source of Life for 2 minutes. | End by returning to the starting position. |

8-STEP INTERNAL STAMINA EXERCISE FOR BUSY MEDITATORS
You Can Do It Anywhere, Anytime...With No Special Gadgets!

Specially-designed for today's busy professionals, this is a shorter variation of the Inner Powers Exercise that only takes 5 minutes. This method does not require special equipment or accessories, and it can be done almost anywhere, anytime. You can do the exercises and breathing techniques in a business suit in your office, at a conference or before going home. This program is available on DVD so you can apply it easily.

I recommend that you try these exercises before proceeding to the rest of this book.

PROCEDURE AND PRACTICE

(see pages 162-180)

Preparation

1. You may follow the DVD video guiding this program.
2. You can achieve best results in a well-ventilated exercise space with plenty of clean, fresh air. Once you have familiarized yourself with the sequence, do it outdoors if possible.

Procedure

1. SHOULDER AND SPINE STRESS RELEASE (10 times): to release tension in your abdominal area, upper body and spine (see page 172)
2. ARM SWING (10 times): to oxygenate your lungs and blood and empower your upper torso (see page 174)
3. UPPER BODY TURNS (10 times in each direction): to release tension in your upper torso and spine and to balance the left and right sides of your body (see page 176)
4. HIP ROLLS (10 times in each direction): to loosen up your hips and flow vitality throughout your body (see page 177)
5. INTERNAL ORGANS EXERCISE (10 times): to detoxify, revitalize and exercise your internal organs (not recommended for pregnant women and people with internal organ problems) (see page 178)
6. EXPANDING SQUATS (20-30 times): for anti-aging, increased will-power and to enhance blood and vitality circulation throughout your body (not recommended for people with knee problems) (see page 178)

   After doing all the squats, stand steadily while concentrating on the top of your head and soles of your feet simultaneously. Breathe slowly and relax for 30 seconds. This technique facilitates the flow of vitality and power in your entire body.

7. **WHOLE BODY STRETCH** (10 times): to align your entire body, release pressure on your spine and strengthen your lower legs and feet (see page 180)
8. **SIDE-TO-SIDE BODY STRETCH** (10 times): to loosen up the sides of your body and further oxygenate your lungs and blood (see page 180)

The 8-Step Internal Stamina Exercise is recommended at least three times a week or, even better, daily before and after work. You can do it after your morning shower before you go to work for more energy throughout the whole day. It is also helpful after a stressful day to revitalize yourself before spending time with your family. I do this exercise after a long flight to successfully beat flight fatigue. You can try experimenting with the program for one week to observe how you feel compared to days you don't do it. This is an ideal exercise before you do meditations because it is short and effective in preparing and conditioning your physical and energy bodies.

To reduce the high impact of awakening internal powers during meditation, especially advanced types, don't forget to do the above preparations.

By spending a few minutes conditioning yourself, you'll prevent days, weeks or months of negative side effects from meditation.

CHAPTER 12

Breath:
The Heart of Meditation

When you can't breathe, nothing else matters.
American Lung Association

In health as well as life, this statement is so true because breath is life. People can go without eating or drinking for a few days or a week, and they can go without sunlight for a month. But most people can't go more than a few minutes without air. Why? Because of the absence of oxygen. This chapter focuses on the fourth preparatory element in Step 1 of the 5-step process for safe and effective meditation that we introduced in Chapter 8: the importance of breath and its proper use. The information and techniques presented in this chapter will be applied throughout all the meditations in this book.

The vitality and energy that vivify and revitalize the physical and etheric bodies, with all their systems and organs, depend on the energy that comes from the air. Air is not just a mixture of oxygen, nitrogen and other gases, but also includes a special planetary life force we earlier referred to as air vitality globules, air *prana* in yoga or *chi* in martial arts. When we breathe air, we breathe the essential oxygen, gases and air energy vitality that energize the physical and etheric bodies.

$$Air = O_2 + N_2 + CO_2 + toxins + air\ vitality\ globules$$

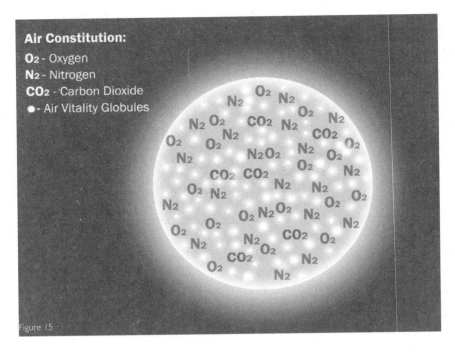

Figure 15

HOW YOUR BODY USES OXYGEN

Let's examine how your body uses oxygen:

- Metabolism: Oxygen is needed for the proper transformation of food nutrients into energy harnessed by the cells in an internal process. The ability to convert food into energy makes the food we eat valuable. People can eat healthy food, but an inadequate level of oxygen in the conversion process, among other factors, can lead to low vitality and malnutrition.
- Oxygen and air vitality globules absorbed properly through the lungs by full breathing techniques enable the blood to displace the toxins in the body effectively, especially carbon dioxide. Also, the absorbed air globules are distributed to the chakras and the etheric body. Therefore, continuous revitalization and detoxification occur automatically.

- Rapid breathing techniques energize and empower the nervous system through the absorption of ions and pranic vitality via nerves in the internal nasal cavity. Therefore, certain rapid breathing techniques can be employed to facilitate this process.

BREATHING AND BODY POSTURE

Posture is one of the most important factors impacting the effectiveness of the breathing process. Proper posture not only determines air intake capacity, but also one's emotional, mental and spiritual aspects. Observe and consider the ways different people sit and breathe:

- Successful and smart people generally sit upright most of the time, especially when they are thinking or doing their most important work. They have better breathing habits except when they get stressed; then breathing becomes more shallow and erratic.
- Depressed people and pessimists have a concave, curled body posture when sitting or sleeping. This creates a compressed diaphragm and reduced lung capacity and oxygen intake, which result in low vitality and reduced power.
- Stressed people and those with anxiety generally breathe through chest movement and expansion while the abdomen is sucked in, accompanied by a shallow and erratic breathing pattern. Again, less air intake means less oxygen and air globules, resulting in poorer health. If this type of person has been exposed to severe stress and anxiety for an extended period, they have the habit and pattern of shallow breathing, even while resting or relaxing. Proper, healthy breathing involves abdominal movement and expansion to draw more air deeper into the lower lobes of the lungs, meaning the abdomen expands, not the chest.
- Insecure and defensive people usually sit with crossed legs and arms. The closed position does not allow them to absorb

vitality from the environment or from the power of ideas during a lecture or conversation. People in this position are not in a receptive mood. These crossed arms and legs positions are not recommended for meditation.

However, this position can be useful on occasion: Crossing your arms and legs is an immediate shielding technique when you are with very negative and stressed people or are in a negatively-charged environment.

KNOW YOURSELF:
What do your posture and breathing style
say about you? Identify your type:

Alert type with upright posture ____
Lazy with laid back, reclining position ____
Pessimistic and worrying type with
slumped shoulders and concave chest ____
Stressed and anxious type with chest
breathing and no abdominal expansion ____
Insecure or defensive type with frequently
crossed arms and/or legs ____

Wrong body posture can create negative physical, emotional and mental health and attitudes, or vice-versa. By positioning your body properly while sitting, standing or sleeping, plus breathing properly by inhaling deeply into your abdomen instead of your chest, greater health and substantial internal power and energy result. The physical exercises and advanced meditations presented in this book always include breathing techniques to achieve the goals of better health and higher energy levels.

BREATHING PATTERNS

Most people exhibit several breathing patterns such as:

- Abdominal breathing
- Chest breathing
- Shoulder breathing

Different breathing patterns are formed depending on health, stress level and consciousness.

ABDOMINAL BREATHING

This natural method involves expanding the abdomen during inhalation and deflating the abdomen during exhalation. Observe the natural breathing of a healthy sleeping baby. The belly expands during inhalation and deflates during exhalation.

CHEST BREATHING

Highly stressed people usually breathe with more chest expansion and minimal abdominal movement. When people have anxiety, anger or high levels of emotional tension, their breathing is shallow and erratic. This tends to congest the heart energy center and also reduces air vitality and oxygen intake. You can observe the breathing of your family members, co-workers or friends to determine if they are stressed or have emotional concerns.

The chest breathing pattern induces anxiety and emotional overreaction, plus it lowers the lungs' capacity to absorb air. Practice abdominal breathing consciously to reverse this habit or use the internal organs exercise method from the Internal Stamina Exercise (see page 178) to develop a habit of natural abdominal breathing.

SHOULDER BREATHING

The respiratory system and body's own intelligence use shoulder breathing automatically in addition to abdominal breathing to draw in more air when the system needs a tremendous amount of oxygen. After a strenuous physical workout like sprinting or lifting heavy weights, your body demands more oxygen and vitality. Therefore, you tend to experience rapid respiration and deep breathing by expanding your upper trunk and lifting your shoulders.

The problem is that if you do not inflate your abdominal area while doing shoulder and chest breathing, you are compressing the diaphragm instead of maximizing your lung capacity, which pushes the lungs upward, causing less air supply.

Breathing, Emotions, Mind and Spirituality: ARE THEY RELATED?

When you are nervous or experiencing anxiety, observe your breathing pattern. Does it change automatically? Yes! When your mind is confused and intolerant, does your breathing also change? How about when you are very peaceful and inward during meditation? How does your breathing behave? Observe people meditating. You can see that they are breathing very slowly and rhythmically.

We can conclude that breathing is a common denominator and connector of all your physical, vitality, emotional, mental and spiritual aspects.

The good news is that you can regulate and control your breathing pattern to regulate your vitality, emotions, mind and spiritual awareness. Spiritual development is also connected to many meditation techniques that require breathing methods to bring in spiritual energy.

The Latin word, *spirare* (to breathe), is connected not only to oxygen or *prana*, but also to the process of breathing spiritual life into the personality.

BREATHING MECHANISMS

To understand the mechanisms of breathing to make it a science, let's consider what medical scientists like Dr. H.R. Nagendra of the Yoga Research Foundation (*The Art and Science of Pranayama*, 1st edition, Vivekananda Kendra, June 1993) say about it. Here's what the scientists and doctors know:

The breathing process is controlled by the respiratory system with several guiding mechanisms and signals from the brain, nervous system and internal respiratory chemical response.

Our respiratory system has two operational functions:

1. Voluntary: Conscious control of breath at will
2. Involuntary: Automatic respiration without conscious mental effort. Respiration is governed and regulated by two main factors:
1. Nervous system control: A group of nerve cells located in the medulla oblongata acts as a respiratory controller for nerves that go to the respiratory organs and mechanisms
2. Chemical control: Lack of or reduced oxygen and excess of carbon dioxide in the blood trigger our breathing apparatus to increase the rate of breathing and depth of breath. Increased amounts of oxygen and a decrease in carbon dioxide will reduce your rate of breathing and signals your nervous system to slow it down.

The neo-cortex, which is the higher center in the brain, is believed to control the lower brain system as well as the body's physiology. The "boss" of the lower brain is the hypothalamus, which has two "assistants":

1. Autonomic nervous system: Responsible for many of the spontaneous functions of the body's programs
2. Endocrine glands: Regulate the majority of hormonal and chemical aspects of the body

Thus, it can be inferred that the hypothalamus and the autonomic nervous system govern involuntary respiration.

The neo-cortex is believed to control voluntary breath and respiration. At will, we can override the program of the hypothalamus and autonomic nervous system control mechanisms. But after a certain length of time, the autonomic nervous system overrides the respiration apparatus.

Esoterically speaking, overriding the autonomic respiration is a big deal: Conscious, deliberate control of breathing patterns through the science of breath, or *pranayama*, brings many changes physiologically, emotionally, mentally, spiritually and in terms of vitality. This is what you will learn in this chapter so you can bring many desirable changes to your body and inner consciousness during the practice of breath control. You can reverse many wrong programs and unconscious bad habits through breathing techniques.

We will not go into detail here about the basic parts of the respiratory system since these are already well-known by many practitioners.

Other Factors to Know

The table below shows the major gases involved in respiration.

GASES	INHALED AIR	EXHALED AIR
Nitrogen	79%	79%
Oxygen	20%	16%
Carbon dioxide	0.04%	4.04%
Miscellaneous	0.96%	0.96%

About 4% of the oxygen we inhale gets absorbed by the body in normal respiration. The volume of carbon dioxide also increases about 4%[6].

Normal rates of respiration are as follows[7]:

Newborn babies	40 breaths per minute
One-year-old	30 breaths per minute
2-5 years old	24 breaths per minute
Adults	10-20 breaths per minute

These rates change according to activity. Meditation, rest and relaxation naturally decrease the breathing rate.

BREATH VOLUME AND LUNG CAPACITY

Lung capacity and breath volumes vary according to body weight, gender, age and health conditions. The total volume of air that can be inhaled into the lungs is an adult average of 4.5 liters (.157 cubic feet), but the average volume in an ordinary breath for a normal person is about half a liter (.0175 cubic feet). Super-athletes, martial artists and advanced yogis have more tidal volume, as it is called in medical terminology[8]. There is also some air that naturally remains in the lungs called residual volume, which is slightly more than 1 liter (.035 cubic feet)[9]. It is also observed that the reserve of the lungs when inhaling is about one-third more than when exhaling, meaning that when you exhale to the maximum, you have a residual volume of air that you can't expel even if you force it.

A portable, computerized spirometer can be used to measure breath volume and lung capacity. If you want to study detailed calculations, refer to Gregg L. Ruppel's *Manual of Pulmonary Function Testing* (St. Louis: Mosby Yearbook, Inc., 1994).

PROLONGED BREATH RETENTION DOES NOT ADD MORE OXYGEN, BUT THERE ARE IONIZING EFFECTS OF PRANA

When holding your breath after deep inhalation, there is no added oxygenation after a saturation point regulated by the surface area of the alveolar membrane and the partial pressure of oxygen and carbon dioxide on either side of the lung membrane.

The oxygen diffusion stops when the pressure of gases is equalized. In some breathing techniques and *pranayama,* there's a chance that carbon dioxide increases its level, but the nervous system and the brain signal systems are educated and programmed for higher tolerance. At controlled levels, increased carbon dioxide in the blood causes altered states of consciousness and also stimulates the brain capillaries to dilate to increase blood supply to the brain. When the carbon dioxide increases to a high level, the incoming surge and gasp for oxygen increase the sense of exhilaration.

The pranic vitality increase and the effect of the turbinal bone structure inside the nasal cavity with rapid inhalation and exhalation as in the Synchronized Breathing Method (see pages 202-204) produce an ionizing effect on the nerves inside the uvula area. This effect tends to radiate to the nervous system and the brain, stimulating expansion of consciousness. Therefore, the retention of breath has   exoteric and esoteric significance, but the technique should be done carefully. Otherwise, there can be negative side effects. Having a trained mentor is important.

INNER AND ENERGETIC SIGNIFICANCE OF THE SCIENCE OF BREATH

Let's study the inner and energetic significance of the science of breath and *pranayama.* We'll classify the procedures and practices in three levels:

LEVEL 1: BASIC BREATHING METHODS
These are very safe and effective methods that do not require much training from an instructor or mentor. They can also be incorporated into self-healing and general meditation procedures easily. The following are included:

1. Inner Purification Breathing Techniques
2. Abdominal Breathing Technique (10:5:10:5 ratio)

3. Chakral Breathing Method
4. Synchronized Breathing Method

LEVEL 2: INTERMEDIATE BREATHING METHODS

These are more powerful methods that activate many chakras and awaken the inner forces and powers of your system. They are still relatively safe except for some precautions for certain ailments. These methods include:

1. Advanced Synchronized Breathing Method™
2. Combination Breathing Technique™ (Basic Level)
3. Alternate Nostril Breathing
4. *Kriya* or Purifying Breathing Methods: *Kapalbhati* and *Bhastrika*

LEVEL 3: ADVANCED BREATHING METHODS

Proper use of postures, locks and *mudras* are important with the advanced *pranayama* techniques. These include:

1. Advanced Combination Breathing Technique
2. Breathing Methods to Awaken the Spiritual Fires with several ratios

Before we proceed to the actual discussion of the techniques, see pages 130 and 131 for meditation postures you will be using in the meditations and breathing practices.

LEVEL 1: BASIC BREATHING METHODS

Let's start with the first level. The methods we will be discussing are:

- Inner Purification Breathing Techniques
- Abdominal Breathing Technique (10:5:10:5 ratio)
- Chakral Breathing Method
- Synchronized Breathing Method

Inner Purification Breathing Techniques

This is a natural abdominal breathing technique to externalize negative feelings, body tension or discomfort, guided by intention. It is a self-guided tool for stress or pain release. It is also a safe, gradual revitalizing technique and fast relaxation method. It is a powerful technique even though it seems simple.

PROCEDURE AND PRACTICE FOR INNER PURIFICATION BREATHING METHOD: 7-10 minutes
1. Sit in a comfortable chair with your spine erect, your feet flat on the floor and your hands in your lap. You may also sit in a lotus or semi-lotus posture with your hands in your lap or arms straight. You may close your eyes.
2. Inhale and exhale slowly for 1 minute and relax. Imagine yourself in front of a beautiful ocean.
3. Externalize body tension as you exhale slowly to the imaginary ocean. Imagine you are releasing of all of your body's discomfort to the ocean (2 minutes).
4. Continue the slow breathing and exhale all your negative feelings to the imaginary ocean (2 minutes).
5. Continue the slow breathing and exhale all your negative and disturbing thoughts to the imaginary ocean (2 minutes).
6. Relax and enjoy the inner peace and calmness for as long as you would like.

This is a very simple and easy technique that has worked for many professionals, parents and ADHD children. My executive clients employ this technique to release their stress before going home. They also use it in between business meetings to align and calm down. This technique slows down your heart and breathing rates and helps normalize your blood pressure.

The imaginary ocean is an important target to release negative energies because energy follows your thought.

10:5:10:5 Abdominal Breathing Technique (5 minutes)

Slow abdominal breathing with breath retention is commonly used in yoga and martial arts. This method will not only calm you down and revitalize you fast, it will also sharpen your ability to concentrate and focus. It is not recommended for pregnant women and those with hypertension or heart ailments because it boosts your internal energy too quickly, which can produce negative side effects.

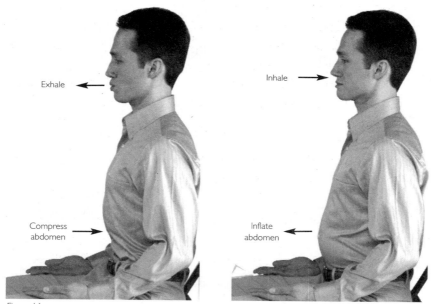

Figure 16

PROCEDURE AND PRACTICE FOR 10:5:10:5

1. Sit with your spine vertical and your feet flat on the floor.
2. Inhale slowly and deeply into your abdomen while mentally counting to 10.
3. Hold your breath for a count of 5.
4. Exhale slowly, deflating your abdomen completely while mentally counting to 10.
5. Hold your breath for a count of 5.
6. Repeat the whole breathing pattern for a maximum of 5 minutes.
7. Do this procedure 3 times weekly or daily as required.

These abdominal breathing methods have been observed to offer the following benefits:

- Rapid increase in internal energy and vitality
- Calming of the mind and emotions
- Rejuvenation of the body

These methods can be used as simple meditations to de-stress, relax and detoxify the body, then to revitalize and rejuvenate yourself. You can do the techniques daily before and after work.

When you concentrate on any chakra while breathing slowly for a few minutes, you activate the chakra and purify and revitalize it and its functions. Let's try a simple technique.

Navel Chakra Breathing Method: 3 Steps to Center Yourself
(5 minutes)

This is a very simple but powerful technique to center yourself quickly, plus awaken your internal stamina. The navel center is where you can gather and alchemize *prana*. It is also a storehouse of synthesized *chi* in the lower part of the aura. When the navel center is very active, your gut instincts also improve greatly.

PROCEDURE AND PRACTICE

1. Sit in a chair in the Egyptian posture, lotus or semi-lotus position. Be comfortable and just relax.
2. Assume the meditation *mudra* (*dhayani*) (left hand on top of right) at the navel.
3. Inhale and exhale slowly and deeply for 5 minutes while mentally concentrating on the navel chakra. Do not visualize. Just focus on the navel point. Do not concentrate too much. Just relax and enjoy.

This meditation *mudra* (*dhayani*) will facilitate the automatic circulation of energy in the front and back meridians while you are charging the navel center and its "storage bins". If your mind gets side-tracked with another thought, focus back on the navel and continue breathing slowly. When done regularly, this technique will automatically center you and your consciousness back from too much thinking or feeling. You also get revitalized with this technique. It is great for sports, including athletic training.

PRECAUTION FOR NAVEL CHAKRA BREATHING METHOD
Do not exceed 30 minutes of the navel breathing method because it will over-energize your sex chakra.

Sychronized Breathing Method
One of the most successful methods I have designed for both material and spiritual applications is the Synchronized Breathing Method. It is a daily routine that I use for many different applications, and it's a favorite of my students and clients.

The Synchronized Breathing Method is a multipurpose breathing technique to:

- Rapidly release stress
- Calm the emotions and mind fast
- Purify and revitalize the bodies and energy centers
- Activate and align the chakras regulating emotional, mental and spiritual energies and faculties

This method was designed after many experiments with the training I received from my early spiritual mentors. Also, while teaching and traveling in India, I encountered several advanced yogis who practice *pranayama* yoga, which literally means "yogic breathing science" in Sanskrit. Several yogic and healing books also mention the two breathing methods we discussed in the previous chapter: *kapalbhati pranayama,* which involves rapid inhalation and exhalation with simultaneous up-and-down head movement and *bastrika pranayama,* which involves rapid compression and expansion of the abdomen during exhalation and inhalation.

Based on my experiments, when I integrated these two breathing styles into one technique, it brought fantastic results: greater detoxifying and revitalizing of the human energy system and rapid calming of the mind and emotions. I have also added chakral breathing to activate and align:

+ The heart chakra for emotional intelligence
+ The *ajna* chakra for mental faculties and stamina
+ The crown chakra for spiritual intelligence and powers

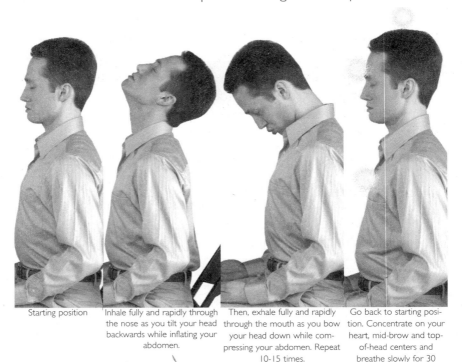

| Starting position | Inhale fully and rapidly through the nose as you tilt your head backwards while inflating your abdomen. | Then, exhale fully and rapidly through the mouth as you bow your head down while compressing your abdomen. Repeat 10-15 times. | Go back to starting position. Concentrate on your heart, mid-brow and top-of-head centers and breathe slowly for 30 seconds. |

Figure 17

Procedure and Practice for Synchronized Breathing Method

1. Sit in a comfortable position with your back straight and vertical in a lotus or semi-lotus position or in a chair with your feet flat on the floor. Close your eyes before you start.
2. Inhale rapidly through your nose as you tilt your head back while simultaneously inflating your abdomen.

3. Immediately exhale quickly through your mouth as you bow your head down while compressing your abdomen.
4. Repeat steps two and three 10-15 times.
5. Just relax with your head vertical and breathe slowly. Concentrate on the top of your head (crown energy center), mid-brow area (*ajna* energy center) and center of your chest (heart energy center) simultaneously while breathing slowly. Do this step for 30 seconds.
6. Use this technique 3 times weekly or daily as required.

PRECAUTION FOR SYNCHRONIZED BREATHING METHOD

The technique is not recommended for pregnant women or those with neck injuries, high blood pressure, migraine, vertigo or severe heart conditions without supervision of an expert. If in doubt, consult a certified safe and effective meditation or yoga instructor before you perform the technique.

This method activates and creates more energy in the crown, *ajna* and heart energy centers, bringing more spiritual energy to purify and revitalize the whole system. This method also stimulates the faculties of love, compassion, creativity, mental stamina, intuition, Divine inspiration, wisdom and universal consciousness in the personality.

Integrating the rapid breathing and activation of the three energy centers surpasses many methods to detoxify the human energy system, still the mind, calm the emotions and align the personality with the Soul. We can achieve great inner powers when empowered by the Soul and when the mind and emotions are calm and centered. This technique has been used successfully by many of my clients who are executives, leaders and spiritual practitioners for stress management and centering meditation.

BENEFITS OF THE SYNCHRONIZED BREATHING METHOD

- ◆ It flushes and purges out any cloudiness, negative emotions and mental disturbances.

- It purifies and revitalizes the pranic or etheric body fast.
- Once your mind and emotions are calm, you are able to concentrate naturally and simultaneously on three areas:
    - Crown chakra point (stimulates spiritual intelligence)
    - Mid-brow chakra point (awakens mental intelligence and power)
    - Heart chakra point (activates love and inner peace)
- This breathing bridges concentration to awareness meditation.

You can start mastering concentration through the Synchronized Breathing Method. It is the ideal tool for all meditators, beginners or advanced!

There are more basic breathing techniques, but the four above are the most important ones for day-to-day use.

LEVEL 2: INTERMEDIATE BREATHING METHODS

This set of breathing techniques involves additional skills using hand *mudras*, simultaneous concentration on three chakras and additional integrated steps. The techniques have certain steps that awaken the *kundalini* fire and Divine light.

The Level 2 methods include:

- Advanced Synchronized Breathing Method™
- Combination Breathing Technique™ (Basic Level)
- Alternate Nostril Breathing
- *Kriya* or Purifying Breathing Methods *Kapalbhati* and *Bhastrika*

Advanced Synchronized Breathing Method (5 minutes)

The Advanced Synchronized Breathing Method has several practical applications:

1. This technique can be used by beginners or advanced medi-

tators before meditating to help purify and increase the rate of vibration in the bodies. The success of calming the mind and emotions and the depth of one's meditative experience depend on the purity and level of vitality in the different bodies. When the human energy system is purified and aligned, it becomes a receptive agent for high incoming vibrations, ideas and transformational energies.

2. To prepare the energy centers and bodies for clear and accurate psychic or intuitional perception and interpretation. These faculties depend greatly on the purity and vitality level of the psychic reader's aura and energy centers. Many psychics give wrong interpretations due to negative contamination in their energetic, emotional and mental bodies. Their perception is colored and influenced by their own emotions and thoughts, sometimes in the form of beliefs, biases, illusions, emotional preferences and personal experiences. Therefore, for "seers" or psychic readers doing readings, the Synchronized Breathing Method can enable more accurate readings and also make psychic faculties and intuition easier to use.

   By activating the crown, *ajna* and heart energy centers, the Divine connection or the "spiritual antenna" is stimulated to a higher degree, thus the Soul or Higher Self can guide the personality better. Divine energy improves the functioning of the mental and emotional faculties. The Synchronized Breathing Method also increases the rate of vibration of the human energy system.

PROCEDURE AND PRACTICE FOR ADVANCED SYNCHRONIZED BREATHING METHOD

1. Sit in a comfortable position, either in the Egyptian posture or the adept's posture (*siddhasana*) (see pages 130-132). Keep your spine erect and just relax. Close your eyes.

2. Put your tongue on your palate with the tongue or *khechari mudra*. Also perform the meditation *mudra* (*dhayani*). Exhale

your air and go to the chin-in position (see page 204).

3. Inhale rapidly as you tilt your head backward (do not over-stretch) and exhale quickly as you bow your head down to the chin-in position. Breathe through your nose at a rate of 60 inhalation-exhalation sets per minute or 1 second per set. Do 30 sets.

4. At the end of the last exhalation, expel all your air while doing the throat lock, root lock and abdomen compressed lock simultaneously. Hold this position for 5-10 seconds.

5. Focus on your heart, mid-brow and crown chakras. Release your throat lock and other locks, straighten your head and inhale fully but slowly. If you expand, let go. Relax, normalize your breath for a few seconds and continue your concentration on the heart, mid-brow and crown centers. Inhale and exhale slowly for about 1 minute.

6. Repeat Steps 3-5 two more times.

7. Repeat Step 3, but increase the inhalation-exhalation rate to 90 sets per minute or one and a half times faster than the original speed. Follow with Steps 4 and 5 (2 repetitions).

8. Repeat Step 3, but increase the inhalation-exhalation rate to 120 sets per minute or 2 times faster than the original speed. Follow with Steps 4 and 5 (2 repetitions).

PRECAUTIONS FOR ADVANCED SYNCHRONIZED BREATHING METHOD

1. This is not recommended for people who smoke, drink alcohol or do recreational drugs. The basic Synchronized Breathing Method is more suitable for them.

2. Do not do this practice if you are pregnant or have neck problems, migraine, vertigo, bleeding ulcers, heart conditions or hypertension.

3. If you feel lightheaded, that is an effect of hyper-oxygenation or hyperventilation, including the ionization of the nerves in the head area. This technique can also make you spacey, therefore before you drive a car or operate any machinery, do the following:

- Hold your hips and do 20-30 squats. Inhale as you come up and exhale as you squat down. Do not over-exert.
- If you are still spacey, jog in place for I minute.

4. If you experience side effects from this practice, stop immediately and consult a meditation expert or certified **WISEmeditation.org** instructor (see Chapter 25).

This advanced form of Synchronized Breathing can stand on its own, or it can be combined with a more advanced meditation in preparation for *samadhi* experience. It is an excellent meditation in itself, combining concentration, *pranayama* and awareness meditation leading to contemplation levels. It is one of my favorites because it is simple, very fast and effective for going to an altered state of consciousness. Even "chattering or monkey mind" practitioners will benefit from this, but it is recommended that you first do the basic level of the Synchronized Breathing Method for three months weekly before going for this advanced level.

Combination Breathing Technique (Basic Level) (3-5 minutes)

This simple breathing technique is very powerful to recover your vitality fast and revitalize your sexual energy and boost energy for physical activities. It combines full abdominal, chest and shoulder breathing for maximum air capacity.

The esoteric significance of this breathing technique goes beyond oxygen intake as follows:

1. When you inhale fully and hold your breath for a longer period of time, there is a surge of Divine light that comes in.
2. When you exhale fully and hold your breath for an extended period of time, the *kundalini* fire gets awakened slightly.
3. There is a large amount of pranic absorption and assimilation during the breathing sequences.
4. This technique prepares your internal energy for a powerful meditation.

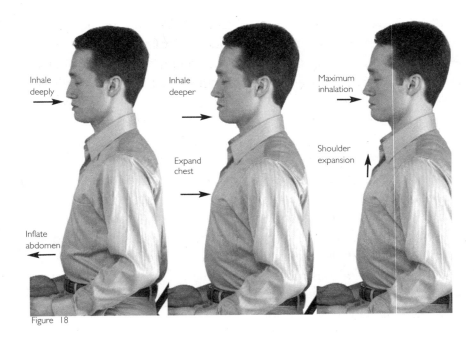

Figure 18

PROCEDURE AND PRACTICE FOR COMBINATION BREATHING TECHNIQUE

1. Sit in a comfortable position with your spine vertical and your feet flat on the floor or in a lotus or semi-lotus position. You may close your eyes.
2. Place your hands in your lap with your palms facing upward. Do the tongue *mudra* on your palate.
3. Inhale slowly and continuously while inflating your abdomen.
4. Continue inhaling slowly, inflating your chest.
5. Continue inhaling until maximum respiration while expanding and lifting your shoulders upwards.
6. Hold your breath steadily for 5-10 seconds.
7. Exhale all your air slowly while deflating your abdomen and chest, and bring your shoulders back down to their normal position.
8. Hold your breath steadily for 5-10 seconds.
9. Repeat this breathing process (steps 3-8) only 5-10 times a maximum of twice a day. Do this 3 times weekly or when high energy is required.

PRECAUTION FOR COMBINATION BREATHING TECHNIQUE

1. This simple breathing technique creates tremendous internal power and a surge of vitality not recommended for pregnant women or people with chest pain, heart ailments, high blood pressure, migraine or headache, bleeding problems, glaucoma, ADHD, cancer or AIDS. If you are not sure, consult your physician before you start this procedure.

2. If you have side effects like acidity, hiccups or extreme dizziness, stop the practice immediately and consult a meditation expert or mentor.

Regulating and sensing the breathing rhythm is an essential part of meditation, especially in *pranayama* or the science of breathing. The Combination Breathing Technique enforces control of the breath breathing pattern from the brain's neo-cortex and mental will-power over the autonomic nervous system and involuntary respiratory control center in the lower section of the brain. By doing this process deliberately, we are re-educating the primitive animal brain instincts with certain new types of consciousness for expansion to emerge. This facilitates new awareness and even physical, chemical, neurological and psycho-spiritual instincts and habits.

There are five components in breathing science:

1. Inhalation, called *puraka* in yoga
2. Holding of breath after inhalation, called *puraka kumbhaka* in yoga
3. Exhalation, called *recaka* in yoga
4. Holding of the breath after exhalation, called *recaka kumbhaka* in yoga
5. Automatic non-conscious stopping or slowing down of breathing, called *kevala kumbhaka*. This happens when you are approaching *samadhi* or a yogic trance stage.

There are three schools of thought on achieving *kevala kumbha-ka:*

1. Through conscious, forceful effort with breath control (*pranayama*)
2. Through the mystical way of relaxing and letting go after deep meditation until a trance-like state of breathlessness
3. Through integration of the first and second schools, which is our approach of combining the science and art of meditation and breathing practices

We will apply several types of breath control ratios in the intermediate and advanced levels of the science of breathing. Again, the important principle to remember is that holding your breath after inhalation awakens your Soul energy, and holding your breath after exhalation awakens your *kundalini* energy and brings in a surge of pranic force. This concept is not clearly included in most yogic books and teachings.

We can offer more complete information in this book because I was so lucky to be trained by a few of the best enlightened mentors in the world who are super-experts in their own fields. One of them, TBJ, a yogic guru, is said to be an immortal in the highlands of the Himalayas. I had one-on-one training with him several times and received priceless teachings in Hatha, Raja and Jnana yoga. I also learned some of the *pranayama* techniques from him. One of my other early mentors is a master of Tantric *kundalini* yoga, Mantric yoga and Zen meditations. He is also an expert in Oriental medicine, internal martial arts systems and hand *mudras*. My other two early mentors, MCKS and MMCN, are the best in their own specializations: healing, psychic powers development and integrated yoga science.

By studying deeply and experimenting with, synthesizing and applying the best of their teachings, the techniques in this book are distillations of their great spiritual lineages. The Bihar School of Yoga, the Yoga *Sutras* of Patanjali and Tibetan Master Dhjwal Khul's teachings also inspired me to search for modern ways to apply their great principles and philosophies.

Kriya *or Purifying Breathing Methods:* Kapalbhati *and* Bhastrika

Before proceeding to the next technique, let me explain the difference between the breathing patterns:

1. *Kriya* breathing is geared to the purifying process of the energy system and chakras. It is very fast and strong because you are doing more than 60 inhalations-exhalations per minute up to 120+. The Advanced Synchronized Breathing Method in its Steps 3, 7 and 8 (pages 202-204) are examples. *Kapalbhati* (nostril forced breaths) and *bhastrika pranayama*, which we'll study after this section, are both *kriya* or purifying breaths.

2. *Pranayama* breaths are different breathing techniques that slow down the breathing rhythm to below the normal rate of 10-20 breaths per minute. Technically, the *pranayama* breathing leads to *kevala kumbhaka* or effortless slow or almost stopped breathing, which characterizes *samadhi* or a deep state of inner experience. Most of the advanced levels of breathing techniques will be *pranayama* methods.

According to ancient teachings in yoga, which I have experimented with extensively and have proven to be effective, if you breathe repeatedly through only one of your nostrils in the balancing breathings knows as *Yogis swara* in yoga, there are certain outcomes such as:

• **Right-nostril breathing:**
  - Increases dynamic activity
  - Increases sexual vitality
  - Improves digestive functions
  - Gives a very optimistic attitude

Slow and very passive people should apply right-nostril breathing daily for about 5 minutes. Sexually over-active or very aggressive people should minimize using this technique. They are already predisposed to a blocked left nostril, and they predominantly breathe with the right nostril throughout the day.

◆ **Left-nostril breathing:**
  - Relaxes and calms you down
  - Improves receptiveness and patience
  - Gradually helps neutralize aggressiveness and superiority complex
  - Provides a more passive and gentle nature

Very gentle and passive people normally are predisposed to left nostril breathing, and generally their right nostril is predominantly clogged. Very aggressive and willful people need the left-nostril breathing technique to calm down.

You can observe that most healthy people have a natural alternation of breathing following what some call the circadian rhythm, which normally alters left and right nostril opening about every 90 minutes throughout the day. The erectile tissues lining the internal nasal passage have a natural intelligence allowing alternate swelling and shrinking of the internal nasal passage to close and open each nostril. If the breathing of the two nostrils balances, you feel a greater sense of inner well-being.

Esoterically, the alternate nostril breathing technique has these functions:

1. Right nostril-controlled breathing stimulates the *pingala* (masculine or *yang* energy) corresponding to the right nostril.
2. Left nostril-controlled breathing stimulates the *ida* (feminine or *yin* energy) corresponding to the left nostril.
3. When the right and left nostrils are balanced through breath control, the *kundalini* energy is induced to flow through the middle meridian, the *sushumna*. Therefore, we need to do the alternate breathing for this purpose.

Right Nostril-Controlled Breathing
(SINGLE NOSTRIL TECHNIQUE) (5 minutes)

1. Sit in an Egyptian posture or any yogic posture or *asana* you're comfortable with to be relaxed.
2. Use your right hand in *nasikaa mudra* (see page 155) with your ring finger and little finger controlling and pressing your left nostril. Connect your tongue to your palate.
3. Press your left nostril closed with your ring and little fingers.
4. Inhale slowly through your right nostril for 10 counts (about 10 seconds).
5. Hold your breath for 5 counts (about 5 seconds).
6. Exhale slowly through your right nostril for 10 counts.
7. Hold your breath for 5 counts (about 5 seconds).
8. Do this for 10 sets of repetitions (Steps 4-7).

This breathing method supports the development of the *yang* or more extrovert nature. It has been used by yoga gurus to help their students lose weight and improve sexual and digestive functions.

Left Nostril-Controlled Breathing
(SINGLE NOSTRIL TECHNIQUE) (5 minutes)

1. Sit in an Egyptian posture or any yogic posture or *asana* you're comfortable with to be relaxed.
2. Use your right hand in *nasikaa mudra*. Connect your tongue to your palate.
3. Press your right nostril closed with your thumb.
4. Inhale slowly through your left nostril for 10 counts (about 10 seconds).
5. Hold your breath for 5 counts (about 5 seconds).
6. Exhale slowly through your left nostril for 10 counts.
7. Hold your breath for 5 counts (about 5 seconds).
8. Do this for 10 sets of repetitions (Steps 4-7).

This breathing method helps enhance your *yin* or more passive nature and has been used by yogis to increase their weight.

Alternate Nostril Technique: Balancing the Ida and Pingala and Awakening and Flowing the Kundalini
(5 minutes)

1. Sit in an Egyptian posture or any yogic posture or *asana* you're comfortable with to be relaxed.
2. Use your right hand in *nasikaa mudra* with the thumb to regulate the right nostril and the ring finger and little finger to control the left nostril. Connect your tongue to your palate.
3. Exhale all your air before you start.
4. Press the left nostril and inhale through your right nostril for 10 counts (about 10 seconds).
5. Hold your breath for 5 counts (5 seconds). Then release your left nostril and press your right nostril with your thumb.
6. Exhale slowly through your left nostril for 10 counts.
7. Hold your breath for 5 counts.
8. Inhale slowly through your left nostril for 10 counts.
9. Hold your breath for 5 counts. Then release your right nosetril and press the left nostril.
10. Exhale slowly through your right nostril for 10 counts.
11. Hold your breath for 5 counts.
12. Repeat the process for 10 sets of alternate nostril breathing.

The idea is to breathe alternately through the right and left nostrils. All inhalations and exhalations are 10 counts, whereas the holding of the breath is 5 counts.

NOTE: If either of the nostrils is blocked, then do the side lying down posture (see page 138) for 5 minutes and open the nostril first this way. Another simple yogic method to unblock a nostril if it is partially clogged is to put a rolled towel or cloth about 3 inches (7.62 centimeters) in diameter underneath the armpit opposite the clogged nostril. You may continue to do the alternate nostril breathing while you have the rolled towel underneath your armpit. Fifteen to 30 push-ups can also help open up the nostrils. If your nasal obstruction is a physical tissue problem, then this is not suitable for you until the problem is resolved or removed.

Variations of the Single and Alternate Nostril Breathing Techniques

1. All above breathing methods: After 3 months of practice, change the ratio of breathing rhythms to 16:8:16:8. Gradually build up the practice to 20:10:20:10 after 6 months of practicing the second ratio. Do not use these higher ratios if they strain you.

2. All above breathing methods: Change the ratio of the breathing patterns to 5:10:5:10:
   - 5 counts for inhalation
   - 10 counts for holding your breath
   - 5 counts for exhalation
   - 10 counts for holding your breath

   After 3 months of practice of the above ratio, you can try 8:16:8:16. Then as you master and stabilize your performance, after 6 months of the second ratio, try 10:20:10:20 ratio. Do not continue any of the new ratios if they strain you. Do not rush. The side effects of over-practice are not apprarently recognizable at first. Do not underestimate the simplicity of this method. The kundalini fire is being awakened. Avoid being "spiritually burned".

3. Special breathing style variation: Interrupted inhalation and exhalation: For those who want more dynamic counting with rhythm and timing, the interrupted breathing style can be used for single nostril breathing or alternate nostril breathing.

   This is how it this special breathing style variation is done:

PROCEDURE AND PRACTICE FOR INTERRUPTED BREATHING STYLE
a. Inhalations:
   - Inhale a little bit, stop.
   - Inhale again a little bit, stop.
   - Inhale again a little bit, stop.
   - Inhale again a little bit, stop.
   - Do up to 10 small interrupted inhalations until you are at maximum capacity.

b. Hold your breath for 5 counts (equal time units with inhalations and exhalations).

c. Exhalations:
  - Exhale a little bit, stop.
  - Exhale again a little bit, stop.
  - Exhale again a little bit, stop.
  - Exhale again a little bit, stop.
  - Do up to 10 small interrupted exhalations at which point you should be out of air.

d. Hold your breath for 5 counts.

e. Continue the 10:5:10:5 interrupted breathing patterns.

    The advantage of this technique is that it gives you a concrete counting rhythm and is easier for some practitioners. This can also apply with variations 1 and 2 above. The longer the duration of the inhalations and exhalations, especially exhalations, the more difficult it is. Feel your way to whatever suits your style: Smooth or interrupted, they both have good results.

Now let's discuss several techniques that require rapid inhalation and exhalation, which are characteristic of *kriya* breathing methods compared to *pranayama*, which are slower like the nostril breathing methods. The two major groups of *kriya* methods are:

- *Kapalbhati*
- *Bhastrika*

Even these two types have many modifications, but we'll only learn and practice the general kinds that are useful for meditation.

Kriya *Breathing Method: Frontal Brain Hyperventilation or Kapalbhati*

This is associated with cranium and forehead hyperventilation using rapid frontal exhalation and passive inhalation. This is opposite from the brain and respiratory system's normal habit. It gives the brain and respiratory system a wider range of experience and neutralizes certain patterns of normal consciousness. It also ionizes the nervous system and the brain and activates the upper chakras, which are purified more than the lower chakras in the process.

The *kapalbhati* is similar to the Synchronized Breathing Method except you are not nodding your head, so this is a substitute for the Synchronized Breathing Method if you have a neck problem.

PROCEDURE AND PRACTICE

1. Sit in a chair with your spine erect. Do the *chin mudra* (index and thumb together).
2. Do the tongue *mudra* by connecting your tongue to your palate.
3. Inhale fast without forcing it, and rapidly exhale out forcefully.
4. Do the complete inhalation-exhalation 30 times.
5. On the last exhalation, inhale fully and slowly. Then hold your breath for 10-15 seconds. Then exhale slowly. Then relax and normalize your breathing for a few more seconds.
6. Repeat Steps 3-5 four more times.

Variations of Kapalbhati: *Single Nostril Breathing*

PROCEDURE AND PRACTICE

1. The same technique as the full *kapalbhati* (both nostrils), but only one nostril at a time.
2. The hand *mudra* and tongue *mudra* are the same as in single nostril breathing.

Variations of Kapalbhati: Alternate Nostril Breathing
(5-7 minutes)
PROCEDURE AND PRACTICE

1. The sitting postures, hand *mudra* and tongue *mudra* are the same as the full *kapalbhati* breathing method.
2. Use the *nasikaa mudra* with the right thumb regulating the right nostril and the ring finger and little finger regulating the left nostril.
3. Exhale all your air.
4. Close your left nostril and inhale more rapidly, but not forcefully, through the right nostril. Then force the air out through the left nostril. Do this breathing sequence at a rate of one inhalation-exhalation per second.
5. Close the right nostril and open the left. Inhale through the left nostril without forcing it, and switch your exhalation to the right nostril by forcing the air out rapidly. The inhalation and exhalation should be one set per second.
6. Do this complete alternate nostril breathing for 15 sets switching back and forth between nostrils.
7. At the last exhalation, inhale fully with both nostrils, then hold your breath for 10-15 seconds.
8. Exhale slowly and relax. Allow your breathing to normalize.
9. Repeat Steps 1-8 for 4 more sets.

The *kapalbhati* breathing method is a fast way to prepare yourself for a higher meditation. It is not as powerful as the Advanced Synchronized Breathing, but it's simple enough to be used by almost everyone. The technique increases the blood's oxygen levels, purifies the upper chakras, especially the head centers, and triggers stimulation of the brain and nervous system.

The complete technique can be applied as follows:

1. Do right nostril *kapalbhati* (5 sets).
2. Do left nostril *kapalbhati* (5 sets).
3. Do alternate nostril *kapalbhati* (5 sets).

Or, do full (both nostrils) *kapalbhati* for 5 sets instead of the above alternate nostril *kapalbhati* technique before any other advanced meditation. This can be followed by *bhastrika*.

Bhastrika *or Bellows Breathing*

This is also a *kriya* or purifying breathing method, but the inhalation and exhalation are enforced and rapid. It purifies the lower auras and chakras more than the upper chakras. It is done with rapid abdominal expansion and contraction at a higher speed than normal breathing. It's good to start at one inhalation-exhalation per second and gradually speed up to 2-3 inhalations-exhalations per second. Breathing is done through the nose.

PROCEDURE AND PRACTICE

1. Sit in a comfortable position, either Egyptian or your preferred *asana*. Do the tongue *mudra*. Close your eyes.
2. Inhale rapidly and exhale forcefully with the power of the abdominal muscles and guided intention. Maintain a speed of 1 inhalation-exhalation per second. Do this 30 times.
3. After the last exhalation, inhale fully and slowly, then hold your breath for 10-15 seconds. Exhale slowly and normalize your breathing for a few seconds.
4. Repeat Steps 2 and 3 four more times.

NOTE: After 3 months of practice, gradually increase the rate of breathing up to 50, but don't do more than that. If you can't tolerate the increasing strain, then stay lower than 50 per set. There's no need to take unnecessary risks of being "spiritually fried". Take it easy, and you'll get there!

Variations: Single Nostril and Alternate Nostril Bhastrika Method

PROCEDURE AND PRACTICE
1. Single Nostril *Bhastrika*: The same as the full *bhastrika*, but involving only one nostril (either left or right) using the basic *nasikaa mudra* (see page 155) to regulate nostril air flow
2. Alternate Nostril *Bhastrika*: The same as the nostril *bhastrika*, but alternate inhaling and exhaling (left to right, right to left)

Combined Kapalbhati and Bhastrika Method

The combination of both *kriya* methods of *kapalbhati* and *bhastrika* is almost a complete system to purify the upper and lower chakras and auras. This is essential preparation for advanced meditation leading to higher experience of *samadhi*.

PROCEDURE AND PRACTICE (25 minutes)
1. Perform *kriya* methods (10 minutes):
   - Full (both nostrils) *kapalbhati* technique (5 minutes)
   - Full (both nostrils) *bhastrika* technique (5 minutes)
2. Do Alternate Nostril Breathing (15 minutes):
   - Right nostril technique (10 sets, 5 minutes)
   - Left nostril technique (10 sets, 5 minutes)
   - Alternate Nostril Breathing (10 sets, 5 minutes)

Best Breathing Combo for Fast Results: Advanced Synchronized Breathing and Combination Breathing Technique

PROCEDURE AND PRACTICE (15-minute strategy)
1. Combination Breathing Technique (basic level): 5 minutes
2. Advanced Synchronized Breathing Method: 10 minutes

This is one of the most powerful combinations to purify all the upper and lower chakras, calm the emotions and the mind, plus boost vitality. The Synchronized Breathing is more advanced and powerful than all the other *kriya* or purifying breathing techniques. It also involves the awakening of the emotional, mental and spiritual centers. This is for more advanced and healthier practitioners.

LEVEL 3: ADVANCED BREATHING METHODS
Now, let's study the Level 3 breathing methods:

- ◆ Advanced Combination Breathing Technique
- ◆ Breathing Methods to Awaken the Spiritual Fires with several ratios

These breathing techniques are advanced because they apply proper use of postures, energy locks, *mudras* and the correct understanding of the ratios of breath retention versus inhalation and exhalation timing. They are also more rigorous and dangerous for beginners to perform. I don't recommend these techniques for beginners and even for more advanced meditators who are not healthy enough – physically, emotionally and mentally – because their conditions might be exacerbated due to the awakening of the *kundalini*, which serves as a fertilizer for both the good and less positive aspects of our character.

Spirituality includes a purifying process, which utilizes the *kundalini* and Divine light to "purge" and burn impurities, even latent ones you don't know you have. This is one of the dangers of excessive speed in development without calibrating what can be handled by the person's daily life and will-power. "Safer and surer" development is recommended for all students and readers.

Before we discuss the advanced techniques, let's evaluate the energy forces that are stimulated in your system by breathing more deeply:

1. DIVINE LIGHT FROM THE SOUL GETS ACTIVATED AND IS BROUGHT
   DOWN BY THE RIGHT TECHNIQUES:
   - Holding of the breath after inhalation
   - Then the crown chakra gets highly activated
2. *KUNDALINI* FIRE SEATED IN THE JUNCTION ABOVE THE PERINEUM
   CROSSED BY THE AXIS FROM THE SEX CENTER TO THE BASE-OF-SPINE
   CHAKRA. THIS IS AWAKENED BY:
   - Stimulation of the navel, sex, base-of-spine, perineum and
     back-of-navel chakras
   - Action of the Divine light to spiritually switch it on
   - Upward siphoning effect of *kundalini* flow due to the bal-
     ancing of the *ida* and *pingala* (feminine and masculine
     energies)
   - Awakening triggered by the holding of breath after exha-
     lation
3. *PRANA* AND ITS RAMIFICATIONS: DIFFERENT PARTS OF THE BODY
   AND ETHERIC BODY ARE ENERGIZED AND REGULATED BY:
   - *Apana*: Pranic energy circulating in the navel down to the
     perineum. This is stimulated by the lower chakras.
   - *Samana*: Pranic energy circulating in the diaphragm, stom-
     ach and solar plexus centers down to the navel — all relat-
     ed to digestion and assimilation of food
   - *Prana*: The energy related to *prana*, respiration and circu-
     lation from the heart-throat area
   - *Udana*: Energy related to the internal middle meridian and
     upward flow of life force
   - *Vyana*: pranic energy responsible for the nervous system
     and overall health of the extremities

So when we are talking about *pranayama* or science of breath,
all these types of *prana* or life-force are being stimulated and circu-
lated.
The chakras absorb many types of *prana* from the environment:
   - Sun *prana* (solar energy)
   - Air *prana* (energy from the air, but empowered by the sun)

- Earth or ground *prana* (life force absorbed from the physical Earth)
- Food and water *prana* (life force absorbed from food and water)
- From other people or the environment

The different *pranas* absorbed by the body from various sources express themselves through the five *pranas*.

Here are a few words of caution when practicing advanced breathing methods:

1. Do not practice with a full stomach. Abstain from eating meals 3 hours beforehand. It is also not advisable to eat one hour after advanced breathing techniques or meditation.
2. Do not do advanced techniques if you are pregnant or have hypertension, heart ailments, glaucoma, bleeding problems, cancer, AIDS, any life-threatening disease or major psychological disorders.
3. Do not drink cold drinks within 2 hours before or after your practice.
4. Do not shower, bathe or swim within 3 hours after you practice. Fires don't like water! Don't mix them until the energies are fully stable or absorbed by your system.
5. Do not overstrain your system. Proceed gradually. Consult a meditation expert or a spiritual mentor, if required. Start at the basic or intermediate level, then go for advanced methods.
6. Study the results and side effects of your practice. Stop immediately if you suspect something is wrong or you have uncontrollable outcomes.

Awakening of the Soul Light and Kundalini Fire:
Advanced Combination Breathing Technique

Better results are achieved if you do the 8-step Internal Stamina Exercise first (pages 186-188).

PROCEDURE AND PRACTICE (15 minutes)

1. Invoke for Divine protection, guidance and empowerment.
2. Sit in a comfortable position, preferably the *siddhasana* (adept posture), *vajrasana* (sitting on the heels) or Egyptian posture if you can't sit on the floor. Close your eyes.
3. Connect your tongue to your palate (tongue *mudra*).
4. Use the all-fingers *mudra* (*brahma mudra*) (see page 155).
5. Inhale and exhale slowly, and relax (1 minute).
6. Inhale slowly, filling up the abdomen.
7. Continue with chest breathing.
8. Finish with the shoulder breathing.
9. Hold your breath without body tension.
10. Execute the throat lock with the head bowing down to lock the energy.
11. Execute the root lock at the perineum to plug the energy.
12. Execute an abdominal compression lock to support your abdomen moving the pressure upward.
    NOTE: Steps 10-12 should be done almost simultaneously and quickly.
13. Hold your breath for 5-10 seconds.
14. Straighten up your head, releasing the throat lock, then release the root lock and the abdominal lock. Exhale slowly as you are releasing all the energy locks. Exhale all your air.
15. Hold your breath for 10-15 seconds.
16. Do the throat, root and abdominal locks simultaneously as you hold your breath.
17. Straighten your head, releasing the throat lock, and then inhale slowly while releasing the root and abdominal locks.
18. Repeat Steps 6-17, but with more smoothness in execution If you are feeling strained, stop, relax and normalize your breathing pattern.

19. Do a total of 10-15 sets and build gradually to 20 sets after 3 months of practice. Do not overdo this technique because it will over-awaken the *kundalini* energy.

Best results are achieved if the Advanced Combination Breathing is done before Advanced Synchronized Breathing or *kapalbhati* or *bhastrika* methods, especially if the meditator is depleted. If the meditator is energetically toxic (stressed or angry, for example), it's better to do Synchronized Breathing first before the Combination Breathing Technique. You can also experiment with doing Advanced Combination Breathing after the Advanced Synchronized Breathing Method. It is a very powerful combination.

Advanced Synchronized Breathing Technique Variation: 16:8:16:8 Ratio

If you experience strain using the Advanced Combination Breathing, try this:

- 16 counts to inhale
- 8 counts to hold
- 16 counts to exhale
- 8 counts to hold

Higher Awakening of Spiritual Fires: 8:16:8:16 Breathing Method

Doing physical exercise first like the 8-step Internal Stamina Exercise is recommended for safe and effective outcomes of your practice.

PROCEDURE AND PRACTICE (10 minutes)
1. Invoke for Divine protection, guidance and empowerment.
2. Sit in a comfortable position, preferably the *siddhasana* (adept posture), *vajrasana* (sitting on the heels) or Egyptian posture if you can't sit on the floor. Close your eyes.

3. Connect your tongue to your palate (tongue *mudra*).
4. Use the all-fingers *mudra* (*brahma mudra*) (see page 155).
5. Inhale and exhale slowly, and relax (1 minute).
6. Inhale slowly for 8 counts (about 8 seconds).
7. Perform the throat lock, then the root lock, then a gentle abdominal compression lock. Hold your breath for 16 counts (16 seconds). Do not strain yourself.
8. Release your throat lock and as you exhale, release the root and abdominal locks and continue exhaling for 8 counts (about 8 seconds).
9. Hold your breath for 16 counts (about 16 seconds).
10. Do 10-15 repetitions of Steps 6-9.

NOTE: Gradually build the repetitions up to 20 sets after 3 months of practice. Do not rush! Remember: Haste makes waste.

The 8:16:8:16 Method increases the *kumbhala* or stoppage of breathing that leads to awakening of the Soul energy and *kundalini* fire to a higher degree. It is advisable to prepare your body and chakras through 5-10 minutes of physical exercise, plus *kriyas* or purifying rituals, including the Synchronized Breathing or Alternate Nostril Breathing to balance your system first. This is a must before awakening your inner fires to a higher degree.

VARIATIONS ON BREATH RETENTION AND REGULATION

Nadi Shodhana Pranayama:
Alternate Nostril Breathing with Faster Awakening of Divine Light and Kundalini *Through 15:20:10:10 Ratio*

This is a very strong stimulation for the Divine light and *kundalini* fire. It is quite risky, especially for beginners, therefore, this is given as training for long-time meditators who have already purified and cultured their bodies, chakras and consciousness. Again, observe the required preparations before you do it like the physical exercises and meditating on an empty stomach.

This advanced breathing technique requires concentration to be able to count properly and perform all the ratios of inhalation, exhalation and holding of breath simultaneously. It's a great training to be able to concentrate on many things at once. But the idea of the *kumbhaka* or stopping of breath is to trigger the awakening of the Divine light and sacred fires. This method requires all of the precautions mentioned earlier with the other advanced breathing methods.

Other Advanced Breathing Ratios

You can practice and experiment with other ratios after years of meditation practice like:

- 5:30:20:10
- 2:4:8:16
- 1:16:4:32

Many very advanced and new designs of breath control are now allowed by spiritual Masters to be revealed in this book to be applied by advanced practitioners globally for spiritual awakening.

In the upcoming chapter on advanced meditation to experience your Soul, breathing techniques with triangulations of chakras will be taught to awaken not only the pranic force, but also the advanced faculties of the power centers in their many combinations.

Awakening the pranic energy alone is not enough. All the other major chakras at the emotional, mental and spiritual levels have to be activated and awakened for them to become bigger pumps of energy. This activation and awakening also make these centers functional for better expression of service.

Most yogic books focus so much on breathing techniques or *pranayama* without understanding the psychology and higher anatomy of the Soul and supra-consciousness. The science of breath has to be practical with deeper esoteric understanding and practical application of the following:

- Construction of the *antahkarana* or cable of light
- The science of chakras
- The science of healing and esoteric blessings
- The science of esoteric service
- The esoteric understanding of the *kundalini*
- Inner world consciousness

I would encourage everyone who studies this book and its teachings to be courageous to go beyond what you already know and challenge yourself to break through limiting concepts and learned information.

When I was teaching in India, even gurus and yogis were surprised by the idea of more than seven major chakras. Even good clairvoyants missed the other five. That's a big deal since it means that most lineages have been teaching so many people for so long without some key data.

My early spiritual mentors in the Philippines, MCKS and MMCN, played an important role in revealing the hidden centers of power in the auras with the help of their guides, and this book builds on their work to offer meditators, yoga practitioners and instructors a more complete picture.

The *kundalini* is a myth more than a reality in some yogic schools and a theory in most esoteric schools. This is the time that the best of the Eastern teachings will be made systematic and practical for the West to catch up with the esoteric teachings, especially meditation and yoga. Many teachers from the East and West are still presenting a mystical and excessively devotional approach to spirituality, meditation and yoga, thereby barring the mental and objective types from learning faster. This is why a practical approach that meets the needs of these types is required.

The next chapters will reveal to you how simple, easy and enjoyable meditation can be! You don't need hours to advance your inner development. You need the right techniques and a systematic, organized approach to a safe and effective path of meditative life.

Part IV:

APPLYING SAFE AND EFFECTIVE MEDITATION

CHAPTER 13

Mastering Your Concentration Made Easy

A Key to Sharpening Your Mind

L earning concentration can be made easier than most people think! This chapter gives you all the information and tools you need for Step 2 of the 5-step process for safe and effective meditation in Chapter 8.

You can master concentration systematically. The untrained meditator has a problem focusing and calming the mind. In most cases, the minds of many meditators and non-meditators jump from one thought to the other. Often the mind is absorbed in a chattering inner dialogue. In many instances, the mind is hyperactive and reacts to a lot of external noises and stimuli. Other people's minds tend to go through spells of daydreaming where they can't concentrate. Why are these things happening?

REASONS FOR THE "MONKEY MIND", "FOGGY BRAIN" OR "BUTTERFLY CONSCIOUSNESS"

Some spiritual teachers call people who can't control their jumpy thoughts "monkey minds", but I call this phenomenon the "cluttered mind". A person with cloudy perception and lack of focus has a "foggy brain". I call a mind that is always dreamy or floaty a "butterfly consciousness". Here are reasons why these happen:

Monkey Mind

There are many feelings in the emotional aura and thoughts in the mental aura. They are circulating all the time, whether a person notices them or not. Clairvoyantly, people's feelings and thoughts are seen as different energy shapes, colors, qualities and intensities. These energy forms are also seen in the chakras, and many of the negative ones are trapped in the energy filters between the auras and in the chakras. When people are very busy in a noisy environment, they don't notice them, but when they are in a quieter meditation space, the person is more receptive to perceive them. So, the emotions and thoughts were always there. Some of them are not positive and of a lower vibration. Where are these disturbing thoughts coming from? Many sources:

- Self-created by the person in this current life or in ancient lives
- Created and projected by other people, including parents and friends
- Picked up from the immediate environment or cultural, national, religious or global affinities. Our personalities live and are submerged in an ocean of continuously circulating thoughts, feelings and psychic energy. A person is like a fish; their condition is determined by the ocean it swims in. In modern cities, these "psychic oceans" are not clean at all.
- Empathizing with the minds and emotions of people we interact with
- Absorbed from media exposure

Foggy Brain

This cloudiness can be caused by head energy congestion or stuck, stale energy in the head aura and chakras. It can also be mental depletion or devitalized upper chakras, including the throat, navel, base-of-spine and sex centers. When people are fatigued, the mind does not function well. Concentration is not easy, and confusion arises. Foggy brain can also be triggered by hormonal imbalances like those that occur in perimenopause and menopause. People who drink alcohol and use recreational drug can also experience foggy brain.

BUTTERFLY CONSCIOUSNESS

When people are spacey and not grounded, they tend to be light headed and unable to concentrate. People with very low will-power can't focus and sustain concentration. In some cases, this condition is caused by over-activated upper chakras relative to the lower centers. The crown, forehead and heart chakras are normally substantially bigger in size than the *ajna*, navel and base-of-spine chakras. This is where the imbalances occur. I usually see these cases in mystics, healers and yogis.

Today, many children are labeled ADD (Attention Deficit Disorder) and have learning disabilities because they are unable to focus in the learning process. Butterfly consciousness is one of the reasons. These types of personalities tend to excel in awareness meditation; they can get out of body anytime during the meditation. Objective, practical people are the opposite. They can concentrate well, but they have a difficult time with the awareness meditation.

What type are you?

What Can You Do to Improve Your Concentration?

Whether you are the monkey mind or the foggy brain type, or have butterfly consciousness, here are my recommendations to unclutter the mind and calm it down:

SYNCHRONIZED BREATHING METHOD™

PROCEDURE AND PRACTICE (see page 204 for illustration)

1. Sit in a comfortable position with your back straight and vertical in a lotus or semi-lotus position or in a chair with your feet flat on the floor. Close your eyes before you start.
2. Inhale rapidly through your nose as you tilt your head back while simultaneously inflating your abdomen.

3. Immediately exhale quickly through your mouth as you bow your head down while compressing your abdomen.
4. Repeat steps two and three 10-15 times.
5. Just relax with your head vertical and breathe slowly. Concentrate on the top of your head (crown energy center), mid-brow area (*ajna* energy center) and center of your chest (heart energy center) simultaneously while breathing slowly. Do this step for 30 seconds.
6. Use this technique 3 times weekly or daily as required.

PRECAUTION

The technique is not recommended for pregnant women or those with neck injuries, high blood pressure, migraine, vertigo or severe heart conditions without supervision of an expert. If in doubt, consult a certified safe and effective meditation or yoga instructor before you perform the technique.

You can start mastering concentration through the Synchronized Breathing Method. It is the ideal tool for all meditators, beginners or advanced! After six months of using the Synchronized Breathing Method or for advanced meditators, you can use the Advanced Synchronized Breathing Method (see Chapter 12, page 204).

NAVEL CHAKRA CONCENTRATION METHOD

(5 minutes daily routine)
This is a very good concentration practice with excellent benefits of internal vitality and stamina, plus centeredness and improved instincts.

PROCEDURE AND PRACTICE

1. Sit in a chair with your feet flat on the floor (Egyptian posture) or use your normal meditation pose like the lotus or cross-legged posture.
2. Do the meditation hand position (*dhayani mudra*) for beginners. Advanced meditators can use the triple finger *mudra*

with thumbs touching the tips of the index and middle fingers and the backs of the index and middle fingers joined at the navel level (see page 154). Relax and be comfortable.

3. Perform the nose tip gazing *mudra* (eyes gazing at the tip of your nose) and relax, but start concentrating (see page 157).
4. Inhale and exhale slowly for 1 minute while continuing the nose tip gazing concentration. Do not over-strain your eyes. Be focused but gentle.
5. Continue step 4 and include sustained focusing on the navel. The navel chakra gets activated to improve instinctive intelligence, internal power and agility.
6. Do this concentration process for 5 minutes.

Zen masters use this as a meditation to center their awareness without leaving the body. It is an important technique for concentration that does not necessarily result in abstraction of consciousness or out-of-body experience, yet it does provide the experience of being present, grounded and centered. This is an excellent tool for decision-makers, martial arts students and athletes, including golfers. It develops super gut instincts and internal sustaining power. That's why we use this in esoteric martial arts training. This is a good meditation for mystics and spacey meditators, as well as a good solution for monkey mind and butterfly consciousness.

SAFE AND EFFECTIVE MEDITATIONS TO PURIFY, ENERGIZE AND CENTER YOURSELF!

The two concentration methods above are simple but relatively advanced meditations when combined. They can be practiced safely and effectively daily and take only 10 minutes:

- Synchronized Breathing Method (5 minutes)
- Navel Concentration Method (5 minutes)

There are other methods to activate inner powers and advanced human faculties, but they are discussed later.

CONCENTRATION TO SHARPEN YOUR MIND

Other practices and uses of concentration-type meditation include the concretizing meditation and understanding meditation. Let's study and practice them.

Concentration on Seed Thought or External Object:
OPEN OR CLOSED EYES

Focus all your attention on one subject. You can pick any topic of immediate significance. For now, let's apply this by re-evaluating your life's vision, mission and plans to move ahead with greater purpose.

Answering focused questions and going through a step-by-step process is key. So aim your focused, uninterrupted attention on details.

Concretizing Meditation
PROCEDURE AND PRACTICE:
(30 minutes to 1 hour)
1. YOUR LIFE'S VISION: *What do you live for?*
    - At the end of your life, what greatness will you have achieved and left behind that will be of big value to others or a greater whole?
    - What one role in your life will create that big difference?
    - What eulogy would you want your loved ones, friends, associates and the world to hear about your life and your contributions to society?
    - If you had only 10 years to live, what could you do up to the end that would bring you both material success and spiritual self-fulfillment?

    Answer these questions mentally or, even better, write the answers and synthesize them when they are totally clear.
2. YOUR LIFE'S MISSION:
    - What goals will concretely physicalize your life's vision?
    - What different objectives in your life support your life's roles and purpose?

- What are your most important objectives to accomplish
  your most noble spiritual goals according to your vision?
  Answer these questions mentally, or write the answers and
  synthesize them.

3. **YOUR LIFE'S GAME PLAN:**
   - What are your immediate plans (now up to 2 years) to be
     able to achieve your life's vision and mission?
   - What are your mid-range plans (3-10 years) to support
     your life's vision and mission?
   - What are your long-term plans (more than 10 years) to
     be able to manifest or accomplish your vision?
   - How will you achieve all of these plans effectively?
   - Who can help you?
   - Where will you get the resources you need?
   - Where will you start?
   - When will you start to do it, if you have not already start-
     ed it?

You can practice mentally mapping the strategies in a general for-
mat, but it is advisable to write them down and clarify all matters by
organizing and charting the answers. Evaluate the strategies many
times and parade the sequence of events mentally from now into
the future and rewind them back from the future to the present
checking the appropriateness of your assumptions and processes.

I use this method for coaching clients and mentoring organizations to penetrate the details without losing sight of the generals
and overall vision. Many people, including meditators, should practice using this concentration method, either to learn fast or to concretize ideas into plans with minimal or no blind spots. This is concretizing meditation with partial use of meditation for understanding.

Meditation for Understanding:
MENTAL COMPREHENSION USING MENTAL CONCENTRATION
Meditation for understanding to comprehend a symbol or idea is another great use of the concentration method.

PROCEDURE AND PRACTICE: *Closed or open eyes method*
(15 minutes)
Let's say that you had a dream where you didn't remember much. You only remember a snake. How can you understand your dream using concentration? You can do this:

1. Focus your mind to understand the meaning of the snake as a symbol. Mentally search.
2. Once you have a few hints, go deeply into each symbol. For example:
   - A snake can mean betrayal or being bitten or poisoned. Mentally analyze, who, what, when and how? Have you betrayed someone or been betrayed?
   - Snakes can mean medicine or cure. Mentally evaluate. Is there somebody who needs healing or a natural approach to improving health? Is there any poisonous experience to heal from a past or present pain or emotional wound? What, who, how, when?
   - Snakes can mean a curse to "walk at the lower ground level" (i.e., be humbled). Are there instances when you were humiliated or put down? Did you do anything to condescend anyone? What, who, how, when?
   - Snakes can mean the spiritual power of the *kundalini* or sacred fire. Is there any spiritual awakening going on in you that is very powerful for which you need to prepare? Or are you in a cycle where your Soul or your spiritual guide is hinting for you to get prepared?
3. Use your mental concentration and focused attention to understand the different evaluations. Summarize your conclusions and understood principles. Validate.

Simple as this may seem, only brilliant people and philosophers use this type of process to understand their dreams or symbols that are shown repeatedly in their daily lives. They also use this technique while in meditation for understanding when problems arise. In the film, "National Treasure", the main character's talent of penetrating the puzzles leading to the treasure is a good example of meditation for understanding through the mind's process.

Use this technique for understanding problems or crises when they arise. After the lesson and wisdom from the problem are learned, the history of mistakes will not repeat itself. The agony of defeat, for example, with the usual questions, Why did this happen? Why me?, should be followed by:

- Why not, and what's the purpose?
- What lessons can I learn?
- What principles did I violate causing me not to deserve better?
- What can I do to avoid repeating the same situations?

Answering these questions by focusing your undivided attention either mentally or through writing is a practical application of meditation for understanding.

Mental concentration for mental penetrating power

One of our best tools is our mind, so let's sharpen it through the whetstone of concentration. We'll use contrasting techniques to differentiate ideas.

PROCEDURE AND PRACTICE

We will study related words, penetrate their deeper meanings and identify their differences:

- What's the difference between pity and mercy?
- What's the difference between sympathy and empathy?
- What's the difference between compassion and dispassion?
- What's the difference between goodwill and will-to-good?
- What's the difference of all of them from each other?
- Which among them do you apply more easily?

By focusing and exerting one-pointed effort to answer these questions, you will come to know your depth, absence of knowledge or assumptions about these terms and behavioral expressions.

As you apply this mental penetration technique, you will notice that there are energy and deeper spiritual links to these words.

Most people will initially assume that they are all emotional or based on the quality of love. Even dictionary definitions are limited or misconstrued in some ways. Therefore, by using your mind for concentration, you can innovate or create deeper meanings for words or behaviors. You can have a mind with surgical precision and super-penetration by mastering this technique.

Concentration allows you to finish what you start faster

Undeviating one-pointed focus on a certain task is an advanced form of meditation through concentration. Executives are good at this. That's why they produce excellent business results.

I had only 10 days to write this book because of my international trips. So when I was in Texas, I focused on finishing it. After writing for five days in a row, I was already done with Chapter 10. By focusing on the sheer need and exclusive attention to the work at hand, we can do magic to finish what we start faster.

I've covered some of the most important techniques for mastering concentration, both for internal subjective use for spiritual meditation and for external purposes like mental comprehension of and concretizing of ideas. I hope this will help you not just in the spiritual approach of meditation, but also in working smarter. Let's turn to awareness meditation in the next chapter as an easy way to learn wisdom.

CHAPTER 14

Awareness Meditation:

Learning Wisdom the Easy Way

There is a major difference between concentration and awareness meditation. While concentration needs mental will and focus, awareness meditation requires passive sensitivity, surrendering receptivity and all-pervading inward attention. By understanding this difference, meditators can learn to experience awareness meditation easily with no struggle. This chapter gives you simple but advanced methods to achieve awareness, Step 3 of the 5-step process for safe and effective meditation in Chapter 8.

The following psychological and energetic strategies will further assist you in the practice of awareness meditation:

1. During meditation, lessen mental focus and gradually transform it into a waiting, passive attitude. Being patient with no wish for performance is the key.
2. Use your feelings and inner sensitivity more. Mystical meditators and women tend to be good at this.
3. Be in a totally surrendering mood with no reactions to anything, including distractions or influence of the five senses.
4. Be flowing and observant of any result in your meditation. Do not analyze if you start seeing the light of the aura, inner colors, symbols or images. Let them pass by, or continue observ-

ing them with no mental analysis. The mental activity will move you back to concentration mode and shuts off your sensitivity.

5. Do not expect anything while meditating. Do not force any event to produce results. The more you have expectations, the less you will experience. Devotional types of meditators are better here than objective and controlling types.

There are many techniques to bring yourself to the awareness stage of meditation or yoga practice. Some schools use sacred words, *mantrams* or chants to help increase the vibration at a subtle state until you are spacey and lose mental control, which is the desired outcome in this meditation state.

What you'll study and practice here is a very systematic approach:

1. Conversion of mental activity into energetic sensitivity and emotional passivity
2. Transmutation of emotional sensitivity and feelings into heightened spiritual consciousness
3. Putting your concrete sequential mind into a "dead end" so your abstract mind has to take over

Awareness Meditation Techniques

HEART-FOREHEAD-CROWN METHOD
(12 minutes, 2 times weekly)
The first technique to awaken inner sensitivity is to stimulate the heart, forehead and crown chakras. This technique starts first with concentration meditation that shifts gradually to awareness meditation.
PROCEDURE AND PRACTICE
1. Sit in a chair with your feet flat on the floor, or use your normal yogic postures or *asanas*. Be sure you are comfortable with your spine erect.

2. Use the meditation *mudra* (*dhayani*) at the navel level.
3. Do the Synchronized Breathing Method 3 times (see page 204), but instead of focusing on the heart, mid-brow and crown chakra connection, concentrate on:
   - The heart chakra (emotional sensitivity and inner peace)
   - The forehead chakra (psychic sensitivity and inner impressionability)
   - The crown chakra (spiritual oneness, higher consciousness and detachment)
4. Continue with two more sets of Synchronized Breathings as in Step 3, but transform the concentration or focusing on the chakras with gentle attention to sustained passive awareness on the heart, forehead and crown centers. The breathing intervals between the 2 sets have to be 2 or more minutes to allow the sensitivity and awareness to evolve naturally.
5. Do another 2 sets if you are still not in passive awareness. In most cases, 5 sets are sufficient to alter your state into a more inward consciousness.

As far as I know, this technique is faster than other methods I've learned even from my early mentors and their lineages. I've taught this to yogis and meditators, and it works faster than the usual yogic *kapalbhati* or *bhastrika pranayama*. The difference is that the three chakras to sensitize your inner consciousness are activated between sets. This is a shortcut to reach the state of awareness meditation that also helps develop inner powers.

THE OPEN HEART METHOD: GATEWAY TO AWARENESS
(10 minutes, 3 times weekly)
This is not about heart surgery! It's about activating your heart center and gradually opening it up to be a fountain of love and peace energy. Love energy circulated in the auras and chakras will melt down mind control.

Let's practice and experience the state of an opened heart. Soothing music with ocean sounds is a good background to facilitate the experience.

1. Sit in a comfortably in a lotus or adept's posture. Sitting in the Egyptian pose or even lying posture are acceptable. Just keep yourself at ease and relax. Close your eyes.

2. Imagine that you are relaxing in front of the ocean. Inhale and exhale slowly and deeply for one minute.

3. Release all disturbing thoughts and negative feelings to the imaginary ocean through an intention of breathing these feelings out as you think about them. Do this for 3-5 minutes. This purifies the emotional and mental auras internally and purges out any undesirable energies that will jeopardize the meditation. Also, negative feelings shut off the heart, so release them.

4. Continue the smooth, gentle inhalations and exhalations, and be aware of the heart center at the mid-chest area. Just have a gentle slight intention to feel the heart center. Feel the sense of peace, joy or sweetness in that area. Don't force it. Let it happen naturally. Be passive and have the attitude of waiting and observing. This technique activates the heart chakra.

5. Opening the heart chakra needs more pleasant feelings, which you can generate as follows:
   - Recall and re-experience happy events in your life. Feel these nice feelings in your heart again.
   - Let your heart center experience that opening and expansion. When the 12 petals of the heart chakra open, the feeling is fantastic!

6. Continue being aware of the heart's pleasant feeling. As you breathe slowly, diffuse your attention to all parts of your body. Just be aware and maintain general attention to all parts of your body without effort. If you are extremely sensitive, you can include awareness of all of your energy bodies. This

technique will rejuvenate and heal you. Do this step for 3-5 minutes.

This type of awareness meditation tends to make you quite calm and spacey, but joyful and content. Ten minutes of this technique will bring such wellness that it's worth doing 3 times a week for 10 minutes per session. I recommend that more willful, objective and practical people do this meditation to offset their excessive use of mental control and manipulativeness. It is also a great technique to release stress and live healthier.

The heart chakra controls the thymus gland, which is part of the body's immune system. Therefore, it is also a must for people who want to activate their defense system and antibodies. People with cancer and those suffering from traumas need this method to help them overcome their problems and enhance the immune system.

Precaution
People who have severe heart conditions should not do this technique without consulting a certified safe and effective meditation or yoga instructor. If you intend to activate and open your heart, make sure you do Step 3, breathing out to the ocean, first. This will decongest your emotions.

The Difference Between Opening and Activating the Heart Chakra
There's a difference between opening the heart chakra and just activating the chakra. Activating the chakra is easy because all you have to do is concentrate on it and breathe slowly. This will definitely increase the chakral size, but it does not necessarily open the heart.

To open the heart or any chakra, soft, gentle awareness, not focusing, should accompany the breathing process. The heart center opens if it is not forced. Recalling happy events or cherishing a past successful endeavor are two of the fastest techniques to open the heart. Do you see the difference? It's not just about a BIG HEART! It has to be an OPEN HEART.

STRATEGIES TO IMPROVE AWARENESS MEDITATION

Most of the practices of awareness meditation and concentration can be empowered even more with better breathing techniques:

1. **COMBINATION BREATHING TECHNIQUE**
   to awaken the Soul and *kundalini* energy. This was explained in Chapter 11, combining three breathing patterns
   - Abdominal breathing
   - Chest breathing
   - Shoulder breathing

2. **ALTERNATE NOSTRIL BREATHING METHOD,**
   which was also discussed in Chapter 12. This aligns the different energies to awaken a balanced flow of the middle meridian, the *sushumna*.

3. **APPLICATIONS OF ENERGY LOCKS (*BANDHAS*) OR SEALS (*MUDRAS*)**
   to control and regulate the flow of energy in the different segments of the energy bodies and chakras

The practical applications of concentration and awareness meditation will be assembled in the meditation techniques in the upcoming chapters. What we are practicing now are bits and pieces and microstrategies as important preparations for the other meditations.

ABSTRACT MENTAL AWARENESS CAN LEAD TO ILLUMINATION

One of the trainings of the mind is to render it still and aware to perceive higher meanings of ideas or principles. Whereas the use of the concrete mind, represented by the left brain, is to sequence or deduct logical data in a linear fashion, the abstract mind is the more creative and philosophical counterpart. So if we concentrate on an idea or concept in a way that the concrete mind reaches a dead end trying to process it, it lets go of control, and the abstract mind takes over.

The abstract mind, the first aspect of the Soul, allows the consciousness to go into the Soul's expanded state. In this stage, the mind is expanded, aware and receptive to higher impressions of inner meaning and wisdom.

Let's experience this concept and strategy through example and practice.

1. Meditate on or perceive the answers to these questions:
   - WHICH CAME FIRST, THE CHICKEN OR THE EGG? Keep on penetrating the question and potential answers (if there are any) until your concrete mind quits. Then let go, and be aware of higher insight from the Soul through the abstract mind. You might go to an awareness meditation if you let go.
   - This technique is used by Zen teachers to uplift the student's critical mind to go to "emptiness" or a "no-answer" state. This is a common Zen puzzle or koan: WHAT'S THE SOUND OF ONE HAND CLAPPING?
   - Since the logical mind does not have data for this question because there's no recorded experience of it, it seeks answers from the higher mind for principles instead of correct answers.
2. Unknown abstract interpretations: Meditate on or search for interpretations of abstract poems. Try this one from William Blake, an English 19th century poet:

> *To see a World in a Grain of Sand*
> *And a Heaven in a Wild Flower*
> *Hold Infinity in the palm of your hand*
> *And Eternity in an hour.*[10]

Practice for 15 minutes. Mentally look at it line by line and penetrate the higher meaning until your mind is open to abstraction. Be aware of your Soul's impression. At a certain level, your concrete mind surrenders and what's left is an empty space, which is awareness.

Whether you get an answer or not, the consciousness is stretched into a wider dimension that is abstract. This is a fascinating point where your wisdom, intuition and inspiration are engaged. If you close your eyes at this moment, you can go into a deeper state, which is called *samadhi* or higher expansion of consciousness.

Learning the right way is the clue. Even the terminology to be used for instructing meditators or readers is important. Wrong use of instructions by interchanging words — "think of your heart", for example, instead of "feel your heart" — can be counterproductive in the learning process. Also, using the words "concentrate" or "focus" when meditators are being guided in awareness meditation is not helpful for their deeper experience. The words "concentrate" or "focus" should be used when giving concentration instruction.

"Sense", "feel" and "be aware" should be used for awareness meditation. In some yogic books and translations of the *Yoga Sutras of Patanjali*, these terms in the meditation state are mislabeled, which blocks the ability to decipher whether to use the will or just be aware of the techniques at a certain level.

Words are like elevators or escalators: They can make you go down or up in your experience. Wrong use of terminology to learn a meditation technique can make you lose so much meditation time and effort, resulting in frustration because your meditation is not working for you.

Let's turn to the next chapter to bring you to an even higher expansion of consciousness in the realm of the Soul or Spirit where you can be merged with the grace of ineffable light and life.

CHAPTER 15

Samadhi:

Not Just for Advanced Yogis

nlightenment or illumination of consciousness is not just a big bang explosion of light, and that's it. It is a continuous, progressive path of growth towards the light. It is wrong to assume that it is a dead end or a permanent culmination of experience. It is indeed a high spiritual achievement, but evolution does not stop there.

To enhance your spiritual development and evolution, this chapter gives practical definitions of *samadhi*, Step 4 of the 5-step process for safe and effective meditation in Chapter 8, and techniques to achieve it faster and more easily than you may have thought possible.

When we talk about enlightenment through *samadhi*, it is about the degree or level perceived. It is a state of consciousness puncturing the greater unknown, sometimes called the "supra-consciousness". In religion, it is called God. In yogic philosophy, it is called Ishvara. Since there are so many layers of consciousness up to the ultra-frequencies of the Universal, Absolute, Infinite, Eternal, Super-Eternal and Ultimate Reality, anyone who declares that their *samadhi* or highest meditation experience is high enough because they have merged with God is really barely scratching the surface of Cosmic Consciousness. Many are just experiencing planetary and Soul level of God-consciousness at the Soul level below the Spirit.

Anything higher than the available knowledge of the personality is abstract, and thus called "higher consciousness" or "supra-consciousness".

The term "absolute" in yogic experience is more of a term where the mind or personality can't explain what's above it due to a lack of labels or coined words or because the experience has no concrete sense yet.

We have to remember that an "abstract experience" of one meditator is already a "common-sense" experience to another, just like the concepts of the chakras, auras and *prana*. To most Western scientists and executives, chakras, auras and *prana* are still abstract, but to yogis, spiritual teachers and good clairvoyants, they are all concrete, common sense facts. Therefore, we can infer that many meditators and authors have mislabeled some of their self-described "advanced" experiences by using incorrect words that pertain to God or higher Inner World consciousness or to the realm of the Soul or Spirit.

With regard to advanced meditators or yogis and enlightened Masters, their awareness of higher world consciousness is also subject to their continuing search for new labels from their esoteric meditations. As we said earlier in Chapter 6 about the Earth as a macrocosm with 49 sub-layers, there are many worlds to explore and puncture in terms of *samadhi* experience.

The intensity and ascent to higher consciousness resulting in bliss, ecstasy or Divine Oneness experienced in *samadhi* is affected by many factors.

FACTORS AFFECTING THE INTENSITY OF *SAMADHI* EXPERIENCE

1. Age of the Soul or Spirit and how much of their awakening is available to be experienced
2. Levels of constructed *antahkarana* or cable of light towards the Soul and Spirit and the level to which it is filled with the alchemized *kundalini* energy and the transmuted personality life substance from eons of experience. This is a technical

requirement that most schools and teachers don't study, yet it is the key and secret to the science of advanced meditation or yoga (Divine Union). Without enough substance of alchemized light inside the "pipeline of the *antahkarana*", even if meditators visualize expansion, it doesn't really work. It's like spending money from a checking account with no funds.

Visualization alone isn't enough. The *kundalini* fire has to be highly awakened and siphoned upward to the Soul through powerful but safe methods. The problem with most modern esoteric schools is that they discuss a lot of theories about meditation with lots of philosophy, but there is no actual spiritual technology to activate the *kundalini*. Most of these groups don't even want to talk about the *kundalini*, or they inhibit themselves not to activate the chakras below the heart.

Here's the problem: The *kundalini* seat happens to be down in the perineum area, thus it gets atrophied or stuck due to lack of attention or stimulation, especially without adequate esoteric breathing techniques and physical exercises to jumpstart it.

No kundalini *awakening, no enlightenment or true expansion of consciousness!*

On the other hand, if the techniques are very powerful through yoga or Chinese chigong methods to awaken the *kundalini* and there's not enough Divine light to alchemize the *kundalini* energy, it is not safe because it builds up without circulating, and this congested *kundalini* energy causes hypertension, abnormal growth of tissues in the body, excessive sex drive or explosions of emotional crises. I call this "psycho-spiritual syndrome", which besets a yogi's or meditator's life, resulting in stunted development and difficult-to-heal ailments.

Also, when the *kundalini* is forced to awaken without the action of the Soul's divine electricity, the outcomes are not properly processed and are very slow, and the aroused energy is "spiritually toxic or too gross" for the absorption of the Soul via the *antahkarana* or cable of light.

I am exposing these conservative, time-robbing and dangerous approaches that slow down development because spiritual groups and schools need to be guided with clearer instructions about the science of the *kundalini*, science of *antahkarana* construction and science of Soul development to bring a more systematic and practical perspective to *samadhi* or deliberate union with the Higher Self or Higher Groups of Beings called The Illumined Ones.

The Soul has many grades of higher frequency matter (relative to the personality auras), and these layers of energy consciousness have their own intelligences and light substance with specific qualities. They are all enclosed and interpenetrated by the different inner worlds of the Earth as a macrocosm.

Therefore, the Soul, Spirit and the Earth planes or dimensions of existence are interrelated. Whatever aspects of the Soul or Spirit are accessed through our *antahkarana*, that's where our highest level of *samadhi* is experienced. This can be labeled as:

- God's love or all-inclusiveness
- God's omniscience or expanded intuitional sense
- God's omnipotence or inner power, will and Divine purpose
- Union with a greater consciousness, which the limited "x-ray of the mind" can't fathom and interpret

Thus, the goal of meditation changes with this perspective:

We meditate not just to achieve this Divine Oneness, bliss, nirvana or ecstasy, but to continually ascend to higher consciousnesses to penetrate a higher vision and purpose accompanied by the empowering intelligence and substance of that plane or consciousness we tapped into.

Most often, the desire to achieve *samadhi* or ecstasy is greater than the aspiration to continue serving our incarnated purpose in our own mundane world. Therefore, we miss the train. We put ourselves on the 10th floor without taking care of the 1st floor and the foundation of the building. This is not be a lasting stable construction or form of development.

Meditation should not be the goal
of spirituality, but a tool
to be able to actualize
greater and greater service.

There's also a need to balance between exoteric duty to the world and esoteric practices and meditation to access the inspiration or "spiritual gas" to serve more. Meditation and yoga should not take too long so that the Karma, Bhakti and Jnana yogis have more time to help and serve others exoterically.

Let's discuss the processes and practices to experience *samadhi* or higher levels of contemplation or consciousness. I'll share some of the easiest ways I've used successfully with my students.

A JOURNEY TO *SAMADHI* OR HIGHER INNER EXPERIENCE (25-30 minutes)

PROCEDURE AND PRACTICE

1. Physical exercise should be done to condition the physical body and auras (5-7 minutes). Refer to Chapter 11 for the Body Therapy or Internal Stamina Exercise.
2. Invoke for Divine protection, guidance and empowerment.
3. Do the meditation *mudra* (*dhayani*).
4. Do 3 sets of the Synchronized Breathing Method (3 minutes) to purify all the auras and calm the mind and emotions.
5. Perform deep breathing techniques for 5 minutes:
   - Inhale slowly and deeply for 10 counts (about 10 seconds).

- Hold your breath for 5 counts (about 5 seconds).
- Exhale slowly and fully for 10 counts (about 10 seconds).
- Hold your breath for 5 counts (about 5 seconds).
- Repeat this sequence for 10 sets.

6. Do 2 more sets of the Synchronized Breathing Method to further purify your energy bodies and chakras and to deepen your stillness and awareness.

7. Perform the deep breathing techniques again for another 5 minutes with the 10:5:10:5 ratio (10 sets, 5 minutes).

8. Do 2 more sets of the Synchronized Breathing Method with a slower and slower speed until you gradually stop. Extend the interval between sets to be aware of your heart, *ajna* and especially your crown center.

9. Just relax and let go. Be aware and do not concentrate or think anymore about the technique. Just be and again let go. This can last for 5-10 minutes.

10. As you surrender and be passive, your Soul or any spiritually-invoked higher being or teacher will support the abstraction of your consciousness into higher experience. Do not expect anything before you meditate. No desire and no mental control are the keys. Be patient. The best illuminating experience usually comes when least expected.

11. Come back to normal consciousness by intention, opening your eyes and moving your feet.

12. Do physical exercise for 5 minutes to ground back, especially if you have to drive a car or go to work. Otherwise, on a vacation day, just continue enjoying your inner experience.

The procedure above is only a sample technique to experience *samadhi* or Divine alignment. It's not totally complete for more advanced meditators. Chapter 20 gives a deeper version of *samadhi* meditation for meditators of all levels, which is available on CD.

MANTRIC SCIENCE FOR SAMADHI

The universal *mantras*, Om, Aum or Amen, have many uses, but the most practical one is to elevate one's consciousness and to increase the rate of vibration of the chanter or practitioner. But it has to be done properly with the right vocalization and breathing technique initially using concentration, then awareness.

The most important time when *samadhi* or expansion of consciousness will happen is in the gap or silence between the Oms. When you're able to be aware as an observer in this silent gap between the Oms, Aum or Amen, that is where the "real stuff" happens.

PROCEDURE AND PRACTICE

1. Sit in a comfortable posture, either in Egyptian, lotus or adept's posture. Just relax and be passive.
2. Invoke for Divine protection, guidance and empowerment.
3. Use the meditation *mudra* (*dhayani*).
4. Do 3 sets of the Synchronized Breathing Method (3 minutes).
5. Perform the deep breathing technique for 5 minutes (10 sets):
   - Inhale slowly and deeply for 10 counts (about 10 seconds).
   - Hold your breath for 5 counts (about 5 seconds).
   - Exhale slowly and fully for 10 counts (about 10 seconds).
   - Hold your breath for 5 counts (about 5 seconds).
   - Repeat this sequence for about 10 sets.
6. Vocalize the *mantra* of your choice from the versions of Om, Aum or Amen. Let's use Om. Inhale deeply before you start, and recite Om until you are almost out of breath with 80% O and 20% M (Ooooooommm). Then inhale slowly and fully. Modulate your sound until it is pleasant to hear. Moderate the volume of your voice without cracking or stretching your voice. Use a middle pitch at first, then go to a higher pitch

later. Sound and vocalize the *mantra*, Om, for 5 minutes (about 25-30 times).

7. Continue sounding the *mantra*, Om, for about 2 minutes, but more gently and with more inward awareness without using the full power of your voice. Simultaneously, with slight intention, be aware of the crown chakra on top of your head. No visualization! Just gently touch it with your mind.

8. Continue with Step 6, but do a silent Om in your consciousness. Be aware not only of the *mantra*, Om, but also of the gap between the Oms. No tension, mental control, expectation or analysis should come to your awareness while you're doing this. If this happens, go back to being aware while sounding the Om verbally. This sequence can take about 2-3 minutes.

9. Continue reciting the Om without expecting results. If something great happens, let go without reactions. Finish the whole technique in 25-30 minutes.

    NOTE: If you are in a shared space and you don't want people to hear you, you can do the *mantrams* silently from the start. The effect of the vocalized *mantra* is more robust to purify and upgrade the frequency of the environment, which can enhance the quality of your meditation. The silent Om is more internal, thus it has an excellent effect for the last segment.

10. Say a thanksgiving with gratitude to the Spiritual Beings, your mentor or spiritual lineage as you finish the whole ritual.

If you don't experience a big expansion or results during the first few attempts, just be patient. Perhaps you don't physically notice what's happening, but energetically and spiritually, big changes are occurring in your auras, chakras and consciousness.

There are seven things that can limit your experience:

1. You're not relaxed, or you're too focused. Just be patient and learn how to be passive in a waiting attitude. Do not exert any effort.

2. You need to activate your *kundalini* more through deep breathing to have fuel for expansion. Just build up the *kundalini's* power as you meditate weekly.

3. Your *antahkarana* is being constructed or filled up with substance. Keep practicing!

4. Your upper chakras, especially the crown and heart, are smaller than your *ajna*, solar plexus or base-of-spine. Do more Synchronized Breathing to awaken the upper chakras.

5. You are not karmically entitled due to lack of service or usefulness of energy accumulated through meditation. Find a spiritual service or learn how to bless out healing energy (see Chapter 16, page 268).

6. Learn humility and respect for higher beings, or acknowledge your Soul and get more plugged in to higher consciousness.

7. You need more practice to have greater gentle awareness on the Om and the silent gap between the Oms. Know how to let go.

This is one of the many Mantric yoga techniques to attain a certain level of experience approaching what we call *samadhi* or yogic progressive ultimate experience.

ILLUMINATION METHOD TO ACHIEVE *SAMADHI*

The state of illumination involves the light of the mind and the process of deep understanding. It is a greater expansion of the world of meaning as compared to the current meaning of existence or a specific topic. From the scientific findings which are already true facts, another principle will deepen the search and penetrate more profoundly into the "matter" or idea. This can be done infinitely, both macrocosmically or microcosmically. The development of the third eye and the *antahkarana* or cable of light are the keys. For the sake of practice, we'll use a meditation technique that I used when I was in grade school. I did this naturally without knowing it was an advanced meditation. I had many expansions of consciousness that even allowed me to become part of the greater whole of the Earth Being and partially beyond. It was so overwhelming that I shut it off when I was a kid. Then I rediscovered the experience when I became a spiritual mentor, but by that time it had become a science of abstract meditation leading to *samadhi* or Oneness with a higher consciousness.

QUEST MEDITATION METHOD: *Who's Bigger and More Powerful?*

PROCEDURE AND PRACTICE
1. Sit in a comfortable posture with your spine erect. Just relax.
2. Do 3 sets of the Synchronized Breathing Method (3 minutes) to purify and calm your emotions and mind.
3. Be playful with your mind and use your creative intelligence and imagination (not concrete visualization). Just let ideas, images or concepts appear or emerge naturally. Let them flow, and entertain the answers lightheartedly with no attachment to their correctness or wrongness.
4. The quest for answers or hints starts from here:
   a. **Who's bigger and more powerful than you?**
      Most probably you pick an answer like your Soul or Spirit or city. Whatever you pick as an answer, be aware that you are enclosed by a bigger being, not only physically, but also energetically. Just play with your imagination and relax while continuing to breathe. Go to the next question.
   b. **Who's bigger and more powerful than your city and you?**
      Let's say your answer is your country. Then allow yourself to be enclosed by that entity or being called your country, including the city you're in. Just allow the game to play itself and relax.

c. **Who's bigger and more powerful than your country, your city and you?**
Let's say the answer is the planet Earth. Then allow yourself to be enclosed by that entity or Earth Being, including your country, city and you. Allow your consciousness to sense that enclosure or Being inside those macrocosms. No analysis of answers. Just enjoy and relax.

d. **Who's bigger and more powerful than the Earth, your country, city and you?**
Let's say the answer is the solar system. Continue awareness of being enclosed with all the other entities.

e. **Continue asking this question and the sense of awareness of being enclosed by a bigger and bigger consciousness.** Other Macrocosmic Beings in order of greatness are:

- Galaxy
- Cosmos
- Universe
- Absolute and Infinite
- Eternal
- Super-Eternal
- Ultimate
- Super-Ultimate
- And beyond...

After some point of being more relaxed and aware of the interconnectedness of you and the endlessly "Macrocosmic All", there's a point where your mental grasp ends without labels and descriptions. Then you go to the illumination that God or Divinity has no mentally realized limit and is all-pervasive and nameless, but has "suchness", "everythingness" and "don't-know-anything-aboutness".

The consciousness expands into realms never tapped even by our illumined ancestors and yogis. There's a point where you are in nothingness relative to the vastness of the Macrocosm, resulting in the ego and personality being Divinely humble, totally surrendering and totally big and powerful without asking to be big and powerful or declaring it.

When you can do this without reading this book, but instead by being guided instinctively and intuitively to merge with the greater whole, this is called *samadhi* beyond the Soul! Or the Soul and Spirit can also be the instruments to experience the *samadhi*.

NOTE: Another concept that can bring your awareness to the illumined state beyond the mind is this series of questions:

- Who created me? God is usually the answer for most people.
- Then who created God?
- When did God even start to create?
- In the very beginning, who created the idea to create?
- What was primordial space before it was filled up with vibration and before creation started?
- Did sound come from light?
- Did light come from vibration?
- Where did vibration come from?
- Where did the intention to vibrate come from?
- Where did the force that put the intention to vibrate come from?
- And so on...

Once there is full surrender and inner awareness of hints and intuitional answers, let this flow without logical strain of the concrete mind. As we mentioned before, when the concrete mind is at a dead end, the abstract mind and/or intuition jumpstarts. This causes the *antahkarana* to be stimulated to vibrate and attract light substance to fill it up, and the Soul starts to awaken from dormancy to potency. Certain inner experiences start to happen.

The mind can be a powerful tool for greater illumination of consciousness to tap into the unknowns. The Jnana yogis like the advanced scientists are very good at this. Being an engineer myself and an esoteric scientist, this is partly how I drill into many undiscovered realms of the "unknown knowable things".

Samadhi and contemplation are not just bliss, ecstasy or nirvana, as most gurus, advanced yogis, Saints and enlightened Sages have declared them to be. Samadhi and contemplation are progressive inner expansions and experiences towards the Light of infinite truth substantiated not only by so-called formless truths, but also representing lower material correspondences.

There's no such thing as going upward to the formless world. The fact of the matter is that the higher the consciousness and the more subtle the plane tapped by our meditation, the denser the pixels of light that occupy it. Matter in the physical plane is grosser yet with fewer pixels of light that substantiate it so it is actually less dense than the higher planes. The body is the grosser form of the Spirit, and the Soul in between is the intermediary. Form or formlessness are illusions or delineations of infinite relativity.

The experience of *samadhi*, then, is relative to what a person has attained and penetrated in terms of truth, Divine light and the deeper harnessed form of existence – upward and downward. Light expands in all directions, not only upwards. *Samadhi* through self-realization is not enough. The realized consciousness has to be self-actualized! Therefore, after the so-called ultimate meditation experience, *samadhi*, follows actual usefulness of the "new you" in service to a higher level and a larger whole. Then meditation and yoga are more meaningful.

CHAPTER 16

6 Post-Meditation Techniques Meditators Should Do

M ost meditation and yoga techniques, including those in books, taught today stop at the culmination point called *samadhi* or contemplation. But there are so many other important steps meditators should do to utilize the excess energy absorbed during intense meditation or yogic breathing. There is also the need for procedures on how to absorb and assimilate the alchemized energy, plus the precautions and guidelines on what not to do after the meditation. My early mentor, MCKS, is a great example of a Sage who knows what he is doing technically and is familiar with the dangers behind meditation. I learned a great deal from him.

The six post-meditation techniques presented here are the final step in the 5-step process for safe and effective meditation we introduced in Chapter 8.

6 Steps to Maximize Your Post-Meditation Experience

Step 1:
ABSORPTION, ASSIMILATION AND STORING OF ALCHEMIZED ENERGIES
During meditation, especially more advanced types, there is an

awakening of internal energy, including *prana* or life force, Divine light and *kundalini* energy. They are alchemized by our system, resulting in an increased boost of power and vitality that we can absorb and save for bigger use. Not assimilating and storing this properly can cause it to go to waste or can cause congestion.

Let's study how to assimilate and store energy properly after meditating:

1. In a meditation position, preferably Egyptian pose, maintain the meditation *mudra* (*dhayani*) while doing the following technique.

2. After you finish your meditation, absorb and assimilate the energy by being aware or by directing attention all over your body and to the different levels of auras while breathing slowly. This will circulate the positive energy quickly throughout the entire body so it can be absorbed. Do this for 2-3 minutes.

3. Another technique is to short-circuit the energy of the whole body by focusing on the crown center, soles of the feet and palms simultaneously while breathing slowly for 2 minutes.

4. Focus on your navel center, and breathe slowly for 2-3 minutes. Then mentally create the intention to absorb, assimilate and store the alchemized energy in your navel centers. Your navel chakra has small secondary chakras around it that collect and store the alchemized energy. These smaller chakras are like silos and accumulators with different energetic

designs, depending on levels of development and use. Most schools and teachers only mention one or two of the minor navel chakras below the navel. But for more awakened esoteric meditators, there are more than two. The storing of alchemized energy is what sets you apart as a more effective meditator from most other meditators.

Step 2:
Releasing Energy Through Blessings (5-10 minute ritual)
This step accelerates your spiritual development. After an enlightening, expanded and highly energized experience, how can you share this power with others and make a big difference in the world without even walking out of your meditation space? You can use the following blessing technique. This technique, with its releasing of positive excess energy, will serve three purposes:

1. Release excess energy that your body can't handle healthily or comfortably. When you meditate, your energy can increase about two to ten times your normal capacity. This excess can overload your body and auras throughout the whole day if it is not normalized. This is one of the missing pieces and dangers of many yoga and meditation schools. They do not release this excess energy after meditation, which is like a plant getting over-watered. Instead of growing, growth gets stunted or the plant dies.

2. Releasing the positive energy to a subject or others for transformational service is a great idea and generates a lot of good karma or entitlement to good things. You can help your family, friends and people in need. Here is an immediate demonstration of the esoteric application of meditation. There are two variations of blessing techniques:

   a. Using your palms or hand chakras to release the healing or transforming energy to specific subjects like your family, friends, co-workers and social, cultural and spiritual affinities

b Visualizing yourself inside your Soul like a big bright ball of light to radiate like a sun to the different target groups

PROCEDURE AND PRACTICE:

- Visualize the recipients of your blessings as smaller people as if they were all in front of you.
- If you are using the palm blessing method, raise your hands with your elbows bent slightly and have a gentle intention to flow the positive energy out of your hands towards the targets.
- If you are using the Soul Radiatory Method, visualize yourself inside the bright light of the Soul and have the intention to radiate to the different recipients like the sun shining over the planets.
- Form a mental intention that only positive energy will flow and go to the subjects of blessings with positive results. Accompany your blessing with the intentions of love, harmony, peace, joy, healing and transformation. Do this for 2-3 minutes for each group being blessed.
- Do not do blessings to a baby or child as an individual. The blessings will be too strong. Group the baby or child with the whole family.
- If you are blessing individual adults, do not exceed more than one minute per blessing.

3. The blessings and releasing technique will allow you to open an additional opportunity to act as a channel for Divine blessings from your Soul, lineage or Spiritual teachers. You become a spiritual pump to help transform many groups,

including your family. Also, by blessing out your excess energy, all your auric and chakral energy pipelines will flow and circulate better to enhance your overall well-being. This blessing after meditation is an indispensible tool for more advanced meditators. It is what brings you to spiritual maturity for the esoteric application of meditation.

PRECAUTION: It is not recommended that people with vices like smoking and alcoholism, recreational drug users and those with infectious diseases and life-threatening ailments bless others. This is not being separative, but it has been observed by clairvoyants that blessings by people with these issues can result in possible contamination of the auras of the subjects of blessings.

Step 3:
THANKSGIVING TO DIVINE BEINGS, LINEAGE OR SPIRITUAL MENTORS

It only takes a minute to do this step properly, but the energetic and spiritual positive effects are tremendous. It's good to maintain a positive respectful attitude to the greater Divine helpers and beings where it is due. These beings do not demand it, but they give their own blessings selflessly for the sake of the meditator or yogi when they are invoked. Proper respect or aspiration to higher ideals or Divine idols is not bad, nor is it a demonstration of weakness. In fact, it is a must for advanced esoteric meditators to connect to a lineage for extra protection, guidance and empowerment. Respect is not to be confused with blind faith or fanatical devotion. They are not the same.

Proper respect is not only emotional, but also includes the right mental perspective and understanding according to one's level of evolution. The right respect and humility are not about an inferiority complex or a pitiful belittling level of consciousness, but are an aligned composure and balanced point of view of ourselves with respect to others.

I recommend this simple closing ritual:

1. Do the *anjali mudra* with both hands at chest level.
2. Mentally salute the Divine God, the Macrocosm, as high as you have realized the being, and your spiritual lineage or teachers (if you have any). Include all the Divine Mentors and Guides of the world, if you want.
3. Silently express with sincerity:
   Thank you for the Divine protection, guidance and empowerment.
4. Absorb the empowerment for a few minutes and just be aware.

This closing ritual is also a time when invoked help is disengaged and the effects of meditation sealed and shielded. It's a great thing to do.

Step 4:
PHYSICAL EXERCISES

The exercises should be simple, short and easy so as not to disturb the balance and circulation of alchemized energy. Any stretching or easy body movements that can facilitate the normalizing of the body after long sitting postures are good. These should include:

1. Eye rotations (10 times in each direction)
2. Neck rolls (5-10 times slowly in each direction, except for those with neck injuries)
3. Arm swings (10 times each direction)
4. Hip rolls (10 times in each direction, except for people with hip and knee problems)
5. Normal squats (10 -20 times, except for people with knee problems)
6. Leg stretching and body limbering as much as your physical health can comfortably allow. No extra strain is necessary.
   Another part of this step is massaging and physically tapping parts of the body:

a. **Head and face:** Use your palms to massage these areas for a few seconds.
b. **Neck, throat and shoulders:** Gently massage these areas to further flow any physically stuck energy.
c. **Stomach, lower back (especially the kidney area)** and abdominal area: Slide your palms downward and tap the liver and solar plexus area to flow any excess energy there.
b. **Legs and feet:** Spend several moments tapping or sliding your palms over these areas. You can press repeatedly on the soles of your feet to trigger the body's energy flow better.

Paying attention to finishing details is important. Practice your mindful meditation by enjoying this moment-by-moment kind regard to your physical body.

One of the most important reasons for the exercise, especially the squats, is to ground yourself after meditation. The space cadet type meditators need these closing rituals more than anyone else. You don't want to drive while still "out there". You need to be properly physically anchored. The physical exercise will do this for you.

Body Squeeze Method

In more advanced training, the "body squeezing technique" is very useful to ground you back from a very high meditation. This is done by breathing deeply, then holding your breath and squeezing the body for a few seconds (5-7 seconds) before you exhale slowly while releasing the body squeeze. Only healthy people should do this. It is definitely not safe for pregnant women or people with heart conditions, cancer, glaucoma, high blood pressure, vertigo and bleeding. Check with a certified meditation or yoga instructor before you attempt to do this technique.

Step 5:
APPLIED ESOTERIC SERVICE

Whatever you do for a living, use the extra power and additional enlightenment you get from meditation or yoga, even in your professional work. Since you are continually awakening spiritually, your exoteric duty and service should also be growing as a sign of inner maturity. There should be a progressive external expression of your added inner progress, otherwise you get bored or experience a sense of apathy.

If a person has meditated or done yoga for years and they have not increased their sense of duty and service to life and others, there's something missing in the development. This lack of increased capacity to serve and being unable to channel greater inspiration can result in atrophied growth or spiritual blockage. I have observed that external service is a must and a demonstration that your meditation is working and your consciousness is expanding.

This is the hidden blockage for many people on the path of meditation and yoga. They spend most of their time in spiritual practice and meditation and very minimal time in application of service. There is a created desire to grow, but not the avenue to sustain growth.
Hours of spiritual practice and meditation are a slower path than if you decrease these hours and increase the external service or contribution to the lives of others.

If a meditator is not happy with their work or is unable to express service through it, they can always find avocations to express what they like to do most and affect a greater number of people. Don't get stuck in the same predicament as spiritual practitioners I know: They are fading away as they grow older without making a big difference in the world.

Guidelines for Choosing Your Service

Plant good seeds in the most fertile ground. Invest your power to serve in the same way. Feeding the poor is a good thing to do. But normal servers can do that without advanced spiritual development. Feeding the minds and Souls of people who are poor in spirit is an even greater thing to do. Being the best in your profession is also another excellent service if done with the purpose of being the light in that career path.

Another rule of thumb is to search for your greatest contribution.

> *Your maximum service and its maximum good karma*
> *generated should go to an activity that has the*
> *greatest influence on world evolution and*
> *human development for the longest period of time*
> *affecting the largest number of*
> *beneficiaries, human or otherwise.*

Meditation is a tool for greater development and service. How you use that tool is what matters most.

> *Service is an expression of inner growth and*
> *development. It is the muscle-building for virtues.*
> *It is the barometer of inner*
> *development and spirituality.*

Step 6:
Self-Mastery

Character-building is a must on the spiritual path because continuing to increase power of energy without the right attitude and alignment to a righteous way can lead to big-time disaster, not only for the person, but also for many others. Many leaders with esoteric training were able to access some secrets of magical powers, but without the development of their hearts and wisdom, they ended up destroying themselves and many victims, causing tremendous suffering.

Self-mastery is not just about love, compassion, altruism or benevolence. As the meditator awakens, these are natural in their character. Character-building also includes honing the required skills and aptitudes, not only proper attitudes, required of their exoteric and esoteric duties.

Attitudes and Aptitudes for Self-Mastery

Attitudes and aptitudes are key ingredients of self-mastery. Attitudes are more subjective, internal and stimulated by emotional and spiritual influences whereas aptitudes have to do with skills development. Skills development pertains more to objective talents and practicality, which are affected by the physical and mechanical aspects of the mind.

Aptitudes are related to a sense of accountability and work. Attitudes are connected to a sense of responsibility and duty.

Self-mastery is not only having the idea of living as a Soul, but also developing the proper aptitudes and right attitudes to express this idea correctly. In self-mastery, we need to distinguish between:
- Things that are not supposed to be part of our path like vices and negative habits. They should be removed from our daily lives.
- Things that are very important and essential to our new path fulfilling a higher purpose like contribution to community life. We should prioritize them.

Self-mastery = Self-realization + Self-actualization

Self-mastery brings a high level of discrimination and discernment to live our greatest life. On a practical level, self-mastery is logical and applies common sense. For example, there are four types of people with regards to self-mastery and aptitude and attitude development. By knowing your type and your family members' and co-workers' types, you can improve relationships and guide next steps for development. Let's explore the four types:

1. PEOPLE WITH GOOD ATTITUDE, BUT POOR APTITUDE
   Those who are more subjective, love-centered Bhakti yoga types have the right attitude, but need to develop the proper aptitude and skills to grow even farther and facilitate greater applied service with more objectivity, practicality and sense of accountability. This will lead to more stable material and financial conditions to balance the inner development.

   Self-mastery includes balance between the two worlds, material and spiritual.

2. PEOPLE WITH GOOD APTITUDE, BUT POOR ATTITUDE
   Those who are more objective, mentally intelligent and Jnana yoga types have great aptitudes and life skills, but are not always equipped with positive attitudes, including benevolence, humility and altruism. For them to grow and sustain real progress, they need to culture their gentler inner aspects and emotional intelligence to facilitate their life's purpose with win-win strategies.

   Balance of personal, professional, social and spiritual aspects of life results in self-fulfillment.

3. PEOPLE WITH POOR ATTITUDE AND POOR APTITUDE
   Those with negative attitudes and no positive aptitudes need a lot of work and learning. They are a pain in the neck of society and the test of the boss in the workplace. They usually get

fired from work or ousted by groups. These people need to be the subject of blessings and transformational work.

4. PEOPLE WITH GOOD APTITUDE AND GOOD ATTITUDE

Those who have good aptitudes and positive attitudes are the more integrated type. They practice a balance of Bhakti, Jnana and Karma yogas in life, not only through typical sitting-down yoga or meditation, but also by working in the hearts of the modern cities with global projects and world service. These people are the leaders of leaders. Some of them don't even know how to sit in a lotus posture and do not use any special *mantra*. Their daily mission is "world service".

Those among these types who are not meditators can improve a lot if they meditate properly and have spiritual mentors and guidance. Even the smartest of them can access greater wisdom and spiritual insight for their next steps through spiritual meditation. They also need to heal their remaining personal issues and neutralize their karmic issues, which they can do through the meditation techniques in this book.

Self-mastery is not only heart or mind development. It is a position of expertise while becoming a purer, more powerful carrier of Divine will-power, Divine love and Divine light. These three aspects of the Divine Macrocosm can be mastered through the eight core virtues mentioned earlier in (Chapter 3 page 44) Let's itemize them again because they are so important.

- ◆ Right inner attitudes can be developed by mastering:
  - Benevolence (selfless loving kindness and compassion)
  - Altruism (selfless generosity and intelligent sharing)

- ◆ Proper aptitudes can be trained by mastering:
  - Objectivity and practicality
  - Will-power and vitality

- Both proper aptitudes and right attitudes can be mastered by application of:
  - Group consciousness
  - Virtue of sacrifice
  - Good health

MASTER YOURSELF THROUGH THE 8 CORE VALUES
Different values help develop your attitudes or aptitudes.

These virtues, discussed in detail in my book, *From Success to Fulfillment*, are either pure expressions or are compounded values and virtues expressed by the application and use of the Divine triangle of will-power, love and creative intelligence. The eight core values for self-mastery form an integrated approach to the Raja yoga philosophy of *yama* (restraints) and *niyama* (observation of virtues) with a modern application that's universally beneficial to both material and spiritual life.

When these core values are applied, they bring not only success, but also self-fulfillment. They are designed to transform knowledge into wisdom. This new presentation of character-building is geared towards more dynamic development of good character rather than a reflective or reclusive style. This new self-mastery approach overcomes the guilt complex of meditators and their over-reactiveness to simple faults or mistakes on the path.

The eight core values have also been designed to cover virtues from different religions and spiritual groups integrating deeper practical values from various cultures. This results in a more disciplined presentation of moral conduct and organizational codes of ethics. The eight core values are organized so that they apply as a teaching for children as well as their parents and adults. When an approach is universal, it can be used for global value development.

The power and development garnered from meditation or yoga have to be used effectively to warrant the investment of time and energy, not only for enlightenment, but also to empower our daily lives of service and contribution to others and the world. What is enlightenment without the actualization of that illumined state? Character-building is a self-mastery, which is a never-ending path in itself.

The yardstick of spiritual maturity
is seen in the greatness and value
of one's selfless service and
the livingness of daily virtues.

CHAPTER 17

Quick Meditations to Start and End Your Day

Whether your day will be happy, successful or miserable can be affected significantly by two crucial factors: your attitude and your quality of consciousness just after you wake up and how you start your day. The first five minutes in the morning before you take a shower or have your first sip of coffee affect how positive or negative you can be throughout the whole day.

Aside from prayers and breakfast, you can apply the 5-minute meditation of goodwill daily in the morning. Do you want to learn this simple but effective 4-step meditation you can do while lying or sitting in bed after waking up?

MEDITATION OF GOODWILL
(5 minutes daily upon waking up)

PROCEDURE AND PRACTICE
1. Spend 5 valuable minutes right after you wake up to greet your day with gratitude for life and the Source of your life. Use the feelings of your heart to express this for 1 minute.
2. Also silently express your good wishes to your family and loved ones, friends, co-workers and people whom you will be meeting throughout the day. Do this for one and a half minutes.
3. Visualize or create the intention of a good and successful day and mentally see your whole day's programs and goals achieved. If you have problems, visualize them being resolved properly. Focus more on the positive outcomes of your day. Do this for one and a half minutes.
4. Mentally say,
   "Life is good! Life is great! I like it!" (1 minute)
   Say this 7 or more times. The more you say it, the more you feel it!
   That's it! Only 5 minutes will make your day!

Let's take a look at an actual experience from someone who uses the meditation of goodwill.

> As a bank executive, I meditate using the meditation of goodwill before my meetings with clients, colleges and even my boss. If the subject to be discussed is a difficult one, I can see the willingness to discuss it openly and without stress if I do the meditation of goodwill before the conversation. And if I am trying to get a deal done with a potential client or an existing one, we come to terms easily, fast and without too much effort if I have done the meditation of goodwill beforehand. This is a great improvement for my day-to-day business.
>
> - E.F., Bank Executive, Puerto Rico

You've just learned a meditation to start your day off well. What about at night before you end your day? Do you want a short meditation technique to have peace of mind and restful sleep? You've got it!

END-OF-DAY TECHNIQUE
(5 minutes daily before going to sleep)

PROCEDURE AND PRACTICE
1. Sit in a comfortable position with your spine erect or in your preferred yogic posture.
2. Do 3-4 sets of the Synchronized Breathing Method. This will flush all stress and negative energies out of your system (4 minutes).
3. Affirm mentally (1 minute):

    "Life is good! Life is great! I like it!" (7 times)

    Say it with deep conviction and certainty.
    NOTE: If you're emotional or have relationship issues during the day or somebody got hurt, use the following 3-7 times:

I am a being of love and kindness. As I ask for compassion,
I show compassion. As I ask for forgiveness from people
whom I've hurt, I give forgiveness to anybody who has hurt me.
Let all be completely forgiven. Let all be free. So it is!

When your energy and consciousness are clean, energized and balanced, your sleep becomes very deep and restful even though it might be short. This is the secret formula I give to my clients with sleep disorders. Experiment doing the end-of-day meditation on some days and don't do it on others. Evaluate the difference!

CHAPTER 18

Beat Your Fatigue and Stress Fast with Meditations and Exercises

The formula to beat your fatigue and stress fast is simple and easy to learn. It is a combination of physical exercise and breathing techniques we've already learned. We just need to assemble them now into a 4-step strategy.

A 4-STEP STRATEGY THAT REALLY WORKS!

1. Internal Stamina Exercise
2. Synchronized Breathing Method
3. Combination Breathing Technique
4. Centering and Navel Breathing Meditation

8-STEP INTERNAL STAMINA EXERCISE: *Only 5 Minutes!*

We already discussed this in Chapter 11, pages 186-188, so let's just itemize the sequence again.

PREPARATION

1. You may follow the Beat Your Fatigue and Stress Fast DVD video guiding this program.
2. You can achieve best results in a well-ventilated exercise

space with plenty of clean, fresh air. Once you have familiarized yourself with the sequence, do it outdoors if possible.

PROCEDURE AND PRACTICE

1. Shoulder and Spine Stress Release (10 times): to release ten-
    sion in your abdominal area, upper body and spine
2. Arm Swing (10 times): to oxygenate your lungs and blood
    and empower your upper torso
3. Upper Body Turns (10 times in each direction): to release
    tension in your upper torso and spine and to balance the left
    and right sides of your body
4. Hip Rolls (10 times in each direction): to loosen up your hips
    and flow vitality throughout your body
5. Internal Organs Exercise (10 times): to detoxify, revitalize and
    exercise your internal organs (not recommended for preg-
    nant women and people with internal organ problems)
6. Expanding Squats (20-30 times): for anti-aging, increased will-
    power and to enhance blood and vitality circulation through-
    out your body (not recommended for people with knee
    problems)
7. Whole Body Stretch (10 times): to align your entire body,
    release the pressure on your spine and strengthen your lower
    legs and feet
8. Side-to-Side Body Stretch (10 times): to loosen up the sides
    of your body and further oxygenate your lungs and blood

INTERNAL STAMINA EXERCISE SCHEDULE

You can do this on its own or with the next three techniques. You
can beat your fatigue and stress easily with higher vitality. This technique also rejuvenates your body and revitalizes your emotions and
mind. You can do it daily before you go to work or before going
home. Stress is contagious! Don't bring it home.

SYNCHRONIZED BREATHING METHOD (5 minutes)

We've already discussed and applied this many times in many chapters, but we're providing the procedure again here so you don't have to look for it.

The Synchronized Breathing Method is a multipurpose breathing technique to:

- ◆ Rapidly release stress
- ◆ Calm the emotions and mind fast
- ◆ Purify and revitalize the auras and power centers
- ◆ Activate and align the energy centers regulating emotional, mental and spiritual energies and faculties

PROCEDURE AND PRACTICE

1. Sit in a comfortable position with your back straight and vertical and your feet flat on the floor. Close your eyes before you start.
2. Inhale fully and rapidly through your nose as you tilt your head backwards while simultaneously inflating your abdomen.
3. Immediately exhale fully and rapidly through your mouth as you bow your head down while compressing your abdomen.
4. Repeat steps 2 and 3 10-15 times.
5. Just relax with your head vertical and breathe slowly. Concentrate on the top-of-head, mid-brow and heart power centers simultaneously while breathing slowly. Do this step for 30 seconds.
6. Repeat steps 2 through 5 three times. You can do this three times weekly or daily as required. The Synchronized Breathing Method followed by nostril yogic breathings or the Combination Breathing Technique bring best results.

PRECAUTION

This technique is not recommended for pregnant women or those with neck injuries, high blood pressure, migraine or severe heart conditions.

Note: If you have a neck injury, substitute the Synchronized Breathing Method with the *kapalbhati* breathing technique instead (page 202-204).

Just about everyone can use the Synchronized Breathing Method as a practical tool to maximize performance in work, relationships and spiritual practices. It will also improve your overall health.

Combination Breathing Method (5 minutes)

We discussed this technique in Chapter 12, pages 210. Here's a review of the benefits:

- Recover your energy quickly during strenuous exercises
- Boost your vitality fast, especially when you are weak or nearly fainting
- Revitalize your sexual energy
- Activate your spiritual energy

The procedure combines full abdominal, chest and shoulder breathing for maximum air capacity and more time for oxygen and air vitality absorption. This protocol also has spiritual significance for advanced meditators awakening their spiritual powers.

Procedure and Practice

1. Sit in a comfortable position with your spine vertical and your feet flat on the floor. You may close your eyes.
2. Place your hands in your lap with your palms facing upward.
3. Inhale slowly and continuously while inflating your abdomen.
4. Continue inhaling slowly, inflating your chest.
5. Continue inhaling slowly until maximum respiration while expanding and lifting your shoulders upwards.
6. Hold your breath steadily for 5 seconds.
7. Exhale all your air slowly while deflating your abdomen and chest, and bring your shoulders back down to their normal position.
8. Hold your breath steadily for 5 seconds.
9. Repeat this breathing process (steps 3-8) only 10 times, a

maximum of twice a day. Do this 3 times weekly or when high energy is required.

PRECAUTION

1. This simple breathing technique creates tremendous internal power and a surge of vitality not recommended for pregnant women or people with chest pain, heart ailments, high blood pressure, migraine or headache, bleeding problems, glaucoma, ADHD, cancer or AIDS.
2. If you have side effects like chest pain, headache, acidity, hiccups or extreme dizziness, stop the practice immediately and consult a meditation expert.

CENTERING MEDITATION: NAVEL BREATHNG METHOD (5 minutes)

As we discussed before in Chapter 12, this is a very simple but powerful technique to center yourself quickly, plus awaken your internal stamina. When the navel center is very active, your gut instincts also improve greatly.

PROCEDURE AND PRACTICE

1. Sit in a chair in the Egyptian posture or lotus or semi-lotus position. Be comfortable and just relax.
2. Assume the meditation *mudra* (*dhayani*) (left hand on top of right) at the navel.
3. Inhale and exhale slowly and deeply for 5 minutes while mentally concentrating on the navel chakra. Do not visualize. Just focus on the navel point. Do not concentrate too much. Just relax and enjoy.

The entire "Beat Your Fatigue and Stress Fast" program takes only 15 minutes of your time, but it will save you from expensive mistakes and challenges in your relationships, which can be triggered by fatigue and spoiled by stress.

Invest not only in your financial life,
but also in your total well-being.

As a PhD candidate in engineering, I was getting little exercise, eating junk food and sitting for long hours studying. That led to a combination of weight gain and energy loss. I always had an afternoon slump that made it hard to concentrate, and my productivity was negligible. I decided to take advantage of living on the 10th floor of a dormitory by climbing the stairs, but I was breathless by the 3rd floor. After taking up swimming, I could make it to the 6th floor before I was out of breath.

I was first introduced to the "Beat Your Fatigue and Stress Fast" DVD in Switzerland. The most amazing result was the instant stamina boost. My energy and alertness are definitely better throughout the day. No more afternoon slump. I have also observed that I can climb 10 flights of stairs without feeling exhausted. If I don't use the DVD in the morning, then I fall back into the afternoon slump, and I get winded easily when climbing stairs.

Since I started using the "Beat Your Fatigue and Stress Fast" DVD, I feel much more capable of concentrating all though the day. These exercises and meditations are really working for me, and I think that everybody can benefit from them.

- M.A., Stanford University PhD Candidate, California

CHAPTER 19

Self-Healing Meditation to Live Healthier, Be Happier and Grow Faster

Healing oneself is not that difficult. In fact, it is fun because in the process of alleviating your pains and discomforts through the self-healing meditation, you are also growing spiritually.

With this technique, you are hitting three targets in one single meditation. How about that? This magical meditation, which has helped countless executives, leaders, parents and people who are recovering from life-threatening diseases, is called the Inner Renewal Meditation™.

I have achieved a completely new level of balance and focus by doing the Inner Renewal Meditation.

- AS, PhD, Clinical Director,
Southeastern Arizona Behavioral Health Sciences

INNER RENEWAL MEDITATION
(3 times weekly): Available on CD

BENEFITS
- For deep relaxation, peace of mind and stress management
- For inner empowerment and spiritual development

- For enhancing your emotional and mental aptitudes and attitudes
- For purifying, unblocking and rejuvenating your different auras
- For improving relationships and healing your past
- For activating the expression of virtues and to integrate the faculties of will-power, love and creative intelligence in your life

PROCEDURE
A. Proper posture
1. For this meditation, the best posture is to sit on a chair with your feet flat on the floor and your hands in your lap. You may also lie down as long as you keep your back aligned.
2. Close your eyes.

B. Inner purifications and breathing: Select any item (numbers 4-14 below) that concerns you.
1. Start with the inner purifications. Free yourself from any physical, emotional and mental negativities or discomforts.
2. Imagine yourself in front of an ocean. What is important is your intention.
3. Breathe deeply and slowly and relax. During exhalation, have the intention to breathe out your negativities and discomforts.
4. Inhale deeply, then breathe out to the ocean any discomfort, tension or pain in your body. Do it many times. Let the ocean absorb the discomforts and impurities (1 minute).
5. Inhale deeply, then breathe out to the ocean stress or emotional pain and discomfort. Let the ocean absorb these negativities (1 minute).
6. Inhale deeply, then breathe out irritability, anger or hatred. Let the ocean absorb the negative emotions (1 minute).
7. Inhale deeply, then breathe out depression, boredom or frustrations. Let the ocean absorb them (30 seconds).
8. Inhale deeply, then breathe out fears, guilt and worries. Let

the ocean absorb the negative emotions (30 seconds).

9. Inhale deeply, then breathe out resentment and anxiety. Let the ocean absorb these negative emotions (30 seconds).

10. Inhale deeply, then breathe out any remaining negative feelings and emotions. Let the ocean absorb all of the negativities (30 seconds).

11. Inhale deeply, then breathe out harmful thoughts against anyone or any being. Let the ocean absorb the negative thoughts (30 seconds).

12. Inhale deeply, then breathe out any mental limitations and blockages. Let the ocean absorb the negative thoughts (30 seconds).

13. Inhale deeply, then breathe out any tendencies of excessive criticism, control and manipulation of others. Let the ocean absorb all of the negative tendencies (30 seconds).

14. Inhale deeply, then breathe out anything that limits your freedom or obstructs your inner development. Let the ocean absorb any obstacles (30 seconds).

15. Relax and enjoy your new emotional and mental well-being.

C. Opening and activating the heart center

1. Now, be aware of your heart chakra at the center of your chest. This is an area where you can experience love, inner peace and inner joy. Inhale deeply and exhale slowly while being aware of the area at the center of your chest (1 minute).

2. As you breathe, silently affirm:

I am a peaceful, loving and joyous person.

Repeat it 7 times as you continue breathing slowly. Create this wonderful feeling of love, joy and peace within you. Express your love, gratitude and respect to your family, loved ones and those who have helped your life.

3. Visualize yourself being more loving and caring to other peo-

ple and their needs. Start with your family and loved ones. Express love to your friends. Express good wishes and respect to your co-workers. Mentally ask for forgiveness from people who have been hurt by you. Also, forgive the people who have hurt you. Experience the love, peace and joy within you.

D.   *Activating your mental stamina and intelligence*

1. Focus on your mid-brow center between your eyebrows and breathe slowly for 1 minute. By breathing while focusing on this center, you can enhance the ability to think more clearly and properly. Inhale deeply and exhale slowly as you mentally say 3 times:

> *I am a creative and intelligent person.*
> *I will use my creativity and*
> *intelligence lovingly and properly.*

E.   *Opening and activating the top-of-head power center for spiritual faculties and to align with the Soul*

1. Focus on the center on top of your head and breathe slowly for 1 minute. By breathing while focusing on this point, you can enhance the ability to acquire more inspiration, Divine understanding and wisdom. Inhale and exhale slowly and mentally say 3 times:

> *I respect the divinity within myself.*
> *I respect the divinity within All.*
> *I respect the greatness of the Supreme Source of Life.*

2. Relax and let go. Enjoy the inner peace and stillness (2 or more minutes).

F. *Absorption and circulation of internal energy*

1. To assimilate the internal energy and vitality, breathe slowly while focusing on your navel (1 minute).
2. To further improve the absorption of energy, concentrate on your palms and soles of the feet as you inhale and exhale slowly for 30 seconds.

G. *Blessing service* (2 minutes)

1. With intention, share some of your positive and loving energy and vitality with your loved ones, friends and anyone who needs help. You may use the following affirmation many times for at least 2 minutes:

> *I humbly offer myself as an instrument to share*
> *love, peace, joy, beauty, creativity, truth and goodwill*
> *with my family, loved ones, friends and co-workers.*
> *So it is!*

Now open your eyes and smile.

This technique is not just a meditation. It is also a healing tool to live healthier, be happier and grow faster! You may adopt it as a regular spiritual practice at least 3 times weekly.

This meditation has helped many successful professionals and executives achieve the state of inner fulfillment. Use it every week; then it is yours to say, "Life is so good! I am balanced and fulfilled!"

The Inner Renewal Meditation has liberated the limitations of my mind and emotions in my relationships. I have become detached from these limitations; moreover, I'm open to an upgraded deeper and more balanced love and a transformation of fulfillment in all my relationships.

- L.G., Teacher, Texas

CHAPTER 20

Advanced Meditation to Experience Your Soul

S elf- and Soul realization are common jargon in many meta-physical schools. They are goals that set most spiritual aspi-rants on their spiritual path. Yet they are also some of the most misconstrued ideals and often turn into a path of illusion rather than illumination. Why? Because Self- and Soul realization are made into end goals rather than a path of livingness as a Soul — today, not tomorrow.

There's a simple modification to traditional yogic approaches. Rather than "kicking out" or rejecting the personality (mind, emo-tions and physical body) like some techniques of yoga that are not "personality-inclusive", let's bring a new psychology that says:

- The Spirit is great! It's the source of Life.
- The Soul is noble! It's the transmitter of Divine light.
- The personality is wonderful. It is working so hard on its own level to facilitate the Soul's evolution!

Instead of saying , as in traditional yoga:
- I am not my body.
- I am not my emotions.
- I am not my mind.
- I am the Soul, the Immortal Self, that Self, I am!

What about also declaring:
- The body is the counterpart of the Spirit.
- The emotional energy body is the instrument of the Soul to express feelings.
- The mind is the Soul's apparatus of creative intelligence.
- The Soul is enclosed, interpenetrated and empowered by the Spirit.
- All layers of our consciousness are but interpenetrating aspects of ourselves – differentiated, but one Being!

I've observed that if a spiritual practice is too puritanical or idealistic, it can sabotage faster growth. The mind, emotions and vitality auras and the physical body have collective intelligence and consciousness sometimes being expressed as the ego, which has a specific quality of responses:

- It rebels and becomes uncooperative if it is rejected as not important and a subject of total obliteration by the Soul.
- It cooperates and collaborates if it is included as a part of the Spirit and Soul – and is seen as important!

The Soul can't grow without the personality!
That's why the Soul incarnates many, many times
for the personality to work for that evolutionary
experience that fertilizes the growth of the Soul.

Therefore, the new psychology of this practical spirituality is:
- The Spirit is very important.
- The Soul is very important.
- The personality is very important.

They all need to evolve together to not only bring Earthly experience (personality) to Heaven (Soul), but also to bring Heaven (the Soul's life) to Earth (personality).

The old concept about the personality bothered me for some-time – and even all the important books of ancient wisdom and yoga have spelled it out in a more idealistic way. The wisdom of modern life is demanding new analysis and deep study on this "experimental principle" of giving importance (I don't mean self-importance in a greedy, self-gratifying, egotistical way) to the contri-bution of the personality, the incarnated person.

I designed a new meditation to experience the Soul and Divine Oneness, the Namascar Meditation™ with the idea of:

- All-inclusiveness (personality light is enclosed and interpene-trated by the Soul light, and the Spirit interpenetrates the Soul)
- Non-rejection of the personality and non-abandonment of the ego
- Expansion of consciousness; all light is not only upward, but also in all directions
- God or the Divine Macrocosm is everything: Good and other-wise...

Let's experience the Namascar Meditation.

NAMASCAR MEDITATION (28 minutes)

GOALS:

1. To facilitate tremendous downpourings of Divine energies from the Spirit to the Soul and from the Soul to the person-ality. This is a self-help technique for healing and transforming oneself.
2. Fast construction of the *antahkarana*, the connecting cable of light: At first, the beginner meditator will build the matrix, and the advanced practitioner will fill it up with substance.
3. To facilitate safer *kundalini* awakening with the Soul's and Spirit's upper energy system being developed first. Proper *kundalini* development helps accelerate you to proceed to your next spiritual step.

4. To allow the beginner to advanced meditator to experience spiritual unity and Divine Oneness with greater Lives and Divine Macrocosmic substance

5. To enable conscious spiritual connections with Divine Beings to accelerate and empower one's chosen service or path

6. Soul's inner salutation to the Spirit or the Divine Self (1½ minutes):
   Be aware that you are the Soul, inside the light of the Spirit, then salute and express your love, respect and gratitude to the Spirit, as if it were your last opportunity to do so. Maintain this awareness for about one and a half minutes. Allow the merging of the personality and Soul with the Divine Self, the Spirit. Be still, be aware and enjoy the merging experience and Divine Oneness.

7. Affirmation of the Divine Self with the "I am that I am" while you are in the experience of the merging of the personality, Soul and Spirit. The Spirit, Soul and personality internally affirm as a whole being at least 2-3 times:

I am the Divine Self.
I am that I am.
I am Divine Will and Power.
I am Divine Love and Wisdom.
I am Divine Creative Intelligence.
I am one with all.
All are one.
I am that I am.

8. After this, just be aware, be still and let go for a few minutes (3 minutes average). Experience Divine Oneness with the Higher Self.

9. Inner salutation to other Divine Beings (2-3 minutes).
   Express your inner respect and gratitude to your spiritual lineage or affinity, if you have any, then to the Great Divine Beings. Know that they are not afar, but rather that you are

enclosed in the light of the Spiritual Beings. This is the right inclusive process. Experience this step without expectations or focusing on desire to connect...Just be aware, passive and receptive. Great inner experiences start in this detached inner state.

10. Inner salutation to the Source of Life, the Divine Macrocosm (2 minutes):

    Know and be aware that you and other Divine Beings are inside this Divine Macrocosm, the Source of Life, and express a sincere and deep sense of respect and gratitude, as if it were your last opportunity to do so. After this step, just let go and allow, with total surrender, any experiences to occur. Before proceeding to the next step, bring your hands down into your lap.

11. Absorption of Divine energy and storing of internal energy (2-3 minutes):

    To absorb and assimilate Divine light into the energy bodies, concentrate on your crown, palms and soles of the feet, and breathe slowly for 30 seconds. Next, focus on your navel centers while breathing slowly and deeply for about 2 minutes to absorb and store the internal energy mentally. Instruct the energies to be absorbed and stored in the system.

12. Transformational and healing service through blessings (6 minutes):

    This meditation produces great amounts of energy, and one of its goals is to share the spiritual energy with groups for transformational service and healing. You may use the following blessing method:

    Imagine yourself as a bright sun and radiate the blessings with the intention of transformation and healing to:
    - Family as a group (2 minutes)
    - Group of friends, associates and co-workers (2 minutes)
    - Your organization (2 minutes)
    - Bigger targets of concern (for more advanced meditators)

SPECIAL REQUIREMENTS AND PRECAUTIONS

As with any science and technology, there are things to avoid and safety measures required for the safe practice of advanced meditations. It is recommended that you observe them properly as follows:

1. Food and oral intake: Beginning practitioners should preferably be semi-vegetarians and advanced meditators should be vegetarian. Pork and red meat are not recommended for advanced practitioners due to the big contrast between the food's energies and Divine light. Pork and red meat have been observed to produce adverse side effects in advanced meditators. This meditation may not be safe for smokers, heavy alcohol drinkers and people who take recreational drugs.
2. Do not bathe for at least 4 hours after meditating.
3. People with neck problems should not do the Synchronized Breathing Method. Substitute it with *kapalbhati* or *bhastrika* methods (pages 202-204).
4. The Namascar Meditation is not recommended for those under 15 and for people with the following conditions: heart ailments, high blood pressure and life-threatening illnesses. However, when a person is near death, this meditation can be used to help the person exit properly with inner peace.

Doing the Namascar Meditation regularly results in the transformation and healing of the practitioner, his or her group and the environment. It offers a great service to oneself, one's family, others and the environment. This technique is recommended once or maximum twice a week, done either individually or in a group. It is a simple, but powerful meditation to take you to your highest potential experiences of self-realization and gradually to your self-actualization. Namascar Meditation is one of your most important tools for achievable enlightenment in this life.

I used to believe that only meditators who practiced for years could achieve self-realization. After a couple of years of classes, my yoga guru told me it would take many more years of sitting every day to control the mind. I was frustrated because, as an executive, I don't have the time or patience to spend hours sitting in the lotus position, trying to think of nothing.

A friend gave me the "Namascar Meditation" CD as a gift. I tried it for a week. It was the best experience I had ever had. The CD starts with a breathing technique that is very easy to follow and in less than five minutes, I was able to clear my mind so I was able to achieve the deep stillness that led to a level of samadhi *and Divine Oneness I yearned to experience.*

Now, I make it a point to spend 28 minutes once or twice a week listening to the Namascar Meditation. It is easy to let go and let my consciousness expand beyond what I ever expected.

I have been surprised to discover that since I began practicing the meditation, I have become more productive at work and the stress no longer bothers me. Not only that, my relationships have become more satisfying and flowing. The peace of mind, intuitional awareness and inner alignment from the meditation are priceless!

- E. M., Business Consultant, Florida

CHAPTER 21

Advanced Meditation:

A Balanced Life with One Foot in Heaven and One Foot on Earth

A balanced and successful material and spiritual life is a great thing! The notion that meditation is only for spiritual purposes is not totally correct. The Divine Alchemy meditation you will experience in this chapter covers many levels of esoteric science practices and advanced meditation techniques to awaken, unfold and develop the maximum potential in spiritual practitioners so they can perform effectively in both material and spiritual life. This advanced meditation awakens your inner powers to unfold a balanced life "with one foot in Heaven and one foot on Earth" – meaning material success with spiritual fulfillment. Why not?

How do we do this safely and effectively? We will activate the power of each chakra through a combination of slow inhalation focusing on the chakra, plus recitation of a *mantra* during the exhalation process.

This mantric technique is done for a few sets per chakra, and some chakras need fewer repetitions than others. The *mantra* to be used is "Om Mane Padtme Hum" (I am that I am). It has many equivalent *mantras* like "Soham" or "Hamsa" in the yogic tradition. If you don't want to use these *mantrams*, you can use different names like "Je-sus" or "Bu-ddha". Or you can skip the *mantra* and just do the inhalation and exhalation while concentrating on each chakra to be activated.

Activating the chakra by *mantra* and breathing techniques results in a bigger, more active and powerful energy center. By activating and awakening the chakras, their latent faculties are also awakened to a higher degree. The functions, faculties and inner powers of the different chakras are described in Chapter 4, pages 84-86).

MEDITATION PROCEDURE AND PRACTICE: 30 minutes
(available on CD as Divine Alchemy Meditation, Level I)
Activating, balancing and empowering your energy centers requires a purer, more refined and flowing human energy system. For best results and inner experiences, first do the "Beat Your Fatigue and Stress Fast" program (see Chapter 18 or the DVD).

PREPARATION: 5 minutes
a. Sit in a comfortable position, either in a lotus or Egyptian posture (sitting on a chair with feet flat on the floor). Do the *dhayani mudra* at the navel. Close your eyes. Invoke for Divine protection and guidance.
b. Perform 5 sets of the Synchronized Breathing Method (15 repetitions each) and during the intervals between sets, do chakral breathing focusing on the crown, *ajna* and heart chakras while breathing slowly for 30 seconds.

CHAKRAL ACTIVATION: 14 minutes
Sounding a *mantra* or sacred words combined with breathing while focusing on the energy centers is one of the most advanced and effective techniques of activating and balancing the energy centers. This method also purifies and revitalizes the energy centers and transforms their consciousness to a higher level.

Here's how to do it: Inhale slowly and fully while concentrating on each chakra. As you exhale, you will chant "Om Mane Padtme Hum, Mane Padtme Hum, Mane Padtme Hum, Mane Padtme Hum" until your air is emptied out. Then inhale again slowly while concentrating on a specific chakra. The sequence of chakras is as follows:

- **Crown chakra:** Inhale slowly and deeply while concentrating on the crown chakra at the top of the head. Continue concentrating on the crown chakra while reciting the *mantra* during the exhalation process. You can do the *mantra* in a whisper if you are around other people. Do this procedure 5 times. Continue this same procedure with the following chakras.
- **Forehead chakra** (at the forehead): 5 times
- *Ajna* **chakra** (at the point between the eyebrows): 5 times
- **Throat chakra** (at the center of the neck): 5 times
- **Heart chakra** (at the mid-chest): 5 times
- **Solar plexus chakra** (at the center of the stomach below the sternum): 4 times
- **Navel chakra** (at the navel): 5 times
- **Spleen chakra** (below the floating ribs on the left side of the abdomen): 3 times
- **Sex chakra** (in front of the sex organs approximately at the bottom of the pubic bone): 4 times
- **Perineum chakra** (point between the anus and the genitals): 2 times
- **Base-of-Spine chakra** (at the coccyx): 5 times
- **Back-of-Navel chakra** (opposite the navel chakra, at the back): 1 time
- **Back Solar Plexus chakra** (opposite the front Solar Plexus chakra, at the back): 4 times
- **Back-of-Heart chakra** (opposite the heart chakra, at the back): 5 times
- **Back-of-Head chakra** (opposite *ajna* chakra, at the back of the head): 3 times. Include the alta major chakra for more advanced practitioners.
- Repeat techniques at the crown chakra: 2 times

BALANCING AND INTEGRATING THE AURAS: 2 minutes
Be aware of your entire energy system (the mental, emotional and vitality levels), and breathe slowly. After 30 seconds, recite the *mantra* 7 times to integrate and harmonize the different layers of consciousness and balance the different auras.

BALANCING YOUR MATERIAL AND SPIRITUAL CHAKRAL TRIANGLES 2 minutes

  a. Developing the objective chakral triangle: Concentrate simultaneously on the *ajna*, navel and base-of-spine chakras while breathing slowly and deeply 10 times.
  b. Developing the subjective chakral triangle: Concentrate simultaneously on the crown, forehead and heart chakras while breathing slowly and deeply 10 times.

STORING ALCHEMIZED ENERGY: 3 minutes
Concentrate on the navel center and breathe slowly and deeply for 4 minutes. The navel centers (including minor navel chakras around the major navel chakra) act as an alchemizer and storer of energy for the aura.

RELEASING EXCESS ENERGY AND SPIRITUAL BLESSING SERVICE: 3 minutes
The entire meditation brings so much positive energy beyond your normal auric capacity. Therefore, it is healthier and safer to release the excess by blessing it out to chosen recipients like family, co-workers and friends. For more advanced esoteric practitioners, you can choose global projects to help transform or empower through your blessings. The release of energy can be done through your hands, or you can use your entire aura to bless. Just imagine the recipients of blessings in miniature in front of you, then release your good intentions accompanied by the blessings through your hands or aura. This ritual can be done for 3-5 minutes.

CLOSING: 1 minute
You may close properly by expressing gratitude to your Soul, Divine Guides or Spiritual Teacher.

PRECAUTION:
1. This meditation is not recommended for those with vices of smoking, alcohol and recreational drugs and people with hypertension, heart ailments, glaucoma, cancer, AIDS and other life-threatening conditions.
2. Best results can be achieved if you do 5-minute exercises before and after the meditation.
3. Do not eat 3 hours before this meditation.
4. Do not drink cold drinks within an hour after this meditation. Cold drinks after meditation can affect your voice, especially with mantric practices.
5. Do not take a bath at least 3 hours after this meditation.
6. Eating heavy meals after advanced meditation when your energy is circulating rapidly is not recommended. Not eating for at least 1 hour after meditation is suggested. A vegetarian diet is recommended for more advanced meditation like this one.
7. Do not meditate in a physically or energetically dirty environment like a highly stressed area or places where people are participating in vices like smoking.

This meditation is powerful for beginners, but it is very safe and effective if you follow the guidelines and observe the precautions properly.

Using the Divine Alchemy Meditation, Level 1 CD to guide your meditation brings different effects and energy because each step and mantric technique is guided by me, so it is easy to use.

The chakral triangles of objectivity and subjectivity are the keys to balancing your material and spiritual life. This special method activates and harmonizes your qualities of power, love and light and is a great technique for both Eastern and Western meditators. It offers you development with one foot in Heaven and one foot on Earth.

I am a certified yoga instructor with an Indian-style lineage and trained at one of the most prestigious yoga centers in the United States. I also have more than 20 years of experience as a trained healthcare provider, which over-developed my concrete mind.

I meditated for more than 10 years, but my experiences were limited to feeling good and revitalization. I never had deep, illuminating experiences. I never saw light during my meditations, and I assumed that I was just too much of a concrete thinker to ever be able to experience what my yoga trainers called samadhi.

That was before I found a meditation CD called Divine Alchemy Meditation that turned out to be 42 minutes that changed everything. I had a powerful awakening. I felt a dense fluid rising through my spine. When I surrendered to the experience, I felt an explosion of light – like an orgasm around my heart. This experience changed my life!

Now, I follow this guided meditation every Wednesday. It not only awakened the seven chakras I learned during yoga training, but also five more that I never heard about before. The meditation's techniques are complete and synthesized. The emphasis on both spiritual and material success has helped me balance both sides of my nature. I recommend this type of approach to yoga and meditation instructors from every lineage.

– L.B., Certified Yoga Instructor, Stamford, CT

CHAPTER 22

Hidden Dangers of Meditation

Every Meditator Should Know

There are so many dangers of meditation, some very esoteric and hidden. Neither meditators nor their physicians are aware that certain symptoms are triggered by "psycho-spiritual awakening". I call this "psycho-spiritual syndrome". My early mentor, MCKS, called some of its symptoms "*kundalini* syndrome".

Psycho-spiritual syndrome is triggered by the different internal forces and inner fires, which are stimulated during meditation or while practicing yoga. This affects the human energy system. The side effects of this process are currently unknown to most health-care providers, especially physicians and psychologists. Several physicians, psychologists and counselors who are my clients, co-workers and students have confirmed many of my findings.

Throughout this chapter, you will find commentaries written by real clients and students to share their experiences applying the techniques I have been researching, experimenting with and validating for over 20 years. It is my hope that these case studies will encourage meditation and yoga instructors and practitioners to experiment themselves with the strategies and methods offered in this book.

I lost more than 23 years of my life suffering from a bizarre combination of physical, energetic, emotional and psychological ailments that could not be cured by traditional allopathic methods, counseling, herbal remedies or yoga therapy. Certain yogic breathing techniques and being energized by certain healers actually exacerbated this group of symptoms.

For years, different types of doctors were unable to diagnose me properly. My symptoms included severe mood episodes, crying spells, fear, deep depression, grief, hypersensitivity to noise, light and odors, extreme cold and hot flashes, severe exhaustion, mental fatigue and reading people's thoughts, even though I didn't want to. I started to worry about my mental stability.

After trying yoga therapy using prolonged breath retention, my symptoms became even worse. I frequently saw people's auras and those of Beings in the inner world. I was also able to see my past lives and accurately predict the future.

After meeting Del Pe, the source of my issues was finally revealed to me. It all began when I was 9 and read about repeatedly squeezing the pubococcycygeus muscle (in the pubic area) in a medical book. This technique is similar to the Kegel method used by pregnant women and is also sometimes recommended for women to avoid urinary incontinence.

Upon the advice of Del Pe, I stopped the technique. No one else understood the myriad of symptoms, their cause or had insight into the appropriate solutions the way he did. Since being healed, I have studied the spiritual sciences, healing and safe meditation systems, and I now help others with similar symptoms.

- A.W., Doctor of Chiropractic, Virginia

As a physician who sees thousands of patients every year, I was frustrated by being so limited in my strategies to cure people with stress, sleep disorders, exhaustion, depression and anxiety. The drugs I can prescribe don't do well at curing the deeper roots of these common conditions, which are pervasive in France. I traveled to five countries in search of alternative approaches to augment my medical practice. I found one complete complementary medicine method, which produced miraculous results by combining Inner Renewal Meditation and energy healing techniques that really work fast and with long-lasting benefits. I studied Del Pe's Inner Powers Healing Science, and I recommend his integrated healing and meditation method to healthcare providers and patients. Now, my patients experience wholeness and are filled with smiles when they leave the clinic where I use both medical practices and this effective natural healing method.

- Dr. A. F., France

Based on more than two decades of studying, researching, validating and teaching healing, meditation, yoga, martial arts and the Eastern wisdom philosophies, I have seen certain dangers and side effects of meditation and yoga repeatedly, some of which my early spiritual mentors had mentioned to me as well.

Traditional behavioral management methods I learned during more than 30 years of professional experience and studying for four graduate degrees, including a doctorate in psychology, did not adequately prepare me to assist people who displayed psycho-spiritual syndrome triggered by spiritual practices. I have encountered in my patients clusters of symptoms like hypersensitivity to emotional stimulus, uncontrollable body twitching, premonitions and feeling contaminated after sex, especially with partners who smoke or drink. I tried all possible traditional approaches, but in vain. It was only after I studied Del Pe's healing methodologies and meditation techniques, that I became effective in dealing with my patients' constellation of psycho-spiritual symptoms effectively. I don't know of any book or strategy that offers such a comprehensive and fast approach.

- S.A., Ph.D, Ed.S., MA, LCDC, LMFC, Texas

Having an opportunity to heal thousands of clients internationally, including yogis, gurus, lamas and advanced meditators, I have noted some syndromes or repeated groups of signs that are related to meditation and yogic practice, leading to certain side effects, some recognized by their physicians and some unresolved by current healthcare methods. Since there are so many cases and variations, let's focus on general evaluation, syndrome classifications and the immediate solutions that have worked to solve the se dangers. There are several groupings:

GROUPINGS OF HIDDEN DANGERS OF MEDITATION

- **PSYCHO-SPIRITUAL:** These affect emotional, mental and spiritual aspects of the practitioner, including the psychic nature.
- **PHYSICAL AND VITALITY:** These affect the physical, chemical, neurological and vitality aspects.
- **WRONG COMBINATION OR SEQUENCE OF MEDITATION OR YOGA TECHNIQUES:** This can affect meditators on multiple levels.
- **PRE-DISPOSED DANGERS FOR ORIENTAL AND OCCIDENTAL MEDITATORS:** Eastern and Western meditation and yoga practitioners have their own sets of inherent dangers.
- **MORE ESOTERIC DANGERS:** Anything very hidden or unknown and factors beyond the mind

PSYCHO-SPIRITUAL ISSUES

There are five major psycho-spiritual issues:

- Psychic syndrome
- Spacey meditator syndrome or yogic syndrome
- Mindlessness syndrome
- Karmic purging syndrome
- Dangers of personality powers

Let's study each issue and their solutions in detail.

Psychic Syndrome

This syndrome is a group of symptoms diagnosed by physicians or psychologists as paranoia, hallucination, being insane or other strange combinations of physical and psychological problems. These symptoms are sometimes short-term and sometimes chronic. Meditation practitioners experiencing this syndrome hear inner sounds and voices, see different colored lights clairvoyantly with their eyes open or closed and see a different world and existence. These people can't shut this off, and in psychically dirty places, they can perceive negative presences and demons or monsters.

> My clairvoyance and other psychic faculties opened up just prior to starting on a more advanced spiritual path. I enjoyed the new powers, but found I could not shut them off. I was constantly "seeing" and intuiting instances of violence and negativity all around me, as well as more positive events. I read people's thoughts and intentions automatically, including their pain. This was a very negative experience, to be able to sense and empathize with people's suffering every day. It was only through some meditations and self-healing practices, as well as awareness about the dangers of opening psychic faculties through Del Pe's book, Inner Powers to Maximize Your Performance, that enabled me to control my faculties and apply them in higher service to a bigger cause.
>
> - W. K., Editor, New York

Many people with psychic syndrome have insomnia because of what they experience psychically while sleeping.

More advanced meditators who understand more about what they see in the inner realm become obsessed with the "inner light" and the extra "inner sight" accessing these scenes of "heavenly movies" in the higher invisible world.

Some more advanced people with psychic syndrome are almost always in ecstasy and out of body watching the inner world. Thus, they become introverts or recluses. The mystical and Bhakti meditators tend to be more affected by this than other practitioners. My early mentor, MCKS, used to call this "mystical syndrome".

EVALUATION OF PSYCHIC SYNDROME

Typical mystical and heart-centered practitioners have very stimulated psychic centers, especially the solar plexus, heart, forehead and crown chakras . Also, their auras are very sensitive and empathic with any type of stimulation, whether it is Soul light, *kundalini* awakening, excessive pranic circulation, other people's energy or environmental forces. Their so-called "weird experiences" after meditation are more of an awakening and stimulation of the inner powers and qualities they already have. They are not crazy. Their ability to see the light of the aura or the capabilities of tuning in to people's negativity and the negative elements of the environment are just psychic faculties.

I heal and mentor many advanced children who have psychic abilities, but were given drugs to shut these abilities off because their pediatricians, teachers and parents don't understand their extra abilities and faculties. A good demonstration of this phenomenon is the borderline tendencies shown in the films, "A Beautiful Mind" and "Suspect Zero". Remote viewers, or so-called "astral travelers", have issues along this line.

The awakening of the *kundalini* fire and Divine light with the application of meditation and certain spiritual practices burns the veils and filters that serve as the curtain between the physical world and the inner world. When these "energetic shields" are damaged, purified or burned (see Figure 11, page 92), the person can see clairvoyantly, which can result in conditions similar to symptoms of paranoia, hallucination and hypochondria. For an untrained psychic, it's hard to distinguish between real and unreal.

If you have the power to read minds and feelings and most of the people around you are negative or abrasive and stressed, how will you live your life? It can be miserable. Some meditators with these faculties suffer through empathy – like Spiderman or the "precogs" in the movie, "Minority Report".

SOLUTIONS FOR PSYCHIC SYNDROME

It's good to have ready-made proactive solutions for unexplainable circumstances that might plague millions of incoming psychic children and awakening meditators. Here's how I have solved psychic syndrome in my own students and clients:

1. Stop the meditation and yoga practices. This allows the person to ground back and adjust their internal and energy conditions.

2. Do 25-50 squats daily (see page 178) to strengthen will-power and physical connection to the Earth. The squats activate the base-of-spine, navel, sex and mid-brow (*ajna*) chakras. These centers will ground a person physically. Psychic types tend to have less will-power and more emotional sensitivity.

   PRECAUTION: This is not recommended for people with knee problems. Pregnant women need to do squats slowly with proper inhalation as they go up and exhalation as they go down.

3. Stomp your feet on the ground as if you were marching or jog in place for 2-3 minutes. The chakras of the soles of the feet are the energy connectors and roots to the Earth. Increasing the flow of Earth ground *prana* neutralizes the excess effect of Divine light and grounds the meditator back. This technique is also good for children with the spacey type of ADD.

4. Release all the extra energy from meditation or yoga by blessing the positive energy out through your hands or directly from your aura (see page 268). Pick a target, like a good cause to bless. When the "Divine overload" is released, the "Divine drunkenness" is solved.

5. Do a lot of gym work with weights, and avoid yogic breathing techniques or postures and *mudras* until things are back to normal. Making yourself more physical diminishes the psychic syndrome.

6. Go to a good energy healer and ask him or her to deactivate or partially inhibit your solar plexus, forehead chakras and sensitive upper chakras. Then have them activate your *ajna*, throat and base-of-spine. But be selective in choosing your healer. (Refer to the directory in Chapter 25). If you are a vegetarian, go to a vegetarian healer. If you don't have vices like smoking, never go to a healer who smokes. Discriminate.

7. Consult your physician or psychologist, and find an advanced healer or spiritual mentor for a second opinion or guidance.

8. Avoid going to psychically negative places, including energetically dirty public places like bars where there is a lot of smoking and drinking. You can get contaminated.

9. Study and analyze what spiritual practices or meditations tend to worsen the condition. Avoid them until your abnormal situation is solved.

10. If you wish to develop your psychic faculties safely, study my book, *Inner Powers to Maximize Your Performance* and understand how to use your talent primarily for healing and spiritual service. Know how to shield your energies, like crossing your arms and legs when you are in an energetically dirty place or with stressed people.

In my path of meditation and spiritual development, one of my issues has been difficulty connecting with people due to my psychic faculties. I have realized that even though I have great capacity for emotional intelligence and magnetism to connect, I keep it shut off because when I connect just a little bit, my heart literally hurts and too many pains and sufferings of the world around me flood into my system. It's like being a sponge in an ocean of negative feelings. I had trouble protecting myself and my aura from being contaminated by others and the environment. Del Pe's shielding techniques and will-power development programs really helped me enjoy my spiritual life without suffering.

- D.G., Corporate Trainer, Texas

SPACEY MEDITATOR SYNDROME OR YOGIC SYNDROME

Many yogis and meditators suffer from this, but they take it for granted because they think it is normal to be on cloud nine after you meditate. This is desirable for people who are in the Himalayan caves or Indian yoga centers, called *ashrams*, or for contemplative nuns and lamas in religious monasteries. But this is not good for professionals, executives and parents like most of you who need to go back to work and make sure that you are not spacey or out of body when you drive, which can cause an accident!

The reasons for spaciness are:

1. Most yogis and meditators practice abstraction meditation, which withdraws the consciousness from the physical senses to inner consciousness. Thus one gets out of body or is spiritually withdrawn. If this is done daily for an extended period of time, one becomes a permanent space cadet.

2. Meditators and healers who are always using their heart and crown centers and less of their lower centers, especially the base-of-spine chakra, are susceptible to lightheadedness and being spaced out. Bhakti yoga and devotional-type practitioners who always connect with and tune in to their guru or spiritual idol are always abstracted by the very high-frequency aura of the teacher. This state feels great, and they prefer to be in that condition rather than face real world situations and going back to work.

   Excessive abstraction meditation (if done daily) may also result in impracticality, financial depletion and difficulty or indifference to material life because of the devitalization and imbalance of the base-of-spine chakra.

3. Yoga and meditation employ body postures, breathing techniques, body locks, hand sealing *mudras* and finger gestures that almost always facilitate the upward flow of energy to bring it up to the Soul and upper chakras. These are:

- Index finger-thumb *mudra* (*gyana mudra*)
- Most *asanas* and meditation postures like lotus, semi-lotus, adept posture, etc. – anything that reverses the soles of the feet to face upward
- Throat lock and abdominal compression upward lock
- Many breathing techniques that hyperventilate the body
- Sacred *mantrams* that increase the vibration of the energy bodies when done excessively and daily, which tends to make the meditator spaced out

4. Practitioners who have small lower centers, especially the base-of-spine chakra, and a small Earth connection to ground *prana* through the soles-of-the-feet chakras
5. Too much fasting and lack of protein and minerals in your diet

The side effects of being spacey are:

1. It can cause accidents and clumsiness.
2. Forgetfulness and inability to focus
3. Disorientation and indecisiveness
4. Financial and material troubles caused by not being able to connect to material life's responsibilities and work
5. Lack of speed in finishing goals and projects
6. Inability to express correctly and communicate properly
7. Unconscious escape from real-life situations, like not solving existing problems and abnegating solutions to others
8. Loss of appetite in many forms: eating, sex, money, etc. leading to impracticality

Thanks to Del Pe, who coached and mentored me, I was able to avoid financial bankruptcy. I am the CEO of the largest newspaper on the east coast of Mexico, as well as two industrial corporations. I had practiced traditional yoga and meditation for many years. Over time, I found myself moving away from my responsibilities managing my companies. I wanted to spend more and more time in my mountain cabin rather than in my city office. I almost lost the businesses I built up over 20 years and also my marriage, which I had enjoyed for a decade. I switched to Del Pe's methods because they enable me to stay materially rooted and spiritually free.

— G. R., newspaper CEO and industrialist, Mexico

Being "out there", having an "out-of-body experience" or being in a spacey altered state of consciousness is a great place to be — in fact, that's my inexpensive type of vacation without having to spend money on a plane ticket, but it should be enjoyed in right moderation and correct perspective that result in balanced material and spiritual achievement, not in a fanatical way.

I met a businessman who used to be a smart executive in Germany touring the foothills of the Himalayas. He never went back because he swung to the extreme by becoming a full yogi. Maybe this was good, but wouldn't it have been better to bring back that extra dose of inner experiences and power to society and make a big difference in the modern world where the real battleground and test of inner development and peace is?

I'm sure many people who read this will not agree. I almost did this myself. Tired of traveling internationally to help people, I almost decided to escape into the Himalayan caves where two of my early spiritual mentors were enjoying their peace. But then I thought that we can flower where we are planted in the cities.

I saw a joke in a yoga magazine that illustrated the importance of not getting too spacey:

Too much chanting Om with the index finger-thumb mudra in a lotus position with an unshaved beard and unwashed robes results in — hOMelessness!

This is a good joke, but it is happening to many spiritual people today who are ungrounded.

SOLUTIONS FOR SPACEY MEDITATOR OR YOGIC SYNDROME

1. Do many deep squats daily or at least 25-35 times, especially after meditation. This will ground you more. It also activates your base-of-spine centers, *ajna*, navel and sex chakras.
2. Stomp your feet repeatedly 20-30 times against the ground. Barefoot on soil is better to absorb ground or Earth *prana* and to establish more of a connection to the physical Earth. Jogging in place is also a good thing to do after meditation, not only to ground, but also for energy circulation.
3. Body squeeze: Stand straight and inhale to half your lung capacity. Squeeze your entire body for 5-10 seconds, then slowly release your breath. Concentrate on the soles of your feet as you exhale slowly.
   PRECAUTION: Pregnant women and people with hypertension, heart ailments, glaucoma, bleeding problems, cancer and hernia should not do this. Consult your physician first.
4. Get an advanced healer to activate your base-of-spine center to be slightly bigger than the crown chakra. Choose the right healer (see Chapter 25).
5. Go for more gym work with more muscle-building.
6. Take karate or chigong classes to increase your physical skills and concentration. Choose good teachers who are not violent.
7. Go for more protein and minerals, especially if you're a vegetarian who does yogic fasting.
8. Meditate without closing your eyes by using the half-closed eyes method. Stop abstraction or yogic meditation or any spacey-type practices until the abnormal conditions are adjusted.
9. Consult a holistic healthcare provider and a good physician and psychologist if you have access to these systems.
10. Stop using the index finger-thumb *mudra* (*gyana mudra*) and

yogic postures that reverse your feet to face upward. These positions withdraw your material roots further and bring most of the meditation energy upward.

11. Change your hand *mudra* to the middle finger-thumb *mudra*. In the use of the *dhayani* or meditation *mudra*, shift it to the variation where the middle finger and thumb are connected (see page 153).

12. Communicate with grounded people and go back to setting your goals and prioritizing your urgent-important activities. Lessen meditation and yoga time in the meantime. Go back to work with deliberate intention. Push against the spacey habits that are already becoming yogic syndrome.

Excessively materialistic people need to swing to the more spiritual practices that will give them balance, and the very spacey mystical and spiritual types of people need to swing back to the material side to be in the center. The key is moderation and balance.

For meditators and yogis who are close to physical death, it is excellent to be in the yogic syndrome mode. But for younger people and growing professionals and executives who still have a lot to offer to physical and social life, you are needed to make a big difference in the material world. Bring your light back to the workplace.

MINDLESSNESS SYNDROME

I know some PhDs and very educated people who used to be very grounded, concrete and smart. After doing yoga and meditation for a few years, they suddenly lost their mental focus and aptitudes. They are now unable to discriminate and make quick, simple decisions.

At first, I wondered why such highly educated people were falling short in their mental processes. You could blame it on Alzheimer's, Parkinson's or neurological disorders, but they are still in their 40s. I later found out that they are practicing "mindlessness" or "going beyond the mind" meditation fanatically. These practices encourage not using the mind, even for simple decisions, but just intuiting and being aware with a perspective that the universe will tell you what you need. This isn't a very practical or economical approach to modern life.

These are the causes of mindlessness syndrome:

1. Wrong interpretation of meditation or yogic teachings: In meditations that teach you how to go beyond the mind, like abstraction yogic meditation and Zen meditation, instructors should include the guideline that:
   - It is during the yogic or Zen meditation that you render yourself mindless or go beyond the mind, but when you have to back to work and back to life, the mind has to be used! Try being mindless when you are driving 65 miles per hour (approximately 137 kilometers per hour) or negotiating with a client.

2. Fanatical teachings from fanatical teachers who think that the mind is the "slayer of the real" (true in some sense) and that intuition and instincts are more important than the mind: There's a time when these spiritual faculties are more useful, but most often, at our level of development, the mind is one of the most useful tools for material and spiritual growth.

3. Yogic syndrome, that spacey by-product of meditation and yoga that can also render practitioners mindless or "not there"

4. Some types of practitioners, like the Bhakti or devotional types, tend to use their emotions, psychic faculties and intuitional nature, which results in bypassing of mental development. They don't want to think or engage in mental details and meticulous mathematical or scientific processes. For the Bhakti or devotional types, their meditation practices might cause them to be too subjective without objectivity and concrete thinking. Their throat and *ajna* chakras are also underdeveloped.

5. Depletion of sexual energy starving the creative mental energy: Some of the Tantric *kundalini* yogis of the lower type

engage in uncontrolled sexual practices leading to excessive release of sexual energy instead of transmuting it. This depletes their vitality and *kundalini*, so the required vitality for the brain and upper chakras is drained and wasted. The mind becomes impotent and loses creativity.

SOLUTIONS FOR MINDLESSNESS SYNDROME

1. Modify wrong interpretation of the Eastern philosophies like Zen and traditional yoga. For maximum use of the mind outside the realm of meditation, challenge old beliefs and increase your understanding of the teachings and practices of Zen and traditional yoga.
2. Get another opinion from other teachers, and learn new techniques to integrate the use of the mind with emotional intelligence and wisdom (See Chapter 25). You can develop at least five intelligences to have a more integrated perspective of life.
3. Do the grounding techniques the spacey meditators were encouraged to do in an earlier chapter to do to ground back (see pages 126, 137, 209, 236-237).
4. If you lack mental aptitudes because you prefer the love-centered approach, challenge yourself to learn Jnana yoga. I have included some techniques in Chapter 13, pages 238-240.
5. Study the chapters on mastering your mental powers in my book, *Inner Powers to Maximize Your Performance*.
6. Conserve, and learn to transmute your sexual energy to revitalize the brain and the mind.
7. Be with mentally active people and harness the habit of using the mind as an instrument of success. Mental creativity and sharpness are contagious.
8. Activate your mind by focusing on the *ajna* and throat chakras while breathing slowly for 5 minutes. This will increase your mental activity immediately if you do it daily for a week.

If you are a Jnana yogi or mental type person, it would be good to practice mindlessness meditation more, but don't lose the mental faculty at work. Balance is important.

KARMIC PURGING SYNDROME

This is common among people who are on the spiritual path. They complain that before they set foot onto the path, their lives were smooth-sailing with no hassles. Then they attend several workshops on meditation, yoga and healing as well as spiritual retreats, where things start to stir up and small problems become crises. Their business becomes more difficult, and then money problems start.

These people claim that before their spiritual awakening, they felt better and their body didn't have any troubles. Now that they are eating cleaner food, meditating and chanting *mantrams,* health problems tend to accelerate and sometimes there are catharses, including more conflicts. Does this sound familiar?

> *I already had some tendencies towards conflicts in my professional life, but when I started meditating and bringing more will-power into my system, I had many blow-ups with family members as well. I was purging and healing years of having repressed my feelings with my family. This was a painful, cathartic process. The more I did yoga and breathing techniques, the more I engaged in conflicts and became irritable. Fortunately, I found the Del Pe's Inner Powers Healing Method, and I became balanced after a few weeks of using its meditations.*
> - J.C., Assistant Vice President, Santander Securities, San Juan, PR

What are the potential causes and triggers of karmic purging syndrome?

1. Divine light is not just an inspirational substance. It is also a purifying and transforming light. Purification entails a process of purging, cleansing and destroying old, obsolete patterns. It

also reveals hidden negativity and "negative karmic accounts" to be healed and balanced in relationship with others. Thus, meditation, bringing purification through the action of Divine light, causes much strife, struggle and so-called crises and pain in the personality. This is more for adjustment to make the personality better spiritual equipment for the Soul to express its higher purpose and goals.

2. *Kundalini* awakening exacerbates both positive and negative habits. We are supposed to be "more holy" when we meditate or do spiritual practices. How come sometimes it is the reverse? Before the "holy state of life" happens, the cleaning up comes first, then empowerment, then enlightenment! That's how a Soul helps a person walk through the holy ground. The problem is that the hardware (body) and the software (energy body, emotions and mind) come with "karmic viruses and program bugs", plus inherited past baggage and negative stuff. The action of the *kundalini* fire burning our energetic impurities has by-products and side effects.

Also, the chakras people are born with have both good and bad in them due to contamination from the ancient past. As we mentioned before, the *kundalini* serves as a fertilizer for the chakras. This is sometimes converted into the acceleration of the the growth of the "weeds" rather than the "flowers" in one's consciousness and energy system. This can cause or trigger the surfacing of impurities in the body called diseases. Accelerated negative karma is usually labeled as bad luck. It is actually energetic purification.

With the *kundalini* more active, negative thoughts and feelings we have created in the aura are also fertilized, thus, they materialize as events even though we already forgot about them. The thoughts and feelings we create do not die fast or fade away because we don't remember them anymore. They usually stay waiting to be harvested – in whatever way we have sown them.

326 HIDDEN DANGERS OF MEDITATION AND YOGA

I never expected when I started meditating that the negative effects of gossiping about people's misery and criticizing people all my life, due to insecurities and negative inherited tendencies of my parents, would be revealed and accelerated as mishaps. I learned that these negative habits were like boomerangs that kept creating loneliness and conflict in my relationships. When I started watching my thoughts and words by applying the self-healing strategies, meditations and virtue development introduced by Del Pe's teachings, my relationships started to flow better.

- H. L., School Administrator, Switzerland

SOLUTIONS FOR KARMIC PURGING SYNDROME

1. Don't stop purging or cleaning up. If the Soul is constipated at the personality level, it is better that the poisons get out than to stay and spoil the consciousness. But you need to do damage control. Use meditations and breathing techniques to continue with the release of these energies of crisis or health and emotional problems. Keep releasing!

2. Continue with your life and maintain your energy and stamina to be able to cope effectively. Go to the gym for a workout and/or use the Beat Your Fatigue and Stress Fast program.

3. Stop your advanced meditation, especially if it is an esoteric meditation that awakens the *kundalini* and Divine light further. That is the last thing you need at this juncture. Do more physical exercises instead, and take nature walks.

4. Lessen your contact with negative people, abstain from going to negative environments and don't rush into major decisions that result from conflicts or anger, especially with irreversible decisions. Be careful not to be impulsive or reactive.

5. Study your crisis carefully and learn the lessons behind the problem. Adjust to the situation properly. Wait and see about better options. Be patient. Be objective and practical in your approach. Use a good expert, coach or consultant for difficult or crucial matters.

6. Learn virtues required to overcome the situation like forgiveness, love without attachment and moving out of lower passion.

7. Donate to a good cause, especially related to your particular condition, and dedicate the good karma or good grace from your donation to neutralize your crisis or problem.

8. Release excess energy every time you meditate and bless others who are in need of healing or transformation. As you show compassion, you'll receive compassion and help. Just be persistent with your effort.

9. Use some of your time for community service or any project that adds value to life and society. Dedicate the good karma of helping others to neutralize the negative events in your life.

10. Understand that spiritual growth requires purification, and purification needs a process and time. Patient persistence is your healer. As the saying goes, time heals.

11. Avoid breath retention techniques and use of the root, abdominal compression and throat locks.

12. Study the techniques in my *Inner Powers to Maximize Your Performance* and *From Success to Fulfillment* books to maximize your performance with integrated solutions. They offer a complete practical guide to live healthier, be happier, work smarter and grow faster — in a wiser way!

13. Choose an esoteric healer who understands the *kundalini* system and color energies in healing. Karmic purging syndrome is a special case that needs special advanced healing. See Chapter 25 to find an esoteric healer who's right for you.

14. Consult your physician for the physicalized aspects of your health problems. Always get a second or third opinion. Discriminate.

15. Find a good spiritual lineage or school, and study with a qualified instructor or mentor. There's no substitute for higher spiritual training. With a lineage or mentor, expensive mistakes and delays of time can be avoided.

*Before meeting a coach-healer trained by Del Pe, I was reading every-
thing I could get my hands on about inner powers and spirituality. I
was doing it indiscriminately and making mistakes because I wasn't
learning techniques from a sense of service. Rather, I was intrigued by
having more power. The types of information offered by the coach-
healer I worked with helped me understand the responsibilities that
come with greater power. I discovered that you could do more in life
with fewer mistakes with the help of a spiritual mentor. Now, I am
able to align to a great purpose and world service empowered by
powerful but safe meditation techniques.*

- Jana, Writer, Budapest, Hungary

DANGERS OF PERSONALITY POWERS

The stimulation and fertilization of the meditator's character by
action of the *kundalini* fire unleashes his/her strengths and weaknesses to a higher degree of power. Here are some of the powers
and qualities that are exaggerated and exacerbated:

1. Certain psychic powers, including but not limited to clairvoy-
    ance, clairaudience, telepathy and precognitive faculties.
    These can be used positively or negatively depending on the
    level of the practitioner's spiritual and heart development.
    There is a real point of possible danger of misusing the
    increased power without character-building.

2. Increased sensitivity to impression through the auras or the
    nervous and limbic system. This is another area of tension.
    The sensitive meditator can empathize too much with other
    people's or environmental negativity, thus rendering him or
    her either too involved and bothered or helpless to aid with
    so much suffering and chaos in the world. This type of per-
    son will not have peace of mind. In the movie, "Suspect
    Zero", the remote viewer psychic couldn't stand the pressure
    of psychically seeing crime everywhere.

    Also, people who are too sensitive sometimes don't know
    how to discern whether the negative thoughts or emotions
    they sense are theirs or from other people or the environ-

ment. They get so confused with their reactions to stimuli. This affects their relationships with their families, especially if the spouse is a smoker, alcoholic or very stressed. If the meditator is vegetarian and their family is not, they get affected with the different type of energy from the members. This variation of spiritual development and energy make-up creates difficulties, resulting in separation or divorce. Or, these sensitive people become anti-social or aloof, not because they don't like people, but because they don't want to be a sponge absorbing people's negative issues and vibrations. Many women meditators and an increasing number of children are like this.

3. Misuse of intelligence and mental sharpness: When you talk to people who are "mentally slow", and you have an acute, sharp mind, you sometimes get bored and instead of looking at the person with good eye contact to listen, you face somewhere else looking at something else. Then the person gets mad at you because they think you are not listening. Your mind is probably just too fast. You lose interest and get impatient with people who are slow or less intelligent. Or you tend to finish what people are saying because you can predict their point so fast and you can even pick up when they're telling a lie. This is good and bad at the same time.

It is not positive when you condescend or belittle people. Arrogance and mental pride are not assets. They push people out and make relationships sour. They bar effective communication. Meditation techniques fertilize our mental growth and make us sharper and smarter, but the lesson of wrong pride is to be humbled. Be careful of this.

Another point is that when the mind is so sharp and creative, we don't discriminate when our reasons are just alibis or when our creative genius justifies even wrong things with manipulative explanations that look seemingly correct. Pride is a veil in itself that can cause expensive mistakes because of a blind spot of the mind.

4. Increased will-power and stamina: It is an exceptional quality to have will-power and stamina, but if you have these too much, resulting in being excessively bossy, then it is not good. If these extra powers are not balanced with love, compassion and conscience, they can be a menace to our growth. A person with this imbalance will have more enemies than friends. That's the danger. This will-power to manifest goals should be accompanied by love and wisdom. Likewise, too much love without will-power is harmful. It also creates lopsided personality power.

SOLUTIONS FOR DANGERS OF PERSONALITY POWERS

1. Study yourself and your personality strengths and weaknesses. Overcome the weaknesses, including pride or inflated ego because of insecurities.
2. Always use personality power for good purposes guided by conscience and service-orientedness. Use meditations that develop the heart if you are too willful and over-critical.
3. Do not belittle or condescend people who are less developed or are underprivileged in the material world. You don't want to be put into their position when the Law of Karma (Cause and Effect) fulfills itself: What goes around, comes around.
4. Study Chapter 7 in my *Inner Powers to Maximize Your Performance* book to train yourself in how to use your talents for greater good.
5. It's best to study with a spiritual mentor to have higher guidance in the use of power. See Chapter 25 to find one who is right for you. But remember this rule: The secrets of handling greater powers are through the virtues of benevolence, altruism and wisdom.
6. Find a group that can balance your qualities of power, love and light.

PHYSICAL AND VITALITY SIDE EFFECTS

There are ten major physical and vitality issues:

- Over-awakening of the lower chakras and contamination
- "Spiritually-fried" meditators and yogis
- Internal coldness felt from inside the body
- Jitteriness, anxiety and nervousness
- Feeling of physical hardness, brittleness or atrophy accompanied by internal tension and energetic strain
- Feeling of exhaustion and weakening of the body
- Oversensitivity to physical light, noise, smells and negative energy of the environment
- Pain during and after meditation or yoga, especially the back or spine
- Body jolts and twitching
- Side effects on certain health conditions

Many of these signs and health issues are common to advanced martial artists, meditators, lamas and yogis. I've even seen these conditions in many gurus and Tantric yoga practitioners and have healed many of them in Asia, India, South and Central America, Europe and the United States.

Let's look at the specific symptoms and their causes.

OVER-AWAKENING OF THE LOWER CHAKRAS AND CONTAMINATION

These people are "over-heating" all the time, even in cold weather. They also suffer from skin rashes and they have poor bowel movement. They have excessive awakening of the lower types of *prana* and the *kundalini*, particularly the red colors that energetically burn the meditator.

SOLUTIONS FOR OVER-AWAKENING OF THE LOWER CHAKRAS AND CONTAMINATION

1. Stop practices that awaken the lower chakras and *kundalini*, especially the holding of the breath after exhalation. This prolonged breath control over-awakens the "heat" of the chakras, especially the lower centers. Martial artists who have this problem should stop their practices, especially squeezing the perineum and doing root locks.

2. Tantric sexual alchemists with these symptoms should stop their rituals and techniques that over-stimulate the sexual energy and sacred fires.

3. Practitioners eating meat who have these side effects should become vegetarians. Meat energy, especially red meat and pork, has lower frequencies with a very reddish-colored vibration. This energy is grosser and tends to block the meridians and exacerbate these over-heating conditions. Cleaner food, as in a vegetarian diet, is a must for advanced meditators and Tantric *kundalini* practitioners.

    I experimented with eating chicken after an advanced meditation once and ended up with skin rashes, a heavy and sluggish feeling, red eyes and high internal heat for days. I had to heal myself and do many physical exercises to decongest and detoxify my energy bodies. I also took salt water baths (1 cup of salt for every gallon of water) for 3 consecutive days. You can try this yourself: Soak in this salt water solution for 30 minutes and then rinse as usual.

4. Regularly drinking aloe vera juice and chlorophyll to help detoxify the body. These drinks are now available in natural health markets.

I never had any intention of becoming a vegetarian, but when I started doing yoga, my body just didn't want meat anymore. I got sick anytime I ate it, especially when I ate pork or other meat after meditating.

- T. K., Nurse, Ireland

"SPIRITUALLY-FRIED" MEDITATORS AND YOGIS

These issues manifest as hardening or atrophying side effects of the body. Whereas excessive awakening of the *kundalini* causes overheating, insomnia, being over-sexed, hypertension, skin rashes, crying spells and abnormal growth of cells in the body, there are several side effects of spiritually-fried meditators and yogis. Let's study each one.

INTERNAL COLDNESS FELT FROM INSIDE THE BODY
(Even When It's Hot Outside!)

This is caused by the excess of spiritual energy or Soul light, which has a cooling effect on the body.

In these cases, people are relatively healthy and don't have anemia or depletion that can trigger a cold feeling or fatigue. The crown chakra is very activated, far more so than the solar plexus or other lower chakras. The sex chakra may be weak or depleted.

SOLUTIONS FOR INTERNAL COLDNESS FELT FROM INSIDE THE BODY

1. Stop any practice that awakens and activates the crown chakra, including long prayers or mantric recitations.
2. Awaken the lower chakras by doing 30 squats twice a day. This will make the base-of-spine chakra bigger. This chakra has a lot of red energy, which stimulates internal heat in the body.
3. Reduce or stop releasing sexual energy through orgasm until you recover from these side effects, and practice moderation in your sex life.
4. Get a healer to activate most of the lower chakras, especially the base-of-spine, sex and navel chakras. (See Chapter 25 to find an appropriate healer.)
5. Take wild Red Korean or Chinese ginseng, and Chinese reishi mushroom. Their natural forms have red energy to warm your body internally.
6. In extreme cases, the crown chakra can be inhibited to a slightly smaller size to decrease the amount of Divine light entering the body through advanced meditation methods.

JITTERINESS, ANXIETY AND NERVOUSNESS

When a meditator's energy is too high from meditation, and if the emotional body, especially at the solar plexus area, is over-activated, the results are feelings of anxiety, nervousness and being jittery. The nervous system's energy is also high-strung and over-stimulated. I have observed that many advanced yogis and meditators do long meditations with no techniques to release excess energy like blessing and healing. They don't usually exercise after long hours of yoga or meditation.

I have also observed that there are cycles that affect their emotional vitality and purging of negative karma every year. Based on my study and validations of ancient wisdom teachings, people have seven cycles of the personality every year and seven Soul cycles every seven years. The period wherein meditators have more of these karmic purging symptoms is 208-260 days after their birthday and the last two weeks up to their birthday.

The person's emotional body is more stimulated, especially the solar plexus and sex chakras, during this time. If the emotional and sexual energy are not expressed properly and/or not used or transmuted to the upper chakras, this congestion causes the disturbing signs of jitteriness, anxiety and nervousness. Some meditators also experience these same symptoms from eating meat and fish. They get congested and contaminated.

SOLUTIONS FOR JITTERINESS, ANXIETY AND NERVOUSNESS

1. Release excess energy through blesssing techniques (pages 268).
2. Do physical exercise, especially the 8-step Internal Stamina Exercise (pages 186-188).
3. Do inner breathing techniques (page 200) to externalize emotional congestion.
4. Become a vegetarian if you are doing advanced meditations and yoga. Meat energy and fish are coarser and easily clog the meridians and chakras, especially the solar plexus.

5. Avoid stressful situations: Stress jams the solar plexus and negatively affects the nervous system and endocrine glands.

Feeling of Physical Hardness, Brittleness or Atrophy Accompanied by Internal Tension and Energetic Strain

These symptoms are caused by excessive will-power substance of the Soul downloaded into the physical and etheric bodies from advanced meditation, especially techniques that penetrate the will substance of the Soul at the *atmic* level (see Figure 9, page 83). This can last for weeks until the condition is normalized.

Solutions for Feeling of Physical Hardness, Brittleness or Atrophy

1. Stop meditating, especially advanced meditation or yogic practices, until your body has adjusted back to normal.
2. Activate the heart, navel, sex and base-of-spine chakras to awaken love, sexual and *kundalini* energy that neutralize the brittleness and willful energy. The Soul's will energy is structured like a diamond, causing the hardened and compacted brittle feeling. The physical and etheric bodies are most affected by this type of Soul energy.
3. Learn how to release by blessing with the excess energy and expel it further through jogging or physical exercises.
4. Get help from an advanced energy healer who has a good grasp about deeper esoteric philosophy and understands esoteric healing.

Feeling of Exhaustion and Weakening of the Body

One of the reasons for these symptoms in meditators and yogis is congestion or excess energy that overwhelms the body. After long hours of meditation in a yogic posture, there's a tremendous increase of energy in the different auras.

If this excess energy turns into congestion in the whole body for a long time like a day, the practitioner will feel tired or fatigued. Then because of this symptom, s/he will meditate more thinking it will improve the condition. What usually happens is that the more s/he meditates, the worse it gets. Why? Because there's more congestion, especially if a person is eating meat and meditating heavily. S/he will become even more congested.

When a meditator is involved sexually with a very "low-vibration" partner who's a good person but with no meditation practice, the meditator also gets contaminated and suffers from congestion. This excess of lower vibration triggers a feeling of exhaustion of the body.

To clarify this situation further, contamination is not just about negative energy, but also the discomfort of differences between the auric frequencies of the interacting parties. The wider the difference in frequency, the more uncomfortable it is to the higher-frequency partner.

Another issue comes when the meditator is sexually overstimulated with *kundalini* fire, which tends to produce increased sexual releases weekly. This causes exhaustion and if the condition persists untreated for a long time, it can cause paralysis or degeneration of muscles.

Solutions for Feeling of Exhaustion and Weakening of the Body

1. Do physical exercises before and after every advanced meditation and yoga technique.
2. Stop eating meat and become a vegetarian.
3. Take a salt-water bath (see page 121), with 10 drops of lavender oil, if available, 3 times a week.
4. Watch for negative contamination from your sexual partner, especially if they are smokers, alcoholics or drug users or if their diet is not compatible with yours.

Oversensitivity to Physical Light, Noise, Smells and Negative Energy of the Environment

As a meditator's aura gets more refined through meditation, sensitivity to negative vibrations from others and the environment will increase. S/he also tends to have oversensitivity to light, noise and smells. In some instances, the oversensitive meditator can even smell cigarette smoke at a distance of 100 feet (30.48 meters).

Why is this? Because the aura has expanded to a greater distance and radius, including other people's auras. For example, the particles of light in the big and expanded aura of a powerful lecturer or teacher interpenetrate the auric substance of the whole classroom. This happens with meditators as they develop.

When a meditator's energy has been re-calibrated and upgraded into more sensitive equipment, the ability to receive and process more subtle data or environmental stimulus is higher, just like a highly sensitive, high-fidelity microphone that can pick up a wide range of sound.

Another explanation of this is that in meditators, especially the mystics and Bhakti yogis (devotional, loving types), their crown, forehead, heart and solar plexus chakras are over-activated compared to the *ajna* (mental will-power and focus center) and base-of-spine (physical power and grounding) chakras. The former sets of chakras stimulate inner sensitivity and clairvoyance, especially the forehead because it regulates the limbic system in the brain, which is the controller of pain and pleasure. Sometimes it is called the emotional part of the brain mechanism. If the will-power is low and emotional energy is high, sensitivity is also high.

I have always been sensitive to cigarette smoke. However, after six years of meditation, I became even more sensitive not only to cigarette smoke, but also to people's body odor and negative energy in the environment. I can smell smokers at a distance, and I feel the pain and stress of people. Del Pe's healing and meditation seminars have taught me to energetically shield and desensitize myself by developing my will-power.

- BC, United Nations Development Program Consultant, Bogotá, Colombia, National Planning Department

SOLUTIONS FOR OVERSENSITIVITY TO PHYSICAL LIGHT, NOISE, SMELLS AND NEGATIVE ENERGY OF THE ENVIRONMENT

There are many solutions to this unpleasant experience of sensitive meditators, but the following are the most practical:

1. Activate the *ajna*, navel and base-of-spine chakras by focusing on them simultaneously and breathing slowly and deeply for 5 minutes, 3 times weekly. After 2-3 weeks of practice, assess your sensitivity. If it is normalized, discontinue the technique. If it still persists, continue doing this chakral breathing until you sense a big improvement.

2. Do 25-30 squats (see page 178) daily for 3 weeks, then gradually decrease to 2 days a week, 3 days apart. This technique increases mental will-power.

3. Don't over-focus when you smell a constant stinking smell or negative vibrations. Stay steady and will it not to distract you. Focus back on what you are doing or switch to another positive "channel" by thinking of a pleasant experience.

4. Visit a good advanced healer and suggest that s/he inhibit or de-sensitize your solar plexus chakra with light bluish-colored light. This is a color you can flow through your hand chakras by focusing on and breathing through the throat chakra. The throat chakra is the source of green and blue energies.

Pain During or After Meditation or Yoga, Especially the Back or Spine

This is not only physical pain, but also emotional pain sometimes resulting in catharsis. But in this section, we'll talk about the startling sudden pain that comes as a result of blockages of chakras and meridians.

When the *kundalini* fire is aroused and is automatically raised upward through the *sushumna* or circulated by the meditation at the back meridian, the strong onrush of this sacred fire is resisted by any blockage in its path. This causes pain or a burning sensation as a side effect. Thousands of advanced yogis and meditators in many groups suffer from this pain. The pain is real, but their gurus don't know that it is a negative side effect or that it is preventable and healable.

Most teachers accept this pain as part of growth and purification, which is true, but in my experience, it can be prevented with exercises that unblock the whole energy and chakra system like the Body Therapy and Inner Powers Meditation method.

When a meditator is emotionally blocked, the solar plexus chakra, especially at the emotional auric level, is clogged and stuck with negative energy. This can result in abdominal pain and catharsis that can last for weeks. I've helped meditators who had crying spells for weeks until they were chronically hysterical and suffered with insomnia. After several healing sessions, the symptoms stopped, and the energy blockages were removed successfully.

Solutions for Pain During or After Meditation or Yoga

1. Sufficient physical exercises like the Body Therapy Exercise or Internal Stamina Exercise to unblock and purify the energy bodies
2. Hire an advanced healer who specializes in advanced esoteric healing for *kundalini*-related pain and disorders.
3. Stop meditation and yoga practices until you understand the problem and have consulted a certified meditation or yoga instructor, holistic health practitioner or physician. If the side

effects are severe, seek immediate medical attention. Advanced healers specializing in healing pain and its origins should be hired or consulted (see Chapter 25).

4. A salt-water bath (see page 121) will help to a certain degree to decongest the aura and energy blockages.

5. Use the Inner Renewal Meditation to help release emotional and mental congestion and negative side effects in the auras and chakras.

6. Do the Synchronized Breathing Method (see page 204) to help release the emotional and mental triggers of the physical pain.

7. Create a habit of exercising before meditation like Internal Stamina Exercise or Body Therapy Exercise.

8. Get a meditation mentor to assist in identifying causes of the pain or to evaluate the type of meditation suited for your health conditions (see Chapter 25).

9. Do not awaken the *kundalini* by breath control or *pranayama* until an expert's advice is available.

Different types of meditation have different purposes and prerequisites. Sometimes practitioners are too eager to proceed to the more advanced meditations and *pranayama*. Make sure your health condition and age are taken into consideration before doing advanced meditation, not only the number of years of meditation or yoga experience.

These sudden spurts and/or periodic jolting, jerking or twitching movements of the body while meditating are a byproduct of the temporary side effects of the *kundalini* flow. They are caused by little energy restrictions in the major and minor meridians and sometimes in the middle meridian called the *sushumna*.

Rotational body movement sometimes experienced during meditation is more of a sensitive response to the upward movement of the *kundalini*, especially in people with big upper chakras and a small base-of-spine center. But the body jolts and twitching can be formed as a physical body habit and can become a daily "abnormal gesture", which is awkward for others to observe in public. I've seen clients who have these symptoms, and it's not easy to stop their body responses. In some cases, pain accompanies these body movements, but they subside after the meditation.

SOLUTIONS FOR BODY JOLTS AND TWITCHING

1. Develop the lower chakras, especially the base-of-spine chakra to ground and strengthen the body. 20-30 squats daily are helpful to increase the lower energy root to the Earth.
2. Activate the base-of-spine chakra by breathing deeply and slowly while focusing on the chakra. This technique is not recommended for pregnant women or meditators with hypertension or cancer. These conditions tend to be exacerbated by the awakening of the base-of-spine chakra.
3. Energy healing, especially extraction of negative blockages along the spine and solar plexus chakras that obstruct the energy flow

SIDE EFFECTS ON CERTAIN HEALTH CONDITIONS

Health risks are exacerbated in certain people when the *kundalini* energy is awakened rapidly and powerfully.

Pregnant Women

The lower chakras in pregnant women, especially the solar plexus, navel, sex, back-of-navel and base-of-spine centers, are more active compared to the upper chakras than when they are not pregnant.

This is an automatic response to the baby's growth. Awakening the *kundalini* further activates the back-of-navel and sex chakra, which can cause eclampsia or higher blood pressure in the mother or can over-energize the baby.

Squeezing the perineum repeatedly to facilitate delivery (Kegel Exercise) is not the safest way for mothers to deliver naturally.

People advocating this technique have not seen the side effects and dangers of this method clairvoyantly. It may cause "energetic frying" of the baby if the *kundalini* awakens because of the "pumping effect" of the muscle movement, which affects the very seat of the sacred fire. This method has a variety of side effects directly proportional to the *kundalini* development.

This common Kegel technique needs to be reevaluated closely to check if there are certain hidden or unknown side effects to babies born of mothers who use this method.

The perineum squeeze is a technique in Tantric *kundalini* yoga to awaken the sexual *kundalini* energy to transmute it to the upper chakras. There's a substantial increase in internal heat and *kundalini* intensity after this technique is done.

I was 35 when I became pregnant with my first child. I was thrilled and very much wanted a natural childbirth. I had practiced yoga and meditation for years and found the most progressive certified midwife in the area. She advised me to do Kegel exercises throughout the day to strength the pelvic muscles. To make the exercises more powerful, she suggested I hold my breath while squeezing the pelvic floor muscles and that I do this dozens of times a day — when I woke up, when I was sitting at a traffic light, before bed. She also encouraged me to do squats every day to open and strengthen the pelvic region. I knew she meditated and studied at one of the finest university's midwifery programs.

I dutifully followed her instructions. As the pregnancy progressed, I became increasingly emotional. I continued doing Kegel exercises several times an hour over the months. I developed Bell's palsy, a nerve condition that resulted in muscle atrophy on the left side of my face. By the end of the pregnancy, I had pre-eclampsia (elevated blood pressure) which required fetal monitoring every week to be sure my child was healthy. Fortunately, she was, and I was able to deliver naturally.

Because I nursed and then had another child, I was not able to take steroids, the only medical treatment of Bell's palsy. My facial muscles remained weak for years. I could barely focus my eyes, which as a writer, threatened my livelihood. I consulted neurosurgeons at a renowned teaching hospital who told me that nerves do not regenerate and they could not guarantee surgery would improve the condition. Then, I sought out chiropractors, homeopaths, herbalists and healers.

A friend recommended I call a coach-healer certified by Del Pe in his Inner Powers Healing science. After many months of healing, the nerves in my face slowly regenerated and my vision returned to normal. The coach-healer brought me to Del Pe, who explained the negative side effects of doing Kegel exercises during pregnancy.

I now practice advanced meditations which leave me feeling centered and balanced so I can raise my children, earn a living and continue my spiritual growth safely — faster than I ever thought possible!

- K. C., Writer, Boston

SOLUTIONS FOR PREGNANT WOMEN

1. Avoid meditation, breathing techniques and rituals that awaken the *kundalini* prematurely during pregnancy.
2. Use meditations that release any build-up of internal energy and stress like the Inner Renewal Meditation.
3. Do gentle physical exercises and simple inner breathing to release negativity.
4. Get advice from a healing expert.

Hypertension

The back-of-navel and most often the solar plexus chakras are active in people with high blood pressure since they regulate blood pressure. *Kundalini* awakening can trigger them to become very active, resulting in sudden uncontrolled hypertension, which can even lead to stroke or other undesirable consequences.

SOLUTIONS FOR HYPERTENSION

1. Use meditations that release stress and congestion, but avoid advanced powerful meditations that surge the energy of the back-of-navel center.
2. Avoid abdominal breathing techniques that emphasize long breath retention, especially holding the breath after exhalation. This technique awakens the *kundalini* rapidly.
3. Improve your diet and try vegetarian food. Advanced meditation usually requires more refined energy from food.
4. Take a salt-water bath to decongest the back-of-navel and lower chakras and to release congestion caused by *kundalini* awakening.
5. Hypertension medication can work temporarily to inhibit the back-of-navel chakra from becoming very active.

Cancer

The lower chakras in cancer patients, especially the solar plexus, back-of-navel and base-of-spine chakras, are very congested with negative energies, plus they are over-activated. The heart and *ajna* chakras are significantly smaller. *Kundalini*, which has red energy, fertilizes the growth of abnormal cells and worsens the existing chakral imbalance.

SOLUTIONS FOR CANCER

1. Avoid breathing techniques that have longer breath retention and any awakening of the *kundalini*.
2. Salt-water baths are recommended weekly.
3. Use the Inner Renewal Meditation to awaken the upper centers and to help release the negative energies from the energy bodies. The *ajna*, heart and crown need to become more active through the Synchronized Breathing Method (page 202).
4. There's a need for more physical exercise that includes oxygenation of the blood like the Internal Stamina Exercise (pages 186-188).

5. Try taking aloe vera juice, chlorophyll juice or wheat grass juice to alleviate the energy congestion. These natural juices have a lot of green *prana* that helps decongest the solar plexus and aura.

I am writing this testimonial not only to warn people of the harm some yogic breathing techniques can do to people with cancer, but with other health conditions, too. I was a victim of untrained yoga instructors whom I worked with a few years ago. When I was diagnosed with ovarian cancer, I started doing yoga therapy. The yoga teacher taught me pranayama *breathing. After a few months, I became really bad because the cancer spread fast even with medical intervention. Fortunately, I found Del Pe, who told me that yogic breathing awakens the sacred fire called* kundalini *and this can accelerate the cancer to grow because of the energetic heat. He also explained that this* kundalini *is a fertilizer for cancer cells to grow faster. I was very angry about the ignorance of many yoga teachers and schools. I learned that many of them are not healers and teach people without knowing the side effects of yoga or contraindications of meditation. Thanks to Del Pe, who knew how to help me in the recovery process, I am now healthy.*

       - P.D., Restaurant Owner, New York City

Glaucoma

The *ajna* and back-of-head chakras in glaucoma patients are congested and full of dirty red energy. These are the chakras that control the eyes. The solar plexus center is very congested with dirty red energy and possibly stress.

SOLUTIONS FOR GLAUCOMA

1. Avoid breath retention techniques, especially advanced meditation methods with long stopping of breath or *khumbaka*. The eye pressure will increase tremendously with these methods.
2. Use the Inner Renewal Meditation to release stress and toxic

energy from the eyes, solar plexus and the rest of the auras.

3. Use the Synchronized Breathing Method (see page 202) to improve the congestion associated with glaucoma.

4. Chlorophyll and aloe vera juice have also been used successfully by my clients. As we mentioned earlier, the green *prana* and vibration of these juices decongest the solar plexus and other affected areas.

5. Avoid red Korean ginseng roots because they emit red energy, which is not good for the chakras of glaucoma patients.

Chronic Fever Not Triggered by Infection

The energetic cause of this condition is excessive dirty red energy in the solar plexus and throat chakras. This dirty energy is also generally distributed throughout the whole aura.

Red energy increases body temperature, especially in angry, stressed people whose solar plexus chakra is very clogged energetically. Even if there is no infection, the meditator always feels feverish and has a higher body temperature.

SOLUTIONS FOR CHRONIC FEVER NOT TRIGGERED BY INFECTION

1. Salt-water baths help decongest the aura and chakras.

2. The Synchronized Breathing Method definitely works to release extra negativity in the aura and awakens the crown chakra, which brings in cold energy (Divine light) to neutralize the situation.

3. Special exercises like the Internal Stamina Exercise should be done before advanced meditation and *pranayama*.

4. Consult your healer or physician for further evaluation and recommendations.

AIDS

Certain types of meditation like the Inner Renewal Meditation are useful for AIDS patients. I have also designed other special meditations that can help them increase their white blood cell count and boosted their immune system.

A meditation to increase will-power and vitality, clean the blood with energy, decongest the lymphatic system and release stress is a must for survival and transformation of those with AIDS.

Solutions for AIDS

1. Avoid any meditation and breathing technique that awakens the *kundalini* because this tends to exacerbate the conditions and imbalances inherent in AIDS.

2. Do the Inner Renewal Meditation or any other meditation that releases stress and psychological issues and awakens the heart, *ajna*, spleen, throat and crown centers. These centers help enhance AIDS patients' ability to fight back against the virus and other negative energy issues. The heart chakra controls and energizes the thymus gland in the chest area, which is responsible for lymphocytes and antibodies.

3. Regular exercise like the Internal Stamina Exercise is recommended to oxygenate the blood, improve circulation of positive energy and quickly release toxic vibrations.

People with Spinal Injury or Herniated Disks

The sudden increase of *kundalini* energy can pressurize the spine and trigger strain and pain in these affected areas, especially with the rush of red energy upward. Since these conditions have weak points in the spine in those with spinal injury or herniated disks, that is where the energy gets blocked and produces either tenderness or inflammation.

Solutions for People with Spinal Injury or Herniated Disks

1. Avoid powerful *pranayama* with long pauses of breath control.

2. Be careful with heavy-duty exercises because they can adversely affect the conditions of spinal weakness. Use gen-

tler yogic methods.

3. Get regular healing from someone who has good decongesting techniques applying colored energy, especially green and blue pranic vibrations.

Migraine or Severe Headache

I don't recommend that people who suffer from dizziness, headache or migraine do advanced meditation and *pranayama* until their conditions are healed. If they do intense meditation, they will exacerbate the congestion in the head area, and the solar plexus chakra becomes very congested with dirty red energy. The awakening of the *kundalini* is not good because the red energy of the sacred fire will bring more energy that triggers more pain and headache.

SOLUTIONS FOR MIGRAINE OR SEVERE HEADACHE

1. Salt-water baths can help alleviate the congestion.
2. Get healing from an expert in pain management and migraine using special colored energies like green and blue. The solar plexus chakra and the affected area(s) should be inhibited.
3. Stop practicing or avoid advanced meditations and powerful breathing techniques.
4. Do Inner Renewal Meditation to heal yourself.

Uncontrolled and Excessive Sex Drive

I have observed this condition in many yogis and meditators who are celibate or who have an active sex life, but conserve energy without a technique to transmute the excess energy. I healed a yoga guru in India who had so much guilt about sex and was celibate for 40 years. Unfortunately, he did not learn how to transmute his accumulated sexual energy upward to his upper chakras. He complained of sexual thoughts all the time. He had wet dreams daily. This made him feel more guilty. The more he suppressed his sexual urges, the more the sexual energy got stuck and congested. In fact, he ended up with prostate cancer. He asked me for healing, but it was too late.

On the other extreme, many Tantric *kundalini* yogis with partners get obsessed with the sexual aspect of their practices, and they can be lost in sexual pleasure. Thus, they can also lose the spiritual component of their yoga. An additional side effect is that they get very sexually depleted, missing the chance for enlightenment. Sexual energy is the spiritual gasoline for illumination. Over-consumption slows down enlightenment!

My sexual nature has always been intense even since childhood, but I repressed it because of guilt from my religious beliefs. My sexual problems really started after I practiced breath control in Hatha yoga. My first exposure to this type of meditation was immediately after I got married, when I was 35. At the same time, I also got exposed to a Chinese herbal medicine expert who recommended that I take red Korean ginseng to improve my sexual performance during my honeymoon week. I took it almost daily. A short time later, I encountered a self-study book suggesting a Tibetan mantra that is sounded with a very long pitch. I think my experimental nature led me to combine all the yoga breathing techniques with the wild ginseng root and the recitation of the mantra a few times a week. At first, nothing happened. But, after two weeks of combined practices, I started to have jolts of electricity rising in my spine and excruciating pain in my lower back. Also, I became sexually insatiable and behaved like a sex maniac. My mind was full of uncontrollable sexual fantasies every day and my dreams were loaded with wild sexual events.

After three months, I got so fatigued and mentally empty because of releasing sexually every day, with or without my wife. In 1996, I saw Del Pe on television on CNBCS's "Alive and Wellness Show" demonstrating an energy healing with a volunteer from the audience. I contacted him immediately and was lucky to receive several healing sessions that saved my life from destruction. With his help and safe meditations, I have grown so much and have become a healer myself.

- F. A., Certified coach-healer, Queens, NY

SOLUTIONS FOR UNCONTROLLED AND EXCESSIVE SEX DRIVE

1. Avoid deep breathing and *pranayama* with long periods of breath retention.
2. Use more bellows breathing or *bhastrika* style (see page 221). Minimize right nostril breathing because this technique triggers more sexual energy stimulation.
3. Get a good healer to help deactivate the sex chakra and transmute the sex energy upwards.
4. Do not lose sight of your goals in Tantric *kundalini* yoga. Conserve your sexual energy for higher experiences and spiritual development by bringing this alchemized energy up to the upper chakras and the Soul.
5. Avoid red Korean ginseng root and any supplements that stimulate heat or *yang* energy.

Dangers to Children

There are two aspects of the hidden dangers of meditation and yoga for children.

They are too young for advanced breathing techniques or powerful meditations or yoga.

Any long pauses of breath control are not advisable because this activates their *kundalini* and can burn their chakras and entire energy system prematurely. Their chakras are still fragile and adjusting.

Seven-year-olds may be taught simple body exercises to train their physical body's resilience and for rhythm, but they should not be activating their chakras and inner fires. Those aged 14 to 20 should not awaken their energy bodies intensely, especially the emotional body, because the emotional and mental bodies are still being constructed gradually. In fact, what they need are techniques to transmute excessive sexual energy to fertilize their upper chakras and mental creativity.

I teach parents, healers, educators and teenagers how to perform this sexual transmutation method to diffuse excessive rising or release of the sexual creative power through normal sex.

Parents or adults meditating near their young children or babies can over-energize and over-stimulate them.

This over-stimulation can cause children to become hyperactive and/or develop insomnia because of the excessive energy radiating from the meditating parent's aura to their children during meditation.

A parent or adult doing an advanced meditation or yoga can have an energy field as big as 10 feet (3.05 meters) or more, and during meditation, the energy, especially the *kundalini* fire, can directly activate the children's *kundalini* through energetic osmosis or empathy. This is not safe at all, especially for babies and toddlers.

In contrast to meditations that can make children hyperactive and sleepless, doing meditations for relaxation near children can make them spacey.

My Indian yoga guru told me meditation could make me calm and energized, which is true, but he never mentioned that when you meditate and do yogic breathing around your children, they can develop insomnia and hyperactivity! I never suspected that my three young children had health issues because of my spiritual practices. I usually meditated just a few feet away from where they were playing. Sometimes, they were even next to me while I meditated. They were unable to sleep properly and were hyperactive. It was only when I discussed this situation with Del Pe that I understood what was going on. I was over-stimulating and over-energizing them with my meditation. After several healings and mentoring sessions, my children's issues started to normalize. Now I help other meditators and their families heal their issues by applying what I learned from Del Pe about safe and effective meditations for families.

- I. R., Medical Technologist, Puerto Rico

SOLUTIONS FOR DANGERS TO CHILDREN

1. Avoid doing advanced meditation and breathing techniques

near young children and babies. Normally, 15 feet (4.6 meters) away is safe enough.

2. If you are a very powerful meditator, your energy field and aura are bigger than your house. Therefore, you have to employ methods to withdraw your auric influence during meditation. Using your will and mental intention, isolate and will your energy away from your children during the course of the meditation. Your aura will be disengaged temporarily not to over-energize your childrens' or baby's system.

3. Meditate outside of the house if your children are home, or send them out with a babysitter or other family member until you are done. Make sure they are safe without your attention for the duration of your meditation.

4. Do not bless your children strongly after meditation. Bless the family as a group instead of only one child or small body absorbing it. If you are not secure with this idea, it's better not to bless your children directly with energy. Just wish good intentions for them and the family without projections of energy. This is safer.

5. Do not rush young children to go for advanced types of yoga, meditation or breathing techniques unless you know the effects of the style or method. Different meditations have different purposes and energy dynamics. I recommend Jnana yoga or yoga for mental development for your children and teenagers, including study of philosophy and ancient wisdom teachings as a start and preparation.

Physical types of yoga like Hatha yoga are acceptable except for the breathing techniques or *pranayama*. Be aware that the physical movement does not reveal the energetic stimulation of the Divine light and *kundalini* fire. Therefore, it is dangerous just to evaluate the effects on your children from a physical perspective. We saw in the previous chapters on *mudras* and body postures that much energetic movement and stimulation are happening to the meditator internally without knowing it.

Be extra cautious choosing yoga or meditation instructors for you and your loved ones. The meditation or yoga instructor should understand these hidden dangers of meditation and yoga. Chapter 25 offers a directory of recommended schools, groups and instructors you can evaluate and choose from.

WRONG COMBINATION OR SEQUENCE OF MEDITATION OR YOGA TECHNIQUES

When yoga or meditation systems are designed by their founders, they are created with safety in mind. The sequence and combinations, in general, are intentionally designed to avoid over-stimulating the meditator through repetitions that energize a certain chakra, gland or organ excessively or over-activate the practitioner's inner powers.

In some cases, the breathing methods prescribe particular maximum sets or numbers of repetitions because exceeding those limits is known to be dangerous.

I have healed a few cases of meditators having spiritual and emotional crisis induced by mixing different techniques from different yoga and meditation styles. They mixed many techniques without knowing their negative side effects when combined improperly.

The overzealous spiritual practitioner thinks that practicing the most powerful technique from each yoga system and combining them will make them powerful and grow faster. This type of curious but ignorant meditator is playing with fire unsafely and can be energetically burned without correct discrimination and guidance from a seasoned mentor.

Like other young American executives, I wanted fast turn-arounds and quick fixes for my goals. I traveled to India, believing it to be the haven of spiritual gurus. I was shopping for a formula for enlightenment from one of the ashrams. I started drinking in college, and at the age of 28, I was still drinking to deal with the pressures of my executive responsibilities. I also ate red meat and fish. When I joined a yoga group, I was so excited to start the advanced yoga breathing and rituals immediately, including the recitation of mantras.

After a few weeks, I started to get congested, developed a feeling of exhaustion, and I became feverish. Also, I experienced shallow breathing, which turned into difficulty breathing almost daily. The guru advised me to do more deep breathing, called pranayama, *in order to release the energy blockage and continue the chanting of* mantras. *The more I did these rituals, the sicker I became, so I returned home to Detroit for a medical examination. The medical exams did not find anything wrong with me.*

I heard about Del Pe's healing system while attending a New Life Expo and arranged for a consultation. Del Pe helped me give up drinking through his amazingly fast and effective Vice Elimination Programs. Now, I have the spiritual teachings I yearned for by following his safe meditation methods. I am able to develop spiritually, but now I don't have to fly half way around the world. I am successfully managing my business and family obligations while incorporating Del Pe's safe meditation practices into my busy schedule, so I am able to enjoy greater professional success while growing spiritually.

- M.R., Executive, Michigan

Here are some cases and problems I've encountered in my work as a healer and mentor:

1. Awakening the lower centers and *kundalini* fire through prolonged chakral breathing on the base-of-spine, perineum, sex and navel chakras, then forcing it to rise through the central body channels without first activating the heart and head chakras and awakening the Divine light. This can cause over-

heating and over-stimulation of the person's lower nature or negative tendencies.

2. Awakening and bringing up the *kundalini* force without purifying the chakras, auras and major meridians through exercises and purifying breathing methods creates crises of excessive emotional purging, physical issues or exacerbation of existing health conditions.

3. Awakening the sexual and *kundalini* energy, then circulating the alchemized energy through the aura of a sexual partner during Tantric sex without exercises and purifying techniques first and without preparing the upper centers for Divine light. This can cause complex side effects like excessive energy congestion sensed as exhaustion and body pain brought by contamination and serious energy blockages, especially to the higher-frequency partner.

4. Interchanging the sequence of breathing techniques with extended periods of holding the breath (*pranayama*) before practicing the purifying breath like the Synchronized Breathing Method, *kapalbhati* and *bhastrika* methods.

5. Over-activating a certain chakra by wrong combination of *mantra*, chakral breathing and color visualization. This can cause severe health or psychological conditions. I healed a meditator who became blind by combining techniques of prolonged concentration and breathing on the *ajna* (mid-brow) chakra while doing all kinds of visualization, especially with red-colored imagery. He was told he could open his third eye fast with this method. Be careful with hearsay and techniques from neophyte trainers who don't use safe approaches or know about the hidden dangers of meditation.

6. Powerful techniques that lack a proper safe sequence:
   - Doing advanced breath control methods like *pranayama* with prolonged holding of breath without using proper throat locks, abdominal compression locks and root locks in the proper sequence. This wrong sequence or lack of technique can cause throat and health issues or deforma-

tion of the abdomen because of the extra pressure caused by the compression of air, *prana* and *kundalini* force.

- Releasing yogic locks (*bandhas*) in a wrong sequence like root lock before throat lock, which can cause over-activation of the lower centers and *kundalini* fire more than the upper chakras and Divine light.

7. Combining techniques that over-develop the sexual *kundalini* energy like taking red Korean ginseng and Chinese reishi mushroom, plus doing martial arts or yogic breath control emphasizing holding the breath after exhalation. When done in combination, these methods over-activate the *kundalini* (heat) without balancing cooling energy from the Divine light. Many martial artists suffer from tumors and indulgence in sex or violent behavior because of this excessive stimulation of the "lower fires" without the balancing spiritual light.

SOLUTIONS FOR WRONG COMBINATION OR SEQUENCE OF MEDITATION OR YOGA TECHNIQUES

1. Do not jump into haphazard experimentation or overzealous practices that improperly combine or change techniques or methods from their original founders without understanding their possible side effects. Consult a meditation or yoga expert or mentor with excellent knowledge of and demonstrated experience with energy science and healing.

2. As a rule of thumb for meditation or yoga practices:
   - First awaken the Divine Light to regulate the powerful effects of the *kundalini* fire by activating the crown and head centers. This can be done through chakral breathing techniques and *mantrams* on the head centers. (See Chapter 21 for the proper *mantrams* and sequences.)
   - Activate the heart center before *kundalini* fire awakening. This step develops a bigger heart to serve as a pump to diffuse extra energy from the *kundalini* awakening instead of the solar plexus emotional center. In fact, with the heart opened during a surge of *kundalini* energy, you can experi-

ence extreme joy at the heart chakra. I call this "heart orgasm".

- Purifying breathing methods (Synchronized Breathing Method, *kapalbhati* and *bhastrika* breathing techniques) are pre-requisites for more advanced *pranayama* and awakening of the *kundalini* fire, including for Tantric sexual practices.

- Do not combine mantric recitation on a chakra with prolonged chakral breathing and color visuals, especially at the head chakras, throat, heart, solar plexus, spleen, back-of-navel, sex and base-of-spine. I would not recommend this combination for more than 10 cycles (inhalation and exhalation) for novice meditators except for the navel chakra to store alchemized energy. The colors red and orange should not be used on any chakra in the head or on the heart and spleen chakras. Green and violet colors are safe, but light hues only. If you do not understand energy color science properly, I would not recommend that you use meditation with colors because there are exceptions to the rules regarding pranic and esoteric colors that most healers and some spiritual teachers do not totally understand yet.

3. Use the following sequence for the yogic locks for safe and effective meditation:

   - When performing deep breathing with holding of breath after full inhalation, execute the throat lock first, then the root lock at the perineum with a partial abdominal compression lock (*uddina*) to prevent abdominal sagging. Without the throat lock, the throat mechanisms like the glotis and vocal cords can be negatively affected by the internal pressure.

   - Release the three locks and internal energy after breath retention with the throat lock released first, followed by the abdominal lock and ending with the root lock. This sequence is important because you need to bring the internal energy upward first to fertilize the upper chakras before injecting the extra energy to the lower system.

4. Develop the upper centers and awaken the Divine light to regulate the lower nature. The use of natural supplemental herbs or Oriental medicine like red Korean ginseng, reishi mushroom or other aphrodisiacs and "shaman's potions" are healthy if you are not sexually over-congested or if your lower centers require a power-enhancer and are not over-active. But if you practice martial arts or a yogic breathing and exercise method that awakens the lower chakras, plus the upper centers are not as active and developed as the lower chakras, there is a danger of lopsided development of the lower nature or attitudes.

    The higher principles of life through the development of the spiritual centers and Divine light like love, compassion and will-to-good should regulate the animal nature. You can still benefit from the natural supplements above by taking the "*yin* types" of ginseng or herbs until you need a more powerful boost of red or "*yang* type" of energy.

5. Use the universal sound, Om or Amen, with the vowels recited with a ratio of 80% of the vowel O or A to 20% of the consonant M or the syllable Men. This mantric ratio increases your frequency and enables you to abstract your consciousness before more powerful meditation practices. Do this for 5-10 minutes to help purify your auras and the meditation environment.

Pre-Disposed Dangers for Oriental and Occidental Meditators

There is a profound difference in temperament between Oriental (Eastern) type people and Occidental (Western) type people. They are pre-disposed to natural strengths, weaknesses, behavior patterns, vices and virtues.

Even though there is more cross-cultural exposure now through migration, international travel and intercultural marriages, there are still esoteric and subjective differences that need to be discussed and elaborated. Understanding these differences will help guide the choice of meditation styles best-suited for people with Eastern and Western constitutions.

An enlightened master, Dhjwal Khul, in his book (as transcribed by Alice Bailey), *Letters on Occult Meditation*, mentions this type of meditation danger:

> *I wish to point out for the guidance of future students and as a prophetic statement, that in days to come when the science of meditation is more comprehended, two factors will be wisely weighed and considered before assigning meditation. These factors are:*
>
> *a. The man's subrace characteristics*
> *b. His type of body, whether it is oriental or occidental*
>
> *In this way, certain disasters will be avoided and certain troubles obviated that are now found in more or less degree in every occult group.*"

The reason for this potential danger lies in the wrong choice of meditation that can exacerbate latent conditions inherent in both types of cultures or races.

There are types of meditations that are best suited for each temperament, and there are certain meditations that are harmful or less effective for both.

I have traveled throughout and lived in many cultures, taught seminars and healed clients internationally. This international exposure enabled me to study and evaluate both Oriental and Occidental cultures, and I have mentored both Eastern and Western students.

Here are some of my general observations as of this period:

1. Eastern meditators have a more mystical and subjective (inward) approach to life and events. They have more heart, emotional, abstract mental and philosophical tendencies. They tend to be more interdependent and group conscious

for their survival and growth. The family and spiritual group is their foremost line of affinity called lineage. They are less corruptible with material and financial attachments, but they have more attachment issues with family and devotion to spiritual lineage.

2. Western practitioners are generally more mental, objective and practical. The concrete mental faculty is stronger and more dominant, thus, they are apt to have a more organized, systematic approach to life. They have better order and structure and mental discipline than their Eastern counterparts. They are more independent, even at an early age, and are more resistant to following a family or spiritual lineage due to lack of devotional energy and tendencies. They tend to move from one yoga or meditation style to another. The Western yogis are either Hatha yoga meditators for the sake of culturing the physical body or Karma and Jnana yoga and meditators, using the concrete mind and career roles as a path. The heart center is developed eventually.

3. The Eastern meditator starts the spiritual path and meditation practices earlier through a spiritual lineage or school. They also tend to start on a vegetarian diet sooner, especially in India. The southeast Asians like the Chinese, Japanese, Korean, Indonesians, Thais and Filipinos are generally introduced to martial arts, psychic development or Oriental spiritual arts as part of their tradition, even at a young age. Those from the Middle East are also stimulated at an early age by devotional adherence to their religion or by mystical arts.

4. The Western meditator starts preparing their body through sports and more competitive activities. As of my current study, I have observed that they become vegetarians and more spiritual after they find their spiritual group or have entered onto a meditation path. They tend to be more diversified by studying and combining many techniques from different schools, both the commercial types and esoteric. They are more flexible but careless and are usually more gullible,

resulting in practicing wrong combinations of techniques. They sometimes mix meditation practices without the guidance of a mentor. This is a big danger.

5. The Eastern practitioner has more discipline with regard to the control of lower appetites and the negative influence of the external senses compared to his/her Western counterpart. The Eastern meditator tends to be more reclusive and inward whereas the Western practitioner tends to be more extroverted and is susceptible to having more vices and addictions from negative commercial influences, including food.

6. Even within the Eastern tradition, sub-races have variations in temperament. For instance, southeast Asians are different from those from the Middle East and the Indian sub-continent. The same applies to the Western tradition. There are many cultural variations within Europe. Italians are more fiery, passionate and explosive compared to the Central Europeans, who are more aloof and less warm. German and Swiss meditators tend towards a more systematic, structured, disciplined science of meditation compared to Russians, who are more mystically and psychically aware.

   In the United States, the West Coast tends more towards a mystical, heart-centered approach to meditation and is generally influenced by the mysticism of Asian and Mexican cultures. The Northeastern United States like New York and New England is more mental, influenced by European culture.

   The aim of this section is not to go into all the details, but to illustrate the effect of cultures, sub-races and temperament on approaches to meditation and lifestyle.

7. In countries like the United States, meditators with a mixture of sub-races and cultures combining the Eastern and Western behavioral patterns require a more integrated approach to meditation and the spiritual path. When the meditator is more advanced or is an advanced Soul, whether they belong to the Oriental or Occidental culture, there's a need to

choose integrated meditation or Yoga of Synthesis. The future advanced children from both East and West will follow this systematic inetgration of the meditation path.

SOLUTIONS FOR PRE-DISPOSED DANGERS FOR ORIENTAL AND OCCIDENTAL MEDITATORS

The different cultures, races and sub-races have their own pre-disposed strengths, weaknesses and behavioral patterns that are exacerbated when the *kundalini* is awakened. A wrong type of meditation practice can negatively induce the practitioner to get worse or over-develop certain tendencies rather than work towards balance or integration.

Whatever culture or sub-race you belong to or have affinity with, there are many variations and ramifications of the different temperaments, and it is complex to design one specific model for each. Therefore, the meditation style recommendations are categorized depending on the following:

1. THE EASTERN CULTURE PRACTITIONER OR MEDITATOR WITH THE FOLLOWING QUALITIES: MORE SUBJECTIVE, HEART-CENTERED, MORE INTUITIVE AND MYSTICAL TEMPERAMENT, PREFERENCE FOR AN INWARD MEDITATIVE LIFE, LESS ACTIVE AND STRUCTURED MIND

   - Start with heart-centered meditation, like Bhakti yoga, but balance it as soon as possible with a mental type of meditation leading to Jnana and Karma yoga applications. It is important not to over-develop the emotional and Buddhic or love-wisdom aspect without the interpretive and organized qualities of the mind. These types must do Karma yoga and practical service in society so they don't escape into a reclusive state in the mountains.
   - Will-power and dynamic vitality have to be developed and maintained to reinforce the activities and qualities brought about by love and intellectual development. This is especially so for more advanced practitioners.
   - Regular exercises should be a part of the routine before

and after meditation to strengthen the body. The typical Eastern meditator prefers to do lotus position and devotional types of meditation for hours. They should ground first through physical exercises before they go back to work.

- Balance the upper and lower centers by not using the index finger-thumb *mudra* with lotus or adept posture. Any excessive upward flow of energy depriving the lower centers of much needed nurturing is not good for more mystical meditators. They tend to become impractical and financially bankrupt if they do not feed the lower chakras compared to the upper chakras. Therefore, I recommend that this type meditates with feet flat on the floor and the triple finger *mudra* (index, thumb and middle finger together) periodically.

- Join meditators and groups that are more mental and business types to harness their more concrete and structured qualities through osmosis.

- The chakral breathing meditation emphasizing the *ajna*, throat and heart breathing technique and the *ajna*, navel and base-of-spine chakral activation is highly recommended.

- Join more sports and competitive activities to develop the will and access "unity through diversity" qualities.

- I recommend the Inner Renewal Meditation to balance the heart, mind and will-power in one meditation method.

2. **WESTERN CULTURE PRACTITIONERS OR MEDITATORS WITH THE FOLLOWING QUALITIES: MORE MENTAL, OBJECTIVE AND PRACTICAL WITH LESS HEART DEVELOPMENT**

- Start or continue with mind development through the weekly Karma or Jnana yoga approach (career path using predominantly mental aptitudes) employing concretizing or understanding meditation techniques explained in this book (Chapter 13).

- As soon as possible, include the "opening the heart

method" to catch up with the heart development and emotional intelligence quality. The heart, forehead and crown centers need to be stimulated with chakral breathing methods to unfold the meditator's subjective (inward) qualities to offset excessive mental and objective tendencies.

- Will-power and vitality should also be cultured for more advanced meditators to develop an integrated faculty of the mind, heart and will-power.
- The Inner Renewal Meditation can help balance the objective and subjective characteristics of the the meditator.
- Study esoteric science and psychology to develop the abstract philosophical consciousness that will balance the objectivity of the concrete mind.
- Interact with mystical and devotional groups to harness their love and subjective nature, but you don't have to stay permanently with them unless you need it.
- Periodically use the Synchronized Breathing Method, index finger-thumb *mudra* and lotus or semi-lotus postures during meditation to bring your consciousness more upward. This is also to activate the upper chakras to balance the lower chakras in the case of people with a materialistic type temperament.

3. **MORE BALANCED MEDITATORS WITH HEART AND MIND DEVELOPMENT** (*any culture*):
- Use the Inner Renewal Meditation to continue heart, mind and will-power development.
- Do Namascar Meditation (Chapter 20) to integrate the personality with the Soul and Spirit consciousness.
- Use the Divine Alchemy Meditation: Activating and Balancing Your Power Centers (Chapter 21), including the awakening of the objective and subjective chakral triangles.
- Practice the Body Therapy and Inner Powers Meditation to harmonize the energies of power, love and light (Chapter 11).

- Evaluate the 12 types of meditation (Chapter 3), and use some of the meditation techniques that you need most. Follow the weekly schedule from Chapter 24, pages 399.
- Observe the effects of the Oriental *mantras* on yourself if you are a Western type. Some of the powerful *mantras* are suitable for Indian and Tibetan types who have been vegetarians all their lives or who started their spiritual preparations at an early age. Some Oriental techniques need a more resilient energy system and supple physical body for them to be safe and effective.

More Esoteric Dangers

Dangers Inherent to the Inner Growth of the Meditator

These side effects of meditation occur as a by-product of inner development and a rapid shift of the meditator's consciousness changing his/her perspective of life. There are four major dangers:

- Shift in family of social dynamics and relationships
- The advanced meditator's increased auric power
- Advanced meditaition with *kundalini* awakening can harm people who smoke, drink and do drugs
- Unsafe channeling meditation and lack of Divine protection

Let's study each of these dangers and their solutions:

Shift in Family or Social Dynamics and Relationships

After a few months of regular meditation, the meditation practitioner's vibration is changed entirely and upgraded with a higher frequency compared to that of non-meditators like family, friends and professional colleagues. This frequency difference leads to totally different ways of looking at things and gaps in communication from both sides, leading to either the meditator being intolerant of the others' wrong priorities or the mismatched criteria of family members and social contacts.

As the meditator shifts to a different diet like vegetarianism required by his or her yoga or meditation practice, the complications add up if family is not vegetarian. This can be solved with good communication.

The meditator's priority shifts to wiser use of his/her spare time and resources also can create family pressures. This shift is motivated by inward experiences like reading spiritual books or being in nature instead of going to the mall or parties. This internal adjustment and sometimes misconstrued aloofness are interpreted as weird or abnormal behavior.

The widening gap between the meditator or yoga practitioner and family and friends can worsen if unrecognized as a potential seed of future crises for the family. I've seen many cases wherein the meditator has separated from their spouse because of this unresolved issue, especially if the meditator continues to accelerate growth and the partner and family do not.

The increased rate of vibration of the meditator's energy system triggers a shift in consciousness, which can cause the gaps of communication and the drying up of relationships.

People responded to me differently as I advanced in my meditation practices. I felt tremendous love and oneness with friends, family and all of life, yet I was perceived as cold, aloof and uncaring. After 10 years of yoga and meditation, I think I became too detached. I didn't hug much because I felt energetically contaminated by other people's stress and issues. I lost some friends and family relationships along the way because I was misunderstood. After mentoring and healing with Del Pe, I learned how to balance the detached nature of universal love with emotional intelligence and the power of the heart to sustain my personal relationships.

- S. J., Executive, Teacher and Coach-Healer, Connecticut

Indifference, Intolerance and Elitism

The meditator's growth towards greater spiritual light and the inward journey to higher consciousness usually manifest as an upgrade of the person's mental and psychic faculties. Several of the newly acquired energy substances from advanced meditation bring the following:

Indifference

The meditator, having a more abstract perspective of life and a different level of common sense, tends to experience life in a more detached way, which can be viewed as non-caring towards other people's events like parties. This is an adjustment that needs to be recognized by both the meditator and the family.

The energetic difference in their auras and minds will widen if the meditator does not help the family members grow or does not involve them in a spiritual practice. When the crown chakra of the meditator is more awakened and active, it triggers this detached attitude, which is first expressed as indifference.

Intolerance towards family and friends

This affects the mental type of meditators more. The mental acumen of the meditator grows faster than that of family counterparts, resulting in sharper and faster thinking capabilities. This increase in mental development can pose a problem for the meditator if s/he becomes mentally impatient or intolerant of others, especially as s/he picks up faults or what they consider stupidity in family members.

The meditator's mind and psychic impressionability like telepathic or precognitive faculties even allow him/her to sense when someone is telling a lie or has negative intentions. In some instances, this intolerance results in conflict and unhappiness in the family. It can even cause separation or divorce if the situation is not curtailed or managed properly.

I never much enjoyed "normal" social events. I always preferred study-ing and reading to socializing. When I started my advanced medita-tion, I became even less patient with what I perceived to be trivial things, and I got impatient with my family for not being interested in learning more about my spiritual path. It became harder for me to interact with them as I stopped eating meat and drinking, which cre-ated a lot of family conflict and discomfort. I'm still developing more emotional intelligence to be able to harmonize family relationships without bending myself away from my spiritual virtues and alignment when I am around my family. I appreciate the healing and meditation techniques I learned through Del Pe's school where I received training to bless and heal my family even at a distance.

- N.L., Executive, Spain

Elitism

Elitism affects meditators with more will-power and mental devel-opment. It is associated with amplification of pride or arrogance on the part of the evolving meditator who is still undergoing character-building. There are some seeds of weakness in the meditator's con-sciousness that are rekindled or stimulated by the action of the *kun-dalini fire*. One of these weaknesses can be arrogance. Since the meditator's mental and instinctive faculties are growing fast, the meditator's sense of extra power can convert into a feeling of grandeur or an attitude of "I am more advanced than you". The meditator can lose the respect of family and valuable relationships as a result.

I wasn't prepared for what would happen to me when I started med-itating. I was always very intellectual, proud of my education and crit-ical in my thinking; it's required for my job. But after I started medi-tating and studying spiritual science, my mental faculties got even stronger, and I became a real pain in the neck to be around because I became an over-critical perfectionist. This resulted in my getting many karmic lessons in humility: problems with money, bad business decisions, having my mistakes pointed out in front of colleagues whom I never wanted to see me as weak. I've had to learn how to fail and how to rely on others for help. It's still not easy for me, but I'm getting there with the help of Del Pe's wisdom teachings, whose meditation integrates the heart and mind.

    - G.M., Graduate of Brown and Harvard Universities, California

SOLUTIONS FOR SHIFT IN FAMILY OR SOCIAL DYNAMICS AND RELATIONSHIPS

1. Work against potential problems or crises ahead of time by understanding these possibilities. To be forewarned is to be forearmed.

2. Establish better communication and criteria for dealing with family members by having a more balanced perspective of spiritual life that includes family, social and material life. For example, as a person grows, the shift to a vegetarian diet has to be explained to family members who are not vegetarian in a more practical, non-fanatical and non-condescending way, pointing out the health benefits rather than using yoga or meditation as an excuse. Educate family and friends without forceful conversions to what you're doing.

3. Gradually introduce your family to meditation or yoga according to their level of receptivity and degree of readiness. Most plants grow only with just the right amount of water; too much watering drowns them. The same holds true with people. Do not force or pull small plants from their roots because you want them to grow fast. Nurture and coach your family with patient persistence.

4. Share simple meditations with your family that can benefit their weekly needs for issues like stress management or relaxation. Teenagers can learn the exercises in this book and inner breathing techniques like the Synchronized Breathing Method to release their frustrations. Help them grow gradually and safely.

5. The adjustment time for the meditator and his/her family regarding his/her sense of indifference or coldness can take from a few weeks to a few years. This depends on how fast the meditator recognizes that this situation is happening and acts wisely and humbly enough to take the right next steps like developing the heart chakra and emotional intelligence, especially in the case of people with lots of will-power and mental development. The Inner Renewal Meditation is an indispensable tool to neutralize growing indifference, pride or elitism in the meditator.

6. Bhakti yoga or devotional types of meditators have to be cautious about excessive inward tendencies that appear as spaciness and worsening impracticality or non-attention to financial details because their type of temperament doesn't prioritize material needs. This is viewed by others as fanaticism and a negative side effect of meditation. This is a partially correct perception because the meditator does a meditation that just awakens love and spiritual consciousness through the heart and crown chakras. The base-of-spine and lower chakras are underdeveloped. Therefore, s/he is unable to focus on financial and material life. This results in an imbalance, which can lead to financial difficulties.

   Several of the meditators who came to me for healing were victims of this scenario. Their spouse left them after they became unemployed and bankrupt. They fell into the famous "no money, no honey" trap.

   I recommend that meditators do 25-30 squats daily or at least 3 times weekly to ground back to real life and not to become too isolated or aloof. The *ajna* and base-of-spine center are "energy software" for practicality and material groundedness.

7. There's a need to realize that conflict and strife in your karmic chain with other family members or friends are opportunities to heal and grow yourself and them as well. The flaws in our character are exposed for these to be worked out, especially in terms of the elitism issue.

8. Request an advanced healer to heal the side effects of negative, unconscious attacks from your family members and maybe the energetic boomerang that came around to them from you.

9. Be patient and do not make drastic decisions about divorce because you and your partner can't stand each other. The adjustments that result from starting to meditate are usually temporary, and they are exacerbated by the seven cycles of your year. For instance, the 52 days after your birthday is usually better in terms of positive perception whereas the 7th cycle, which is 52 days before your birthday is the most challenging time of your year, especially about two weeks before your birthday. This science of life cycles needs to be employed to help meditators and their families chart the best and worst times of the year. (See Chapter 25 for coach-healers and coach-consultants specializing in charting life cycles.)

Dangers of the Advanced Meditator's Increased Auric Power

This a very important matter to understand from the meditator's perspective. With regular advanced meditation, the increase in their energy level and auric perimeter of influence is accompanied by more will-power development. This tremendous energetic influence can extend to more than half a mile (0.8 kilometer) radius of influence.

For very advanced meditators and yogis, it's significantly bigger. These meditators, especially those with direct group karmic and auric affinity, are subjected to this vibrational stimulation, including indirect awakening of the *kundalini* fires of other people within the meditator's aura.

The meditator's energy, especially the will-power and *kundalini* energy, during and after intense meditation can adversely affect others. The meditator's aura acts like a fertilizing power to people's auras and chakras. This fertilizing effect activates both the positive and negative qualities in others. Just like agricultural fertilizers, the "weeds" sometimes grow faster than the flowers, meaning the "bad stuff" gets stimulated to grow usually faster than the virtues.

This is one of the reasons why when an advanced meditator is not around, his or her family is calm with no tension, but when s/he is around doing more advanced meditation, there are chaotic or negative reactions from the family members. Also, the family members can feel uneasy or jittery because of over-exposure to high-powered energy and *kundalini* force.

I have observed that when I have highly-awakened *kundalini* during an advanced esoteric meditation, it over-stimulates our staff and students, which expresses in both positive and negative reactions. But when I withdraw the extra will-power and *kundalini* energy from their auras, they start to normalize in a few minutes.

Most advanced meditators and yoga instructors are not familiar with these side effects, and most people blame the over-reactions on stress or a bad day. There are also side effects produced in the environment and neighborhood. You might want to observe after an advanced *kundalini* awakening meditation what the reaction is of the people immediately within your radius of influence.

SOLUTIONS FOR DANGERS OF THE ADVANCED MEDITATOR'S INCREASED AURIC POWER

1. Do not do advanced meditation, especially intense awakening of the *kundalini*, near family members or other people who are non-meditators. This prevents direct impact and energy osmosis with their auras and chakras during meditation.

2. Do not bless people and family with energy that is empowered with will substance. With your intention, withdraw the extra will-power from your blessings before you radiate your energy to your targets.

3. With an act of will, isolate and withdraw your auric influence from your family and neighborhood while meditating and for about 12 hours after meditation.

4. Switch from a mental style to more of a heart centered style, and use more emotional intelligence (harmonizing attitude) in dealing and communicating with others.
5. Don't hug your family members, especially your children, immediately after an intense advanced meditation.

Advanced Meditation with *Kundalini* Awakening Can Harm People Who Smoke, Drink and Do Drugs

Simple relaxation meditations and inner breathing techniques to detoxify the body are suitable for people with the above vices, but prolonged intense meditation that awakens the sacred fires of the body are dangerous.

When the *kundalini* awakens through intensive breathing techniques like advanced *pranayama*, this internal force will push itself along the meridians upward, and any blockages in the chakras and meridians caused by the negative vibrations from smoking or the other vices sometimes create a high-pressure energy jam in the whole system, especially at the back heart, solar plexus and back-of-navel of smokers.

For alcoholics and drug users, the auric and chakral energy filters that protect the systems are partially torn and damaged. It is dangerous to magnify these conditions because they can worsen the mental and emotional upheavals alcoholics and drug users already have like hallucinations, paranoia or confusion. The *kundalini*, as we said earlier, acts like a fertilizer of both good and bad qualities.

Solutions for Advanced Meditation with *Kundalini* Awakening That Can Harm People Who Smoke, Drink and Do Drugs

1. Use only relaxation meditation, the Synchronized Breathing Method or the Inner Renewal Meditation weekly.
2. Avoid intense deep breathing techniques that emphasize breath control. These awaken the *kundalini*.
3. Do daily exercises to detoxify the side effects of taking in toxic substances like drugs, alcohol and tobacco.

4. Take salt-water baths at least 3 times a week.
5. Consult your healer, physician or psychotherapist for other health measures and treatment.
6. Seek out advanced healers to extract energetic contamination and blockages and to get revitalized.

DANGERS DUE TO UNSAFE CHANNELING MEDITATION AND LACK OF DIVINE PROTECTION

One of the steps for a safe and effective meditation is invocation for Divine protection, guidance and empowerment before starting the advanced meditation practice. Not only will this give spiritual protection, it allows more effective circulation of energy from the Soul to the personality, which is required for the proper awakening of the *kundalini*. The Divine light that comes with the protection also has a cooling effect on the energy system.

When a meditator uses advanced techniques with intense internal force, the body and energy centers are subjected to "high-voltage" situations that include a fiery burning process. The Divine light will descend to all the auras, resulting in purification and transformation.

Another hidden danger unknown by most meditators is the presence of a negative group of invisible beings and the many forms of invisible elementals that are attracted to disturb or, in extreme cases, "take over" or possess the meditator if s/he is not properly protected. We have to include here the notion that as your auric light gets brighter, it is more visible in the Inner World to the "evolutionary and involutionary" seers.

There are negative forces of the planet that have an esoteric plan to hamper planetary and human evolution. I was thinking of not including this because it is not commonly known by most meditators, but for the sake of warning fanatical advanced meditators, it is now included.

Many advanced meditators do not believe in these invisible forces, but they are a reality. Since you have not proven or disproven the idea, let's consider it as a possible dangerous factor, more for the advanced meditator. The protection invocation is very simple, so why take the unnecessary risk of not using it?

Channeling meditation is the most risky because the channel, during the meditation, can be in a trance or out of body, so many of them are not conscious of what's happening. In a few instances I have encountered and healed, the meditators almost couldn't come back to their bodies because "somebody" or "some entity" was there inside. I had to de-possess or exorcise these types of people for a few hours.

This channeling meditation is also dangerous to clairvoyants. In fact, they are the most targeted by the negative beings or even by playful discarnates who take over the clairvoyant's personality for their own negative ends. This is not to scare meditators. This is intended to inform about remote possibilities and put them into proper perspective.

For more than two decades of occult meditation and studying esoteric traditions, nothing went wrong until one day when I was meditating at Machu Picchu in the mountains of Peru, claimed to be ancient ruins of pre-Incan origins. I think I was very contaminated with the negativity of the remnants of the past civilization where conflicts destroyed the city. I think my chakras became so open and vulnerable after an esoteric ritual that I felt my aura enveloping the whole place.

After this expansion, I started to experience psychic attacks from negative forces, including from the past of the place. I went home devastated and completely drained physically and emotionally. I had trouble sleeping, as well as bouts of panic and depression. I never experienced anything like that before going to the ruins.

I sought out many healers and tried psychotherapy. But no one was able to improve my energetic condition until I found one of Del Pe's trainer healers in Colombia and was able to meet with him. It took many sessions of healing to diffuse the negative entities and repair my chakras and auras. The healer understood what happened and explained it to me. As one becomes lighter, it is easy to become a target of the negative side, so it is important to be careful where you meditate. Not all ancient ruins are sacred! The healer also to taught me how to shield my aura during meditation. This is essential for advanced meditators. I am so lucky I was able to get out of this predicament with the help of a true healer-mentor.

- C. D., Teacher, Rhode Island

SOLUTIONS FOR DANGERS DUE TO UNSAFE CHANNELING MEDITATION AND LACK OF DIVINE PROTECTION

1. Always invoke (silently or verbally) for Divine protection, guidance and empowerment before you do advanced meditation or esoteric practices.
2. Learn how to shield all your auras with energy, including the location where you're going to meditate.
3. Burn sandalwood or sage incense and let the aroma spread around your space to purify it energetically. Meditate in a clean environment.
4. Avoid shortcuts like not exercising and not performing the inner breathing to clean up and release energetic, emotional and mental toxicity. When you are clean of negative vibrations, it is more likely that there's no attracting force in you that brings the negative entities.
5. It is helpful and a safeguard to have a spiritual lineage, especially a spiritual mentor who automatically offers spiritual protection and guidance when they are involved.
6. Be with your spiritual groupmates and co-workers when you are doing extra-intense meditation. Groups with a good healer make you safer and more secure. Find your spiritual groupmates and study this book for more in-depth details.
7. A lifetime of character-building and inner reflection to release obsolete negative patterns will help greatly.

EXTRA PROTOCOLS THAT CAN FACILITATE YOUR SAFE AND EFFECTIVE MEDITATION

1. Follow the guidelines for preparing yourself properly without careless shortcuts. Study this book deeply on the dangers of meditation and yoga.

2. Use only the recommended duration for certain advanced meditations and breathing techniques. Do not be too intense or too eager to go beyond the recommended repetitions of *pranayama* breathing or the Combination Breathing Technique. The powerful effects of mixing techniques from different schools and groups might be dangerous because they can be redundant in stimulating certain powers, internal forces or qualities, resulting in lopsided development. For example, too much heart, forehead and crown chakral awakening will make a practitioner softer and more inward, but s/he can end up too *yin* or passive.

3. Certain guidelines are very important:

   a. No heavy meals or food 3 hours before advanced meditation and breathing techniques, especially the Combination Breathing Technique or advanced *pranayama* with abdominal compression locks or *bandhas*.

   b. No heavy meals within 2 hours after intense meditation. The energy is high and intensely activating and can stimulate the solar plexus (activated during the meal) more than normal. Also, the circulation of energy will be affected when the concentration of body functions is directed at the stomach and solar plexus chakra during digestion.

   c. No bath, shower or swimming, especially in cold water, within 3 hours after intense meditation or awakening of the *kundalini*. Do it before meditation. Water and energy fire don't mix well. Furthermore, good energy after you meditate can be washed out by water and wasted.

   d. Conserve your sexual energy after an advanced meditation because the alchemized energy will be used for higher purposes and as Soul fuel. Also, if your *kundalini* force is too intense, it might over-awaken the *kundalini* of your partner who is not prepared. S/he will get sick or congested or overwhelmed unless both of you know Tantric *kundalini* methods and you're at the same level of consciousness. If you do know these methods, you can empower your experience with safe Tantric techniques using sexual alchemy.

e. I cannot over-emphasize physical exercise before advanced meditation, including lighter exercise after meditation.

f. Do not engage in smoking, alcohol or drugs, especially before undertaking advanced meditation. It is not safe!

g. Use the proper hand *mudra* at the right spot. If you do the *dhayani* (meditation) *mudra* at the sex level for hours, you tend to be extremely sexually-aroused and congested. So maintain your hand *mudra* at the navel.

This chapter has shared the most common dangers of meditation and yoga for both beginners and advanced meditators. As a result of my experience with these dangers, I designed a complete healing system, Inner Powers Healing, that can help practitioners heal psycho-spiritual syndrome and *kundalini*-related problems.

Meditation is becoming so mainstream, commercialized and popular that instructors are more in demand, but have less time to prepare themselves with higher qualifications. This is a potential danger that is already being experienced by many meditators today, so Chapter 25 gives you criteria and resources to help you the choose the right yoga or meditation style and instructor for your needs.

CHAPTER 23

World Meditations for Global Transformation, Healing and Alignment

Generally, meditation is regarded as a personal path or an individual activity, but in its highest usefulness, it can be applied as a group event or global undertaking for a specific spiritual purpose.

When people group together to pray or meditate with focused intention, the power is amplified and has longer lasting positive effects on the individual as well as the group.

Today, different groups and networks of fellowship meditate to support a spiritual cause or to act as a channel for spiritual energy sensed to be flowing or available for that period. Religious groups have their own special group events to celebrate seasonal rituals. Even the United Nations has started to schedule different group meditations for world peace and other global concerns.

Esoteric circles have full moon group meditations qualified by the constellation's energy stimulating the Earth during the month. During the full moon time, the Earth is closest to the sun, therefore the forces stimulating the Earth are highest. Many spiritual and astrology groups also celebrate group meditations during new moons.

The natives of every culture have sensed the power of group invocation expressed through their ceremonial magic and rituals since time immemorial.

There are, at present, many group meditations that are worth mentioning here. Some of them are monthly rituals to receive and transmit spiritual energies available periodically. Most of these meditations and festivities are useful during the period of transition from the Piscean period to the new era called the Aquarian period. The Piscean period is characterized by idealism, martyr complex and sectarianism. Our religions and present and past wars are representations of this period.

The Aquarian period is qualified by pragmatism, objectivity and group consciousness. The new global business, technology and more universal spiritual movements are an initial manifestation of these qualities, although they still lack the proper rhythm and new organizational order and structure of a true Aquarian lifestyle.

Since there are so many group meditations and monthly rituals celebrated by different movements, I'll only include a few important ones in this chapter.

The Roman or Gregorian calendar is not as consistent as the ancient calendars based on monthly full moons. Therefore, we'll use the rhythm of the full moons named after constellations to qualify our major group or global meditations.

The esoteric groups and movements, particularly those affiliated with the Theosophical Society (www.theosociety.org) and Lucis Trust Arcane School (www.lucistrust.org), have established group meditations celebrated internationally.

For the present needs, I have sensed that there are very important global celebrations in the period of transition to the new Aquarian period. Even though the styles of most groups are still colored by the older Piscean system, I anticipate that newer spiritual groups will align to new meditation rhythms and rituals. Currently, I still encourage meditators to join the following three great world events yearly. The recommended meditation procedures for these events are available online at **www.WISEmeditation.org.**

Easter Full Moon Meditation

This is an important Western event commemorating the initiation of Jesus the Christ, an avatar of the Piscean style of love and teachings on the path of spiritual initiation symbolized by his birth, baptism, transfiguration, crucifixion and resurrection. Thus, in the Christian teachings, he is the light, the way and the truth for humanity to emulate to be spiritually raised from normal, everyday life into the Christ consciousness through the process of spiritual initiation.

The Easter group meditation is best done on the first full moon of spring under Aries, usually in April. Groups generally need to focus on and access the available energy to overcome old ways and destroy obsolete forms of lifestyles, resulting in personal discomforts. This is a form of crucifixion and renunciation of negative egotistical patterns. Self-auditing and transformation of the personality is equivalent in the Christian tradition to renunciation and fasting. Then the resurrection aspect of Jesus, not the suffering aspect, is supposed to be the culmination of Easter.

The new Aquarian period will celebrate the triumph of the will and purpose of the Soul, the Christ within, over the personality's mundane life. This is a path to overcome suffering in the long run.

The real value of Easter full moon meditations and rituals is transformation — transformation through love intelligently applied with new plans and strategies. Therefore the devotional Bhakti style of meditation of the older system should be augmented by the "mental concretizing meditation" (Chapter 13) to plan and organize the next positive steps of the personality. Heart and mind development are keys to the new Easter Celebration.

Wesak Full Moon Meditation

This is originally an Eastern and Oriental celebration, but it is gaining recognition by different esoteric groups globally. It is usually called Vaisakha by the Buddhists because it honors the Buddha.

The Wesak full moon is one of the highest and most important full moon global meditation events, not only because it channels the energy of wisdom and enlightenment, but also because the esoteric circles acknowledge this as the special time when the group of Enlightened Masters, led by the Christ, receives the yearly Divine Purpose and Will substance for the planet through the Buddha from the planetary will center. Shamballa is the esoteric name given to this point where the Divine Will and Purpose of the planet are anchored.

The global Wesak meditation is usually done on the May full moon day or during the full moon of Taurus, which sometimes occurs in April. It is also celebrated two days before and after the actual full moon day.

Proper preparation through fasting and cleansing meditation is recommended before the full moon, plus special blessing rituals to channel these powerful energies and Divine substance for a few days. Group spiritual initiations or enlightenment experiences can happen during this time.

Goodwill Full Moon Meditation

The Tibetan Holy Master, Dhjwal Khul, expressed through Alice Bailey's writings the need for humanity to develop right human relations for the golden age of global peace. But the energy of goodwill has to first spread out in the consciousness of human beings around the world.

This energy of goodwill and the will-to-good are variations of the virtue of love that the Christ and other founders of religions have emphasized in their teachings. In our modern life, it has to be a more practical love with intelligent action and service.

This event is called World Invocation Day or the Festival of Humanity by the Arcane School (Lucis Trust). It is celebrated on the full moon of Gemini, usually in June. It is a high time to invoke, receive and express goodness, benevolence, altruism, humanitarian service and unity. The meditations should focus on these virtues, and the groups should express them with practicality.

MONTHLY GROUP AND GLOBAL MEDITATIONS THAT CAN CHANGE THE WORLD

Predominant qualities of energy are available during certain months and full moons to be accessed and channeled by meditators or humanity. These special types of planetary and cosmic vibrations have certain colors, qualities and usefulness categorized according to the seven types of forces or cosmic rays. These seven kinds of rays or energy qualities fertilize humanity's spirituality, personalities and behaviors. Each month during full moon days, these periodic energies are at a maximum planetary precipitation. Thus, we can tap into these qualities through individual or group meditations.

As of this current period of global development, certain types of virtues or attitudes can be developed faster and their vibrations accessed during these macrocosmic influences and rhythms. The full moon virtues and qualities below were validated by a trained clairvoyant in March 2005 and are expected to run through 2035.

Aquarius Full Moon (usually January or February):

    a. **Virtue of will-power and vitality** with accompanying qualities of:
- Will-to-good according to higher purpose
- Will to group consciousness and alignment
- Synthesis and integration
- Fearlessness and detachment
- Transformation
- Positive destruction to creatively construct

    This is a great time to harness the force of will-power and stamina.

    b. Anchoring of the **Aquarian Invocation annually:**
This world invocation newly channeled by my esoteric school is a landmark for the Aquarian period to anchor the initial principles of the new era. It is a universal declaration of what has to come during the Aquarian period. The detailed discussion of this Invocation is available at **www.WISEmeditation.org** with a CD version.

THE AQUARIAN INVOCATION

The New Divine Power of the Great Ones
anchors Aquarian Life.
The New Divine Love of the Great Ones
harmonizes all Kingdoms.
The New Divine Light of the Great Ones
transforms Humanity's consciousness.
The New Divine Purpose of Shamballa guides the Great Ones.

The New Divine Will of Aquarian Life
organizes substance into the Center.
The New Divine Love of Aquarian Life
magnetizes consciousness to the Center.
The New Divine Light of Aquarian Life
transforms all planes of the Earth.
The Synthesizing Force of Shamballa integrates the
New Divine Power, Divine Love, Divine Light into One.

The Aquarian Invocation can be used in group or global meditations on any day or in any month, but the anchoring and transmitting of the maximum energy is available on the Aquarian full moon.

The term "Great Ones" refers to the group of enlightened Sages and Masters, whereas the word Shambhalla denotes the group of Divine Beings who are the custodians of Planetary Purpose and Will.

Pisces Full Moon (usually February or March):

    a. **Virtue of sacrifice:** You need this to become a legend. The accompanying qualities are:
- Humility
- Sensitivity and compassion
- Industriousness and one-pointedness
- Intuitive and psychic nature
- Self-sacrifice for a higher cause
- Courage and commitment

Aries Full Moon (usually March or April):

    a. **Virtue of good health** with accompanying qualities of:
- Freedom from limitation, including diseases, at multiple levels
- Inspiration, enthusiasm and dynamism
- Speed with rhythm and timing
- Transformation and renewal

Taurus Full Moon (usually April or May):

    a. **Virtue of wisdom** aligned with Divine Purpose. The accompanying qualities are:
- Resilient adherence to spiritual purpose
- Love with discrimination
- Alignment to truth
- Illuminating consciousness with synthesizing will
- Group consciousness

Gemini Full Moon (usually May or June):

    a. **Virtue of goodwill and will-to-good** accompanied by qualities of:
- Spiritual unity and harmony
- Adaptability and versatility
- Loving-kindness with inclusiveness
- Mental creativity

Cancer Full Moon (usually June or July):
   a. **Virtue of altruism** accompanied by:
      - Service-orientedness
      - Courageous heart
      - Sensitivity and compassion
      - Intuitive and psychic tendencies

Leo Full Moon (usually July or August):
   a. **Virtue of creative adaptability** accompanied by qualities of:
      - Resilience
      - Fighting spirit to achieve goals
      - Generosity and compassion
      - Ambition

Virgo Full Moon (usually August or September):
   a. **Virtue of discipline and constancy** accompanied by:
      - Capacity for details
      - Methodical and systematic aptitudes
      - Discrimination with balanced perception
      - Good order and structure

Libra Full Moon (usually September or October):
   a. **Virtue of objectivity and practicality** with accompanying qualities of:
      - Alignment and balance through fairness and justice
      - Diplomacy
      - Open-mindedness
      - Sociability

Scorpio Full Moon (usually October or November):
   a. **Virtue of harmony through contrast** with accompanying qualities of:
      - Resourcefulness and efficiency
      - Harmony through contrast and conflict
      - Capacity to liberate through struggle
      - Courage and motivational ability

Sagittarius Full Moon (usually November or December):
  a. **Virtue of benevolence** with accompanying qualities of:
    - Gentleness with inclusiveness
    - Generosity with friendliness
    - Sincerity with straightforwardness
    - Capacity to be happy and fulfilled

Capricorn Full Moon (usually December or January):
  a. **Virtue of group consciousness** with accompanying qualities of:
    - Practicality with reliability
    - Sense of responsibility
    - Business acumen
    - Patience and persistence

There are a few special events where group and global meditation can be observed:

January 19: World Religion Day
Proclaimed by the Baha'i world faith to promote interfaith cooperation and understanding

April 7: World Health Day
Declared by the United Nations to promote health and well-being

May 15: International Day of Families
Declared by the United Nations for families

June 5: World Environment Day
To safeguard and nurture the environment

September 10: World Healing Day
A global event linking people to raise world consciousness and promote healing

September 21: International Day of Peace
Declared by the United Nations

Generally October: Yom Kippur
The Day of Atonement which follows the Jewish new year. It is the most solemn of Jewish holidays and a time of fasting, confession of transgressions, prayer and meditation.

Generally October: Ramadan
This normally occurs in October and begins when the unaided eye first views the crescent moon. It is a commemoration of the revelation of the first verses of the Quran, the Islamic Holy Book.

October 10: World Mental Health Day
This is sponsored by the World Federation for Mental Health and the World Health Organization.

October 24: United Nations Day
This is the founding day of the United Nations.

October 25: Festival of Diwali
This is the Festival of Light for the Hindus, Sikhs and Jains, especially in India. It is a celebration of good over evil.

October 26: Interreligious Day of Prayer for Peace
Created by Pope John Paul II in 1986 to promote the gathering of people from different faiths to work together for peace and justice

November 1: All Saints' Day
This is the time when Christians recall and contemplate the lives of the Saints.

December 10: Human Rights Day
This commemorates the signing of the United Nations Universal Declaration of Human Rights.

December 25: Christmas Day

Christiandom celebrates this as the nominal birth date of Jesus, which is estimated to be in the winter using the Gregorian calendar.

RECOMMENDED 30-MINUTE MEDITATION FOR GROUP MASTERY OF VIRTUES: *Receiving and Channeling the Energies of Full Moons and Predominant Virtues Monthly*

1. Do physical exercises for 5 to 10 minutes. I recommend the 8-step Internal Stamina Exercise (pages 186-188). (5 minutes)
2. Perform the Synchronized Breathing Method 4 times (pages 204) (5 minutes).
3. Think about and focus on the predominant virtues and qualities of the full moon period (3 minutes).
4. Invoke these virtues and qualities and be internally receptive. You can also internally salute, with respect and gratitude, the Divine Beings who embody these virtues or qualities, just by mental intention. Do this for 5 minutes.
5. Channel the good qualities and virtues of the full moon and, with intention, radiate or bless these qualities to your loved ones, group or people who need the virtue. Do this for 5-10 minutes.
6. Think of ways to express the virtues daily and mentally program that you are already expressing them (5 minutes).
7. With strong intentions and expectancy, absorb and assimilate the new qualities received.

Mantric Meditation Method: 27 minutes
(available on "Om of Virtues" CD)
This meditation method is used to channel and distribute energies
and virtues during the full moons:

1. Listen or chant with the guided mantric meditation.
2. The energy substance and quality of the virtues will be
   absorbed and channeled during the process of chanting or listening to the "Om of Virtues".

The **WISEmeditation.org** Website (www.wisemeditation.org)
offers detailed procedures and updated information on the different weekly, monthly and yearly group and global meditations. Please
visit the site and join us to use meditation as a tool and strategy to
help global issues and to bring transformation to the world. In this
way, meditation becomes a path of service bringing a meditator or
his/her group into global usefulness.

CHAPTER 24

Weekly Schedules for Safe and Effective Meditations to Live Your Greatest Life

When a meditator understands the science and art of meditation and knows its dangers and things to avoid before, during and after meditation, then s/he will be safer and more effective to pursue a lifelong meditation path.

Because there can be so many hidden dangers of meditation and yoga, it's a good idea for parents to guide their children in selecting the right meditation and instructor for their age and purpose.

This book is not designed to scare the millions of current meditators or yoga practitioners or discourage the hundreds of millions of prospective aspiring meditators. In fact, it is meant to encourage people to learn and experience meditation without preventable casualties and to be comfortable to include meditation as a part of their weekly life.

There are many types of meditation that can be used weekly, depending on your needs. They have to be sequenced and combined properly to produce synergy of their power, resulting in balanced results.

In this chapter, we arrange the meditations covered in this book from simple to more intense advanced meditations. The meditation menu also indicates the appropriate age and special features of recommended users.

These meditations for weekly use can benefit both beginners and advanced meditators, including meditation trainers and yoga teachers. They do not only deal with the *pranayama* or visualization aspects. Rather, they offer simplified integration of the different yoga aspects, including the science of Soul development.

The meditation schedules provide many benefits like:

1. Morning and night meditations to align yourself
2. Self-healing meditation to live healthier and be happier
3. Meditations to master concentration and sharpen your mind
4. Meditation to develop awareness and mindfulness
5. Meditation to develop wisdom and your abstract mind
6. Meditation to experience your Soul and *samadhi*
7. Divine Alchemy Meditation to activate and empower all the chakras
8. Advanced breathing meditations
9. Complete abstraction meditation, yogic method

SPECIAL NOTE:
Spiritual blessings and healing service are built into most of the major meditations. Therefore, they are not classified as a separate meditation. They are the final steps after advanced meditations to release excess energies. The more advanced esoteric meditations will not be included in the weekly schedule because they need to be taught directly to the student by a highly qualified spiritual mentor for the meditation to be safe and effective.

RECOMMENDED MEDITATIONS AND THEIR WEEKLY SCHEDULES

MEDITATIONS TO OPEN AND CLOSE YOUR DAY

Goodwill Meditation: 5 minutes in the morning after waking up

- Technique for right human relations
- Refer to Chapter 17, page 280

End-of-Day: 5 minutes at night before sleeping

- Technique for releasing negative energy, achieving peace of mind and having a restful sleep
- Refer to Chapter 17, page 281

Both meditations safe for: teenagers and adults

SELF-HEALING MEDITATIONS FOR OVERALL WELL-BEING AND HEALTH MAINTENANCE

Inner Breathing Meditation/Simplified Method: 10 minutes anytime you require self-healing, or do it Mondays and Fridays

- Technique to release stress, anger, fear, grief, guilt, frustrations, traumas, phobias and to alleviate hyperactivity
- Refer to Chapter 19, page 290

Safe for: young children (guided breathing for 8-12 years old), teenagers and adults (even with vices and addictions)

Inner Renewal Meditation: 42 minutes guided by CD. Mondays and Fridays are good.

- Technique to release negative energies and negative emotional and mental issues
- A fast method to develop physical instincts, emotional intelligence, abstract mental faculties and intuition

- CD-guided meditation is very helpful for people with life-threatening diseases to release emotional and mental block-ages
- Refer to Chapter 19, page 291

Safe for: 18 years old or older (some special requirements)

MEDITATION TO MASTER CONCENTRATION AND SHARPEN YOUR MIND

Navel Breathing Method: 5 minutes daily or Tuesdays and Thursdays

- Meditation to align and center yourself quickly
- Technique to improve instincts and internal stamina
- A must for decision-makers and athletes
- Refer to Chapter 18, page 287

Safe for: 18 years old or older (no major dangers)

Meditation with Seed Thought: 15-30 minutes anytime or Tuesdays and Thursdays

- Technique to penetrate the meaning of ideas
- Meditation to concentrate on topics or objects of attention
- Excellent training of the mind to improve decision-making, problem-solving and tactical planning
- Refer to Chapter 13, page 238

Safe for: students, teenagers and adults (no known dangers)

MEDITATION TO DEVELOP AWARENESS AND MINDFULNESS

Open Heart Method: 5-15 minutes anytime or Thursdays and Sundays

- Activates and opens the heart to enhance the love nature
- Enhances inner sensitivity and awareness
- Revitalizes the immune system through the thymus gland
- Refer to Chapter 14, page 244

Safe for: teenagers and adults (without heart ailments)

Mindfulness Method: 30 minutes anytime or Thursdays and Sundays

- Training to be aware of the moment and experience being-ness
- Refer to Chapter 14, page 244

Safe for: teenagers and adults (no special requirements)

MEDITATION TO DEVELOP WISDOM AND THE ABSTRACT MIND

Abstract Mental Awareness: 15-30 minutes anytime or Saturdays

- Training to abstract and understand principles behind events and concrete data
- Meditation to understand the essence of things
- Refer to Chapter 14, page 248

Safe for: teenagers and adults (no known dangers)

Wisdom Meditation: 15-30 minutes anytime or Saturdays

- Meditation to understand the nature of life and events
- Refer to Chapter 14, pages 248-249

Safe for: teenagers and adults (no known dangers)

MEDITATION TO ACTIVATE, BALANCE AND EMPOWER THE CHAKRAS

Mantric Meditation Method: 42 minutes on Wednesdays (guiding CD available)
- Activate and balance all chakras through inner breathing and *mantras*
- Technique to develop and balance chakras for material (objective existence) and spiritual (subjective existence)
- Refer to Chapter 21, pages 303-308

Safe for: vegetarians 21 years old and older who have already meditated regularly for 6 months with no addictions, vices or severe health conditions. It is not recommended for pregnant women or people with heart ailments, hypertension, cancer, AIDS or other life-threatening ailments.

MEDITATION TO EXPERIENCE THE SOUL, DIVINE ONENESS AND *SAMADHI*

Divine Oneness Meditation: 25-30 minutes on Wednesdays

- Experience expansion of consciousness and Divine Oneness
- Refer to Chapter 15, page 259

Safe for: 21 years old and older. Not recommended for people with addictions, vices or severe health issues.

Namascar Meditation: 28 minutes on Sundays (guiding CD available)

- Experience the Soul and *samadhi*
- Technique to integrate your personalilty, Soul and Spirit
- Experience deep stillness, bliss and serenity
- Refer to Chapter 20, pages 297-301

Safe for: 21 years and older with no addictions, vices, hypertension, heart ailments, cancer or life-threatening diseases. A vegetarian diet and regular exercises are pre-requisites to avoid side effects of high-energy stimulation brought by the meditation.

GENERAL ADVANCED METHOD

Divine Oneness Meditation: 1 to 1½ hours on Wednesdays
Combine the following in proper sequence:

- ◆ 8-Step Internal Stamina Exercise (pages 186-188)
- ◆ Advanced Synchronized Breathing Method (pages 202-204)
- ◆ Advanced Combination Breathing Method (pages 210)
- ◆ Meditation on the Oms and silent gaps (pages 257-259)
- ◆ A few minutes of silence and letting go
- ◆ Post-meditation practices (Chapter 16)

Safe for: 21 years and older following a vegetarian diet with no vices, addictions, hypertension, heart ailments, cancer, AIDS, life-threatening diseases or pregnancy.

Advanced Pranayama Meditation: 15-20 minutes on Wednesdays
Combine the following in proper sequence:

- ◆ 8-Step Internal Stamina Exercise (pages 186-188)
- ◆ Single Nostril Breathing Method (both nostrils) (page 217)
- ◆ Alternate Nostril Breathing Method (page 216)
- ◆ Advanced Synchronized Breathing Method (pages 202-204)
- ◆ Advanced *pranayama* or breathing. Select from among:
  - 10:5:10:5 Ratio (page 201): 6 months
  - 16:8:16:8 Ratio (page 227): 6 months
  - 15:20:10:10 Ratio (pages 228-229): 6 months
    Practice each ratio 6 months to 1 year before you shift to another ratio. Mastery of the basics without strain, undue force and risk is the key to successful advanced meditation.
- ◆ Meditation on the Oms and the silent gaps (pages 257-259)
- ◆ Post-meditation practices (Chapter 16)

Safe for: 21 years and older with no hypertension, heart ailments, cancer, AIDS or other life-threatening diseases. Not for pregnant women or people with addictions or vices. Recommended for vegetarians and more advanced regular meditators. Do not combine this method with other advanced *pranayama* techniques as they might duplicate the stimulation of the *kundalini* resulting in dangerous situations. The negative side effects are sometimes not immediately apparent, but can accumulate into a serious health problem over time.

INTEGRATED WEEKLY SCHEDULE
General level for beginners who want to follow a regular discipline

	AM/PM	Monday	Tuesday	Wednesday	Thursday	Friday	Saturday	Sunday
Meditation to open and close your day	AM	5 min	5	5	5	5	5	5
	PM	5 min	5	5	5	5	5	5
Self-Healing Meditation: - Inner Breathing Method (anytime or Mon and Fri)	AM	10				10		
	PM							
or: - Inner Renewal Meditation	AM							
	PM	42				42		
Concentration Meditation: - Navel Breathing Method	AM	5	5	5	5	5	5	5
- Meditation with Seed Thought (anytime or Tues and Thurs)	PM							
	AM							
	PM		30		30			
Awareness Meditation: - Heart Method	AM			10				10
	PM							
- Awareness/ Mindfulness	AM			30				30
	PM							
- Abstract Mind Meditation	AM						30	
	PM							
- Wisdom Meditation	AM							
	PM						30	
Advanced Meditation: - Meditation on the Oms	AM			25				
	PM							
- Namascar Meditation	AM							28
	PM							

Safe for 21 years or older. Consult a meditation expert for more accurate assessment and recommendations. Some techniques from the list can be done by teenagers (refer to detailed schedules earlier in this chapter).

Advanced level meditators: After 1 year of general level or for current advanced meditators

	AM/PM	Monday	Tuesday	Wednesday	Thursday	Friday	Saturday	Sunday
Meditation to open and close your day	AM	5 min	5	5	5	5	5	5
	PM	5 min	5	5	5	5	5	5
- Inner Renewal Meditation	AM	42				42		
	PM							
Concentration Meditation: - Navel Breathing Method	AM	5	5	5	5	5	5	5
	PM							
- Meditation with Seed Thought (anytime or Tues and Thurs)	AM							
	PM		60	60		60		
Awareness Meditation: - Heart Method	AM				10			10
	PM							
- Awareness/ Mindfulness	AM				30			30
	PM							
- Abstract Mind Meditation	AM							
	PM						45	
- Wisdom Meditation	AM							
	PM						45	
Advanced Meditation: - Advanced *Pranayama* Meditation	AM							
	PM				45			
- Meditation on the Oms	AM			25				
	PM							
- Activating and Balancing the Chakras (Mantric Science)	AM							
	PM			45				
- Namascar Meditation	AM							28
	PM							

Safe for 21 years or older. Do not practice the advanced meditation portion if you are pregnant or if have serious health problems, addictions or vices or are not vegetarian. Consult a meditation expert for other recommendations. Most advanced meditation schedules should be done with a mentor.

Note: All basic meditation can be done independently for different purposes and goals. The two charts of weekly schedules are designed for meditators who want to make it a discipline and who plan to accelerate their inner and external growth for a balanced material and spiritual life.

The mastery of anything in life requires constancy of aim and effort. This is true discipline that brings inevitable excellent results. Making meditation a practical way of life will bear great fruit of success, good health, abundance and spiritual fulfillment.

With a powerful awakened personality, inspired by
an illumined consciousness and empowered
by the wisdom of the Soul,
there's no big thing in life that you cannot achieve,
especially in the name of greater service.

Let's make meditation a spiritual solution to a material world. Best wishes for your inner journey!

Part V:

Directory of Safe and Effective Meditation and Yoga Instructors, Centers and Schools

CHAPTER 25

How to Choose the Right Meditation or Yoga Instructor for You

This chapter is not just for the purpose of listing groups, schools, centers and instructors of meditation and yoga, but also gives tips on how to choose the right yoga style for you. By right style, I mean a safe and effective meditation for you, your loved ones, your corporate team or your group.

The list compiled in this chapter is a directory of current credible instructors, schools, centers and organizations.

There are a growing number of meditation and yoga schools and instructors internationally, some very commercial, many publicly accessible, many with Internet-based education on meditation and a very few really esoteric advanced meditation groups and secret spiritual societies with their own rituals.

Therefore, millions of meditation and yoga practitioners might be endangering their health, relationships or careers and wasting valuable time and money without knowing the dangers of practicing meditation or combining different yoga techniques without understanding their potential side effects and immediate solutions.

Selecting the Right Style and Instructor for You

Probably the most important question now is how to select the right meditation style and instructor for you and other people in your life.

Here are my recommendations for how to select a safe and effective meditation style and trainer:

1. **Study and evaluate your type of temperament** Are you a love and devotional type, a mental type, a will-power type or a combination of any or all of them?
2. **Assess your health conditions.** Can your health only handle simple relaxation techniques, or can you do advanced esoteric methods? Re-read the sections throughout the book on the different types of meditation.
3. **Match your temperament type and health conditions with the meditation style. For example:**
    a. **Love or devotional type or Bhakti yogi style:** The easiest path is bhakti yoga or the art of meditation. But if you are already a long-time meditator, you might need to shift to the mental type meditations and the science of meditation, emphasizing "eyes open" concretizing meditation for more balanced development employing the mind.

    At a certain level of development, you also need to incorporate a meditation that develops will-power and the *kundalini*. There's a relationship of developing will-power with the awakening of the *kundalini*. The more awakened the *kundalini*, the more you need will-power to sustain and advance it.
    b. **Mental type personality, the Jnana yoga style:** You might need to master the science of meditation specializing in concretizing meditation and meditation for understanding and wisdom to fully develop the mind. This would be followed by the balancing of the heart and mind to culture

the love and wisdom aspect in you, which is provided by love type meditations, including the awareness and mindfulness meditation.

As you develop yourself further through heart and mind development, you should venture into culturing your will-power through higher abstraction meditation and esoteric meditations. This will complete your integration of Power, Love and Light through the Yoga of Synthesis.

c. **Will-power type personality:** Practitioners with this temperament usually go for martial arts practices, *pranayama*, Raja yoga or Tantric *kundalini* yoga methods. They usually want faster energetic practices to awaken the inner powers. Many of them tend to be esoteric and like to play with their sacred fires. As a result, many are also spiritually burned.

Their style includes speed and high will-power concentration. This meditation includes a lot of physical exercises, *pranayama* with varied grades of intensity and *kundalini* fire awakening techniques, including Divine Alchemy methods.

The next step for this group is to catch up with their love and wisdom meditation to hone their hearts, emotional intelligence and conscience to not misuse their rapidly increasing power. It is very important to offset at an early stage the misuse of power, sex energy and mind control, which is the seed of failure for this group.

The mental types of meditation like concretizing and meditation for understanding and wisdom should be built into the weekly routine since the will-power types need mental development to implement their external roles and karma yoga.

d. **More integrated advanced meditators:** These types need to assess which aspects of their development need balancing and are required for their bigger service or next steps. I have a weekly schedule for this group, but since I am unable to include the very advanced techniques of the

Yoga of Synthesis in this book, the training for this level is given through one-on-one mentoring with me or qualified spiritual teachers or through the **WISEmeditation.org** esoteric curriculum.

When evaluating your temperament, whether you are the love-devotional, mental or will-power type, you need to periodically refer to pages 1-16 to study your preferred meditations with respect to their usefulness.

Choosing the right safe and effective meditation for you also requires:

1. **Interviewing the potential meditation trainer, yoga instructor or spiritual mentor.** There's no substitute for direct question and answer interaction with potential teachers, either in person, by phone or by email.
2. **Knowing exactly what you need.** Do you need to prioritize your stress or health issues, mental faculty development or faster inner development? Once you know your priorities, it is easy to select a suitable meditation, mentor or trainer.
3. **Experimenting with and studying the effects and results of your chosen style.** Is it safe and effective for your needs? Intelligent evaluation through direct experience is an indispensable requirement.
4. **Periodically evaluating if your relationship with your chosen meditation mentor or trainer is working with efficient chemistry.** This is a major test because even with the best style or trainer, if you are not matched properly together, the learning process is impeded.
5. **Re-assessing and studying the need for more advanced steps or increased power in your meditations.** As you grow, you have to be promoted to a more powerful and advanced practice. Otherwise, you'll get bored or saturate your development if your energy load or meditation tools are not pushing your progress or stretching your potentials.

Effective meditation means that it is a calibrated practice that prepares you for your next level of development and satisfies your present needs. Put regular calibration into your three qualities of Power, Love and Light and how to balance your inner experience and their outer expressions of your life. Adopt this book's weekly schedule or a combination of safe meditations based on Chapter 23's weekly schedule.

Meditation is an easy and effective tool to live your greatest life...as long as you know the safe and effective ones for you.

DIRECTORY OF MEDITATION GROUPS, SCHOOLS, CENTERS AND INSTRUCTORS

CERTIFIED MEDITATION INSTRUCTORS

An increasing number of meditation instructors are being certified by **WISEmeditation.org**. The following specialists are currently certified **WISEmeditation.org** instructors who can be reached locally by telephone or internationally via info@wisemeditation.org. Please see www.wisemeditation.org and the MDP Organizations section in the back of this book for more information.

- **Renu Agrawal**: Meditation to Heal Fatigue, Stress and Sleeplessness; Meditation for Smoking Cessation and Vice Elimination (Hindi, English), Stamford, Connecticut, USA, Tel: +1-203-570-7528
- **Fernando Alzate**: Meditation to Heal Pain (Spanish, English), New York, New York, USA, Tel: +1-914-417-7310
- **Linda Bliek**: Meditation for Smoking Cessation and Vice Elimination, Meditation to Heal Asthma and Emphysema, Norwalk, Connecticut, USA, Tel: +1-203-820-6089
- **Juan Colon**: Meditation to Overcome Professionals' Fatigue, Stress and Sleeplessness, Meditation to Overcome Professionals' Addictions, Vices and Their Side Effects

(Spanish, English), San Juan, Puerto Rico, +1-787-645-2392

- **Eliana de la Torre**: Meditation to Heal Fatigue, Stress and Sleeplessness (Spanish), Guayaquil, Ecuador, Tel: +593-998-82440
- **Enid Flores**: Meditation for Work-Life Balance, Meditation for Weight Loss (Spanish, English), San Juan, Puerto Rico, Tel: +1-787-319-2002
- **Antoine Francois**: Meditation to Heal Pain, Meditation for Smoking Cessation and Vice Elimination (French, English), Grenoble, France, Tel: +336-122-31035
- **Karina Gonzalez**: Meditation to Overcome Professionals' Fatigue, Stress and Sleeplessness, Meditation for Family Healing (Spanish), Guayaquil, Ecuador. Tel: +593-998-90997
- **Luiza Grandchamp**: Meditation for Holistic Education, Meditation to Heal ADHD and Learning Disabilities (Portuguese, English), Houston, Texas, USA, Tel: +1-713-398-4121
- **Melissa Gurry**: Meditation for Family Stress Management, Meditation to Heal Children at Risk, South Windsor, Connecticut, USA, Tel: ++1-203-205-8760
- **Suzanne Jarvis**: Meditation to Heal Family Issues, Meditation to Heal Psycho-Spiritual Issues, Houston, Texas, USA, +1-832-754-7743
- **Bruce Jolly**: Meditation to Overcome Professionals' Fatigue, Stress and Sleeplessness, Oak Ridge North, Texas, USA, Tel: +1-832-381-6225
- **Tricia Kennedy**: Meditation for Life-Threatening Illnesses, Meditation for the Dying Process, New York, New York, USA, Tel: +1-917-836-9575
- **Debra Kirsch**: Meditation to Heal Women's Issues (peri-menopause, menopause, sexual issues), Houston, Texas, USA, Tel: +1-832-797-6338
- **Frances Leal**: Meditation to Heal Fatigue, Stress and Sleeplessness (Spanish, English), Houston, Texas, USA, +1-832-498-8437

- **John Mercede**: Meditation for Inner Powers Development, Meditation to Heal Emotional and Mental Issues, Easton, Connecticut, USA, Tel: +1-203-459-8076
- **Bruno Pozzallo**: Meditation to Heal Hyperactivity and Attention Issues, Meditation to Heal Depression (Italian, Spanish), Guayaquil, Ecuador, Tel: +593-978-23735
- **Victor Rivera**: Meditation for Holistic Education, Meditation to Overcome Educators' and Students' Fatigue and Stress, Cayey, Puerto Rico, Tel: +1-787-557-9279 (Spanish), Puerto Rico
- **Nelta Rodriguez**: Meditation to Heal Fatigue, Stress and Sleeplessness, Meditation to Heal Family Issues (Spanish, English), Ponce, Puerto Rico, Tel: +1-787-642-5474
- **Claudia Rothbell**: Meditation to Overcome Professionals' Fatigue, Stress and Sleeplessness; Meditation to Heal Anger, Fear, Guilt, Grief and Depression, Oak Ridge North, Texas, USA, Tel: +1-832-381-6126
- **Kain Sanderson**: Meditation for Inner Powers Development, Meditation for Smoking Cessation and Vice Elimination, Inner Powers Martial Arts, Oak Ridge North, Texas, USA, Tel: +1-832-928-8689
- **Suzette Santos**: Meditation to Heal Hyperactivity, Attention and Learning Issues; Inner Powers Martial Arts (Spanish, English), Houston, Texas, USA, Tel: +1-832-928-9466
- **Alan Simberg**, PhD: Meditation to Heal Addictions, Vices and Their Side Effects, Oak Ridge North, Texas, USA, Tel: +1-832-797-6240
- **Lorena Sion**: Meditation for Aptitude and Attitude Development, Guayaquil, Ecuador, Tel: +593-997-790790
- **Sandra Sion**: Meditation to Overcome Professionals' Fatigue, Stress and Sleeplessness, Meditation for Work-Life Balance, Meditation for Smoking Cessation and Vice Elimination (Spanish, English, German), Guayaquil, Ecuador, Tel: +593-422-96967

- **Donna Sommers**: Meditation to Heal Women's Issues, (peri-menopause, menopause, cancer, pain), Madison, Connecticut, USA, Tel: +1-203-589-5064
- **Bibiana Vasquez**: Meditation for Advanced Human Faculty Development, Self-Healing Meditation for Executives (Spanish, English, French, Portuguese), Silver Spring, Maryland, USA, Tel: +1-240-481-3533
- **Jenna Wayne**: Meditation for Visionary and Intuitive Faculty Development, Meditation for Work-Life Balance (English, Spanish), Oak Ridge North, Texas, USA, Tel (toll-free within US): 1-866-667-8337, Tel (outside US): +1-832-928-8837
- **Carolyn Wilder**: Meditation to Heal Emotional and Psychological Issues, Conroe, Texas, USA, Tel: +1-936-520-2497

MEDITATION CENTERS, SCHOOLS AND ORGANIZATIONS

WISEmeditation.org partners with GLOCEN, ESOCEN and MDP Global Resources to provide additional meditation training, services and products for specific groups. For more information about these organizations, see the MDP Organizations section at the end of this book.

The following meditation centers, schools and organizations were selected as well-known institutions whose major offerings include meditation instruction and/or resources. The author does not vouch for whether these organizations currently train or certify safe and effective instructors and disclaims all responsibility for effects of applying these organizations' techniques and practices.

ARCANE SCHOOL
New York, USA
Tel: +1-212-292-0707, www.lucistrust.org/arcane/

BIHAR SCHOOL OF YOGA
Bihar, India
Tel: +91-6432 232870, www.keepfitwithyoga.com/biscofyo.html

GLOBAL CONSCIOUSNESS PROJECT
Email: rdnelson@princeton.edu, noosphere.princeton.edu

HIMALAYAN INSTITUTE
Pennsylvania, USA
Tel: +1-570-253-5551, www.himalayaninstitute.org

INTERNATIONAL SIVANANDA YOGA VEDANTA CENTERS
International
Email: HQ@sivananda.org, www.sivananda.org

INSTITUTE FOR INNER STUDIES
Makati City, Philippines
Tel: +63-2-819-1874, www.pranichealing.org

INTEGRAL YOGA INTERNATIONAL
Virginia, USA
Tel: +1-434-969-3121, www.yogaville.org

INTERNATIONAL RESEARCH INSTITUTE OF ZEN BUDDHISM
Kyoto, Japan
Tel: +075-811-5181, iriz.hanazono.ac.jp/index.en.html

INTERNATIONAL YOGA FEDERATION
International
Email: fiy@yoganet.org, fiy.yoganet.org

MIND & LIFE INSTITUTE
Colorado, USA
Tel: +1-303-665-7659, www.mindandlife.org/index.html

NAROPA UNIVERSITY
Colorado, USA
Tel: +1-303-546-3500, www.naropa.edu

SELF-REALIZATION FELLOWSHIP
California, USA
Tel: +1-323-225-2471, www.yogananda-srf.org/

SIDDHA YOGA INTERNATIONAL FOUNDATION
New York, USA
Tel: +1-845-434-2000, www.siddhayoga.org/

THE CHOPRA CENTER AT LA COSTA RESORT AND SPA
California, USA
Tel: +1-760-494-1600, www.chopra.com/

THE THEOSOPHICAL SOCIETY
International
Email: intl.hq@ts-adyar.org, www.theosophical.org

THE VIVEKANANDA KENDRA YOGA RESEARCH FOUNDATION
Bangalore, India
Tel: +26528822, www.vyasa.org

THE URALS CENTRE OF WILL-TO-GOOD
Ekaterinburg, Russia
Tel: +7-343-330-61-15, bailey1.narod.ru

TRANSCENDENTAL MEDITATION PROGRAM
International
Tel: +1-888-532-7686, www.tm.org

UNICORN FELLOWSHIP
Quezon City, Philippines
Tel: +632-454-0145www.sufi-isis.org

UNIVERSITY OF THE SEVEN RAYS
New Jersey, USA
Tel: +1-201-798-7777, www.sevenray.com

Quick References:

MEDITATION SOLUTIONS FROM MDP ORGANIZATIONS

ISSUE/NEED	SOLUTION
Working smarter	*5 Intelligences of Highly Developed People* (upcoming book)
Culturing inner powers and higher human faculties	*Inner Powers to Maximize Your Performance* book
Mantric yoga and use of sacred sounds	The Science of Mantrams and Sacred Sounds seminar (ESOCEN) Chantrams of Transformation CD
Material and spiritual balance	Om of Virtues CD
Advanced human energy anatomy and spiritual technology	*Spiritual Technology for Advanced Inner Development* (upcoming book)
Self-mastery through 8 core virtues	*From Success to Fulfillment* book Om of Virtues CD
Protecting and cleaning negative energy from the environment	Chantrams of Transformation CD
Unblocking your energy system and building vitality and stamina	Body Therapy and Inner Powers Meditation DVD Beat Your Fatigue and Stress Fast DVD
Fatigue, stress and sleeplessness management	Beat Your Fatigue and Stress Fast DVD Inner Renewal Meditation CD
Samadhi meditation to experience your Soul	Namascar Meditation CD
Self-healing and balancing the heart, mind and will-power	Inner Renewal Meditation CD
Activating and balancing your energy centers	Divine Alchemy Meditation, Level 1 CD
Psychic faculty development	*Inner Powers to Maximize Your Performance* book
Finding the right meditation and instructor for you	WISEmeditation.org
Smoking cessation and vice elimination	ESOCEN or GLOCEN Eliminating Vices and Their Side Effects Program

END NOTES

[1] Hodson, Geoffrey. Yogic Asccent to Spiritual Heights. (Manila, Philippines: Stellar Books, 1991), p. 41

[2] Research for Religion and Parapsychology Conference, "Yoga and Oriental Medicine". March 1, 1979

[3] Ostrander, Sheila and Schroeder, Lynn. Psychic Discoveries Behind the Iron Curtain. (Englewood Cliffs, NJ: Prentice Hall, Bantam Edition, 1971), p. 217

[4] Ibid, p. 216

[5] Saraswati, Swami Miranjananda. Prana, Pranayama, Prana Vidya. (Munger, India: Bihar School of Yoga, 1994), p. 211

[6] Nagendra, Dr. H.R., Pranayama: Art and Science. (Bangalore, India: Vivekananda Kendra Yoga Research Foundation, 1993), p. 47

[7] Ibid, p. 48

[8] Saraswati, p. 25-26

[9] Ibid

[10] Blake, William. "Auguries of Innocence" in The Complete Poetry & Prose of William Blake. Lines 1-4. (New York: Anchor Books, 1988) p. 490

[11] Bailey, Alice. Letters on Occult Meditation. (New York: Lucis Publishing Company, 1950), p. 110

MDP Organizations
Founded by Del Pe

The World Institute for Safe and Effective Meditation (**WISEmeditation**®) is an international organization founded by Del Pe for the advancement of safe and effective meditation worldwide.

WISEmeditation Services:

- ◆ **Training and mentoring programs** for the public on the science and art of meditation through:
  - Free mini-consultations
  - Online learning
  - Teleconferences/teleseminars
  - Seminars/workshops/conferences
  - Specialized training/mentoring programs
  - Basic, intermediate, advanced and post-advanced meditation programs as an inner development path
- ◆ **In-person or distant healing programs** to heal the side effects of meditation and yoga
- ◆ **Individual, group and global meditations** for transformation, healing and alignment
- ◆ **Development of meditation curricula and customized programs** for groups, families, schools, healthcare systems, corporations, governmental institutions and non-governmental organizations
- ◆ **Offsite retreats** for inner renewal, rejuvenation and personal transformation applying the science and art of meditation
- ◆ **Certification programs** for meditation instructors, coach-healer-mentors and centers
- ◆ **Technical support and consultations** to help establish meditation rooms/centers inside organizations for work-life balance and stress management
- ◆ **Establishment of WISEmeditation centers** internationally
- ◆ **Research and scientific evaluation** on the healing and transforming benefits of meditation
- ◆ **Directory** of recommended safe and effective meditation instructors, meditation coach-healer-mentors and schools/centers for meditation
- ◆ **Products** for safe and effective meditation

GLOCEN® is an international organization helping executives, professionals, leaders, teams and organizations maximize performance and balance life to work smarter, live healthier and grow faster. Its core philosophy applies Eastern wisdom and Western practicality to bring success and fulfillment in all areas of life.

GLOCEN offers seminars, coaching-mentoring, corporate healing, visionary intuitive consulting, offsite retreats and career certification programs.

SEMINARS AND TRAINING PROGRAMS:
- Health, Vitality and Stress Management Strategies
- Aptitude and Attitude Development Strategies
  - Advanced Human Faculty Development
  - Enlightened Wisdom and Visionary Leadership
- Success and Self-Fulfillment Strategies:
  - Family and Work Life Balance
  - Integrated Time and Life Management
  - 8 Core Values to Transform Success Into Fulfillment

COACHING-MENTORING SERVICES:
- Balancing Your Life Program
- Vitality and Stress Management Solutions Program
- Addiction and Vice Elimination Program for Executives
- Addiction and Vice Elimination Program for Families
- Healing Couple's Issues
- Healing Children's Issues
- Family Yearly Life Cycles
- Strategies to Transform Modern Families
- Family Stress Management Program
- Maximizing Intimacy in Relationships Program
- Yearly Life Cycle Program for Professionals
- Time Management Strategies
- Mastering Time and Life Management
- Family Stress Management Program
- Urgent Crisis Management and Solutions
- Fast Decision-Making and Problem-Solving Program
- Maximizing and Balancing Spiritual Life
- Inner Power Martial Arts Program for Stamina, Will-Power and Instinct Development
- Aptitude and Attitude Development Programs
- Spiritual Mentoring for Success and Fulfillment

CORPORATE HEALING PROGRAMS:
- Corporate Stress Management
- Corporate and Group Addiction and Vice Elimination Programs
- In-House Corporate Centers for Vitality and Stress Management
- Mental Powerhouse and "Think Tank" Teams

INTUITIVE VISIONARY CONSULTING PROGRAMS:
- Intutive and Visionary Business Assessment
- Intuitive Charting of Future Corporate Trends, Potential and Options
- Visionary Development of Organizational Vision, Mission and Pioneering Projects
- Intuitive Scanning of High-Level Job Candidates for Potential Seeds of Failure and Success
- Intuitive Scanning of Employees for Effective Team-Building and Management
- Intuitive Scanning to Identify High-Risk and High-Reward Projects

OFFSITE RETREATS:
- Health, Vitality and Stress Management Retreats
  - Addiction and Vice Elimination and Revitalization
- Aptitude and Attitude Development Retreats
- Success and Self-Fulfillment Retreats
  - Inner Renewal and Spiritual Journeys to Special Places
  - Family and Work Life Balance
- GLOCEN Career Development and Certification Retreats

CERTIFICATION PROGRAMS:
- Health, Vitality and Stress Management Strategies
- Advanced Human Faculty Development
- Enlightened Leadership
- Family and Work Life Balance
- Goal-Setting and Integrated Time-Life Management
- Success and Self-Fulfillment Strategies

ESOCEN® is an international, pioneering organization specializing in healing sciences, family transformation, holistic education and advanced spiritual development. Its core philosophy applies Eastern wisdom and Western practicality to balance material and spiritual life to live healthier, be happier and grow faster.

ESOCEN offers seminars, coaching-healing, retreats and career certification programs.

SEMINARS, TRAINING AND CAREER CERTIFICATION PROGRAMS:
- Healing Science
- Family Healing and Transformation
- Holistic Education for the New Generation
- Spiritual Training and Development

COACHING-HEALING-MENTORING SERVICES:
- Healing Stress, Fatigue and Sleep Disorders
- Healing Addictions/Vices and their Side-Effects
- Healing Pain and Its Origins
- Healing Women's Health Issues
- Healing Emotional and Mental Issues
- Healing Sexual Issues
- Healing Hyperactivity, Learning and Attention Problems
- Healing Life-Threatening Illnesses
- Healing Psycho-Spiritual Syndrome
- Family Solutions and Strategies
- Parenting Advanced Children
- Family Healing and Transformation
- Optimizing Performance for Educators
- Optimizing Performance for Students
- Holistic and Wisdom Education for the New Generation
- Balancing Your Material and Spiritual Life
- Inner Powers Development
- Mastering Esoteric Psychology
- Mastering Esoteric Science
- Spiritual Coaching-Healing and Mentoring for Leaders
- Mastering Esoteric Leadership

RETREATS:
- Custom Retreats
- Corporate Retreats
- Retreats to Special and Sacred Places

MDP Global Resources® is a multimedia company producing products to help maximize personal and professional performance, enhance inner development and foster group consciousness. The company supports programs aligned with global transformation and advancement for humanity.

MDP Global Resources serves clients and organizations through:

Books:

- *Inner Powers to Maximize Your Performance*
- *From Success to Fulfillment: Applying the Wisdom of the Himalayan Masters*
- Upcoming 2006 and 2007 Titles:
  - *The 5 Intelligences of Highly Developed People*
  - *Spiritual Technology for Advanced Inner Development*

CDs:

- Chantrams of Transformation™
- Divine Alchemy, Level I: Activating and Balancing Your Power Centers™
- Inner Renewal™ Meditation
- Meditation Music with Mantric Affirmations™
- Namascar Meditation™
- Om of Virtues™

DVDs:

- Beat Your Fatigue and Stress Fast™
- Body Therapy and Inner Powers Meditation™

For Further Information or Services

WISEmeditation, GLOCEN and ESOCEN conduct coaching, consulting, seminars and training programs in in-house and public venues in over 15 countries. Renewal and Stress Management Centers in several countries provide on-going support and nurturing for graduates and members. Our international team is dedicated to serving and assisting our clients on a personal and continuous basis after seminars or consulting engagements.

Please write or call:

WISEmeditation: www.wisemeditation.org /info@wisemeditation.org
P.O. Box 9393
The Woodlands, TX 77387 USA
Tel: +1-832-444-2793 / Fax: +1-936-273-9230

GLOCEN: www.glocen.com / info@glocen.com
ESOCEN: www.esocen.com / info@esocen.com
MDP Global Resources: www.mdpglobal.com / info@mdpglobal.com
P.O. Box 7947
The Woodlands, Texas USA 77387
Tel: 1-800-352-6014 / +1-936-273-9153 / Fax: +1-936-273-9230